TO
SERVE
THE
PEOPLE

UNIVERSITY OF NEW MEXICO PRESS   ALBUQUERQUE

TO SERVE THE PEOPLE

MY LIFE ORGANIZING WITH CESAR CHAVEZ AND THE POOR

LeRoy Chatfield

WITH JORGE MARISCAL

© 2019 by the University of New Mexico Press
All rights reserved. Published 2019
Designed by Mindy Basinger Hill
Composed in Adobe Caslon Pro and Meta Pro
Printed in the United States of America

Library of Congress Cataloging-in-Publication Data

NAMES Chatfield, LeRoy, 1934– author. |
Mariscal, George, author.

TITLE To serve the people: my life organizing with Cesar Chavez
and the poor / LeRoy Chatfield with Jorge Mariscal.

DESCRIPTION Albuquerque: University of New Mexico Press,
2019. | Includes bibliographical references and index. |

IDENTIFIERS LCCN 2019015591 (print) | LCCN 2019021651 (e-book)
|
ISBN 9780826360885 (e-book) | ISBN 9780826360878 (jacketed cloth)

SUBJECTS: LCSH: Chatfield, LeRoy, 1934– | Chavez, Cesar,
1927–1993—Friends and associates. | United Farm Workers of
America—Biography. | Labor leaders—United States—Biography. |
Political activists—United States—Biography. | Mexican American
migrant agricultural laborers—History—20th century. | Labor
movement—United States—History—20th century. | Social justice—
United States—History—20th century. | United States—Social
conditions—1960-1980.

CLASSIFICATION LCC HD6509.C48 (e-book) | LCC HD6509.C48
C54 2019 (print) | DDC 331.88/13092 [B]—dc23

LC record available at https://lccn.loc.gov/2019015591

COVER ILLUSTRATION LeRoy Chatfield with Cesar Chavez
in Porterville, California, 1965. Chatfield had just bailed Chavez
out from the Tulare County jail. Photographer unknown.
Courtesy of the Chatfield family.

We dedicate this book to the young organizers who,
     even as we write these words,
are doing the hard work of listening to the People—
the homeless, refugees, students,
the undocumented, farmworkers,
the undervalued of every color—insisting they
be treated with dignity and given
the opportunity to achieve a better life.

If we aspire to be good, we must ceaselessly work
     to serve others,
serve them in a perfectly disinterested spirit.
     If we hear people crying in distress,
we should immediately run to them and help them.
     After doing what was needed
we should feel that it was all a dream.
     Mahatma Gandhi

One of these [volunteers] was LeRoy Chatfield, who withdrew from the order of Christian Brothers and left his job as a Catholic high school principal in Bakersfield to tackle an endless series of top-level tasks. Intense, dedicated, bright, and efficient, Chatfield was easily identified by his tall, gaunt frame, blue eyes, and blond hair.

Jacques Levy   CESAR CHAVEZ: AUTOBIOGRAPHY OF LA CAUSA

I learned a lot working under LeRoy Chatfield. I saw him as a quiet person with a lot of passion for confronting injustices and making them right. He taught me to not be afraid of those in higher positions and how to confront and solve problems.

Gloria Serda Rodriguez   UFW

You were our teacher. . . . You were sincere and you modeled for us the importance and meaning of our work. We learned to do what would seem impossible in order to help make better the lives of the farmworkers. You did it, LeRoy. You did everything possible to help the boycott accomplish its goal and I am certain you helped develop many great and committed leaders in the process who have gone on to "change the world" in countless and untold ways.

Maria Fuentes   LA BOYCOTT

LeRoy was and will always be one of our star mentors from the movement at its peak.

Richard Ybarra   UFW

CONTENTS

PREFACE

Welcome.

I call my writings "Easy Essays," a title I borrowed from Peter Maurin, who was a French Christian Brother and who, with Dorothy Day, founded the Catholic Worker Movement in 1933, the year before I was born. Peter Maurin passed away in 1949 at age seventy-two and Dorothy Day in 1980 at age eighty-three, exactly my age as I write this preface.

Maurin wrote his Easy Essays in verse—always about social justice—and published them in the *Catholic Worker* newspaper. I was a longtime faithful subscriber to the newspaper and read it cover to cover. Antiwar actions, conscientious objectors, social justice, civil rights, labor rights, feeding the hungry, Houses of Hospitality for the poor, back-to-the-farm movement— the topics went on and on. I soaked it up. The cost of the newspaper was one cent per issue—and still is. Of course, readers who admired the Catholic Workers' commitment to voluntary poverty and service to the poor supported their work financially.

My Easy Essays—now numbering well over two hundred—are not erudite literary material, uniquely profound, or the product of academic training. I wrote them without any expectation that a handful of them would be published in book form. I have Professor Jorge Mariscal to thank for that honor.

The essays that follow are written using everyday words in simple sentences to tell a brief story, recount a childhood memory, or explain social issues I have thought a lot about or discussed with people with whom I have worked and admired. More often than not, the subject matter of my writing is the shameful absence of social justice I have personally witnessed at various times in my life and my response to it.

Of course, essays of this nature will reveal more about me than I wish, but since nothing can be done about it except to not write them, this discomfort falls into the painful category of unintended consequences.

If any of these essays prompt—or provoke—you to think about the importance of social justice in our society and its absence in your own life experience, so much the better!

Very nice to make your acquaintance.

LeRoy Chatfield   CESAR CHAVEZ DAY   MARCH 31, 2019

ACKNOWLEDGMENTS

To my wife of fifty-two years—Bonnie Burns Chatfield. The luckiest day of my life was the day I met Bonnie Burns in Bakersfield, California. The smartest decision I ever made was in San Francisco, when I asked her to marry me. She answered: "Are you sure you want to get married?" I said: "Yes!" Working in the movement, raising a young family, providing and promoting educational opportunities, being politically active, building a professional career, welcoming the grandchildren—the list goes on and on. Until you meet Bonnie, you have not met Superwoman.

In memory of my parents, Raymond Chatfield (1914–1970) and Lucille LaGrande Chatfield (1912–1997), who supported my desire to leave home at age fourteen to pursue my Catholic education.

In memory of my friends and colleagues, Cesar Estrada Chavez (1927–1993) and Helen Fabela Chavez (1928–2017), who founded the farmworker movement in 1962 and lived in voluntary poverty for thirty-one years, dedicating their lives to work for social justice for farmworkers. They changed the course of my life and that of millions of others.

In memory of Daniel Delany (1934–2015), who, along with his wife, Chris Delany, founded Loaves & Fishes in 1983 to feed the hungry and shelter the homeless in Sacramento, California. The Delanys infused Loaves & Fishes with the philosophy of the Catholic Worker Movement—nonjudgmental hospitality. Since its founding, Loaves & Fishes has served more than 7.5 million full-course, home-cooked noon meals to the homeless and hungry residents of Sacramento.

To Governor Jerry Brown, the longest-serving governor in California history, who invited me to work in his first election campaign. After his election, he gave me the opportunity to work in various capacities in his administration, but the one I enjoyed the most was his assignment to build the California Conservation Corps. Governor Brown will be best remembered for passing landmark legislation to protect the rights of farmworkers to bargain collectively with their employers, for recently signing Senate Bill 1437 to amend the 168-year-old felony murder rule, and for granting more than two thousand pardons and commutations to prisoners—because justice had been served and because they earned and deserved to be given a "second chance."

To Jennifer Szabo, a very young Sacramento State whiz tech graduate I met fifteen years ago. Jennifer designed and formatted the website of the Farmworker Movement Documentation Project (farmworkermovement. org) and then patiently taught me how to prepare documents, videos, audio files, and photographs and upload them to the site, thereby re-creating the history of Cesar Chavez and his farmworker movement from 1962–1993. The young will forever teach the old.

To University of California, San Diego, Professor Emeritus Jorge Mariscal, who offered encouragement and support during my ten years of work creating the Farmworker Movement Documentation Project. Without Professor Mariscal's guidance and expertise, this book—*To Serve the People*—would not exist.

LeRoy Chatfield

Mil gracias to LeRoy Chatfield for his lifetime of commitment to the struggle for justice and equality. His efforts not only bettered the lives of hundreds of students, farmworkers, and homeless people, but they also provided us with the Farmworker Movement Documentation Project—an invaluable resource for students and scholars—as well as the thoughtful and insightful essays that make up this book. Throughout his life, LeRoy made history and then wisely ensured that that history would never be forgotten.

Thank you to the anonymous reviewers at the University of New Mexico Press, whose suggestions make this book more reader-friendly. Our thanks go as well to Clark Whitehorn at the University of New Mexico Press, who showed enthusiasm for our project from the first moment we met, and especially to Marie Landau for her superb copyediting skills.

Finally, my gratitude, as always, to my family—Elizabeth, Emma, and Sam—and to our departed canine loved one, Sally, and current canine companion, Tate. No matter what, I return to all of you for refuge.

Jorge Mariscal

ABBREVIATIONS

LC/PH   LeRoy Chatfield responses to questions from scholar Paul Henggeler in 2002–2003. Henggeler was a professor of history at the University of Texas–Pan American (UTPA; renamed the University of Texas Rio Grande Valley in 2012). Henggeler passed away in 2004.

[Name], FMDP, [Date]   Individual essays by union members written for the Farmworker Movement Documentation Project. https://libraries.ucsd.edu/farmworkermovement/.

[Name], FMDPd, [Date]   Group online discussion posts, initiated by Chatfield for the Farmworker Movement Documentation Project, December 2004–January 2005.

Levy   Levy, Jacques E. *Cesar Chavez: Autobiography of La Causa.* New York: W. W. Norton & Company, 1975.

Matthiessen   Matthiessen, Peter. *Sal Si Puedes (Escape If You Can): Cesar Chavez and the New American Revolution.* 1969. Reprint, Berkeley: University of California Press, 2014.

Organization is sacrificing. Successful organized effort always means that the people who do the most work and have the most initiative often get the [least] credit and at critical times are asked and required to submerge their individuality and yield their judgment to the desire of others.

W. E. B. Du Bois LETTER TO R. C. HUDSON, 1927

Let me say first that whether a person is born an organizer, or learns to become one, you never recover from it.

LeRoy Chatfield FMDPd, DECEMBER 19, 2004

Introduction

JORGE MARISCAL

The lived experiences represented in these collected essays are complex. If they were to be reduced to a few basic ideas, the quotations above would serve us well. The pilgrimage of LeRoy Chatfield has been a long road that weaves its way through multiple collective projects designed to better the condition of "the least of these." The intention of the volume is to mine the stories that bring this pilgrimage to life in order to illuminate lessons that can be used by the dedicated organizers of the present and future—those organizers who may get the least credit and who will never recover from the disappointments and the joys of their commitment to justice.

The through line across Chatfield's journey is an unwavering focus on organizing communities so as to expand their agency—what Ella Baker called creating "vehicles of power." Once that agency is directed against the structures of inequality, windows of opportunity for change begin to swing open. Because of Chatfield's personal formation, the commitment to organize for change consistently required that movement participants who chose to walk the organizer's path, especially those in positions of leadership, do their best to maintain their discipline, their integrity, their humility, and their humanity.

First and foremost, it is our hope that activists of the present and the future can incorporate into their own work some of the lessons laced throughout the thirty-six essays that make up this volume. Once adapted to the new context, these antecedents may be helpful for furthering the goal of social justice for workers, students, the poor, and others. Lessons found here may serve as warning signs alerting us to the tensions and miscalculations that emerge in every social movement. Chatfield reminds us, "A movement is a series of trade-offs. If the results are negative, life goes on, and one has to make the best of it under the new circumstances" (FMDP4, December 22, 2004). In other words, the world *failure* is irrelevant with regard to social movements because in every "defeat" are sown the seeds of actions to come within different conditions of possibility. As legendary activist Elizabeth "Betita" Martínez once put it, "It's a long struggle [for social justice], but there are traditions that get set, there are concepts that get established, there are visions that get put out, there are dreams that get dreamed, and just having those in our lives and our minds is a victory in itself."[1]

For those of you making the commitment to explore this book, please be advised that you will not find in these pages a standard biography, an organizational history, or even a strict linear chronological narrative. Rather, in a dialectical ebb and flow across time, you will observe one individual's commitment to progressive change and social equity from the second half of the twentieth century to the present. It is a unique story with regard to the specific details of one man's life. But it is not unique insofar as it resonates with the lived experience of so many activists who chose to remain behind the scenes, anonymous insofar as they refused to claim personal credit for what the collective had achieved. From the vantage point of today's celebrity culture, such quiet dedication and sacrifice may strike some readers as quaint or even foolish. But today, in the chaos of our media-saturated celebrity cacophony, there are organizers quietly going about their business to bring forth a more equitable and just society.

The essays that follow are woven through the dense fabric of postwar America and postwar California in particular. They contain contemporary observations juxtaposed with retrospective reflections, as the narrator looks back and attempts to understand the meaning of each moment in order to interpret its lessons for the present. Chatfield's vision surveys past events as part of a continuum that constitutes what some have called "the good fight"—that is, the calling to devote one's life to the pursuit of equality for all. The social issues that concern him have not been resolved. The struggles represented here have not ended and in fact will likely never end. If the arc of history does indeed bend toward justice, it is only because committed activists over time are pulling it in that direction.

Within each piece, the protagonist's voice is center stage. At times, it may be accompanied by two supplementary sources: 1) the recollections of other actors who participated in the same events, and 2) short intrusions by the editor designed to provide the reader with additional background. In the first category, I have taken the liberty to select actors whose recorded reflections shed additional light on issues illuminated by Chatfield's observations.

The essays on Cesar Chavez and the farmworker movement touch upon events that have received extensive scrutiny in recent years. We have chosen not to enter into that vast bibliography. Rather, in my parenthetical comments for this section, I have included only two journalists—Jacques Levy and Peter Matthiessen—simply because both were physically present at key moments in the history of the movement and because their published accounts are based on taped interviews and contemporaneous notes. With regard to models that inspired the format of our text and the inclusion of supplementary editorial comments, two classic studies were the most influential: Levy's 1975 *Cesar Chavez: Autobiography of La Causa* and Stokely Carmichael and Ekwueme Michael Thelwell's 2003 *Ready for Revolution: The Life and Struggles of Stokely Carmichael (Kwame Turé)*. By allowing the voices of movement participants to "speak for themselves," while an editor provides historical background for the reader at key moments, both books construct vibrant narratives that allow the reader to enter now-distant periods of committed social praxis.[2]

A GENEALOGY OF COMMITTED ACTION

LeRoy Chatfield, the primary actor in this book, was an acute observer of the process by which an individual chooses to subordinate her or his desires to a greater good. Very early in his life, he was inserted into collective structures that subordinated personal goals and desires to broader communitarian projects. From the time he became a member of the Christian Brothers at the age of fifteen, he learned how to negotiate the movement between a life of contemplation and a life of social praxis. He explains this transformation in a short essay titled "Brother Misfit" (not included in this volume):

> From August of 1949 until August of 1953, this monastery [Mont La Salle] located on the steep hillside vineyard properties west of Napa was my home. For the first two years, my only contact with the world outside was a monthly visit in the monastery garden picnic area with my family and a three-week visit home in August; for

the last two and a half years, only a monthly visit on the monastery grounds. Regardless of the section of the monastery to which we were assigned, Christian Brothers in training were expected to be in the world but not of the world, and the reality was that unless one walked the seven-mile mountainous road down to the town, it was a world separate and apart.[3]

Eventually leaving the secluded world behind monastery walls, Chatfield, now Brother Gilbert, would venture out into the broader society as a teacher and organizer; soon after, he would take up his role in the farmworker movement of the mid-1960s. And then, as the revolutionary period of the Vietnam War era subsided and the rise of the conservative Reagan reaction slowly began to roll back many of the victories that had been won, Chatfield devoted himself to the homeless and the disenfranchised, that is, those left behind by the dominant ethos of the emerging neoliberal regime—"greed is good."

Richard Ybarra, the longtime personal assistant to Cesar Chavez, recounts a time when a group of international visitors came to Delano. Eager to understand where Chavez "fit" in the political landscape, one guest pressed him, asking, "How would you describe your political philosophy?" If I had to label myself, Chavez replied, I would have to call myself "a radical Catholic."[4] In many ways, this term describes the foundation of LeRoy Chatfield's lifelong mission. At its core, the commitment was premised on "respecting the dignity of others" and working to nurture and sustain that dignity. These are the values that extend across Chatfield's entire career. The importance of a moral vision, the commitment to act upon that vision, and the discipline to not waver from the assigned task are values that appear often in the following pages. At the same time, it should surprise no one that having begun his career in a religious order, the dynamics of hierarchy, leaders, and disciples would inform much of the work he would undertake and the approach he adopted to complete it.

While it may be true, as Chatfield often says, that he was a "true believer" in various authority figures, we might also view his dedication as a strong commitment to the vision that the person in charge embodied or, better yet, as a gift for being able to negotiate the tightrope that leads from the leader's actualization of the vision and back again to the vision itself. Whether we are reading about the first Brother Gilbert, from whom he took his religious name, or the deeply religious pacifist labor organizer Cesar Chavez or the former Jesuit novice–turned–politician Jerry Brown, what permeates all of Chatfield's writings is his strong belief that a "leaderless" movement, a concept experimented with by a few organizations in the 1960s and in vogue today with many young activists, will always lack a key ingredient (perhaps the key ingredient) for successful organizing. The issue of the relationship between leader and movement is one that has vexed many movements and one that cannot be easily resolved.

Chatfield's decision to leave the Christian Brothers in 1965 was not a simple one. But rather than being a deviation from his original intention, the shift from Catholic educator to volunteer in an incipient labor movement was a logical continuation. Much has been written about the function of Catholic ritual, especially in its Mexican variations, that marked the culture of the farmworker movement—the Mass, the fast, Nuestra Señora la Virgen de Guadalupe. What the essays that follow reveal is LeRoy Chatfield's central role in the development of that culture. Perhaps no other person was more responsible for coordinating the public acts that transformed Cesar Chavez's religious impulses into tools grounded in Catholic doctrine and history with the purpose of organizing people across a wide range of varied beliefs. The impact of the first public fast for nonviolence in 1968, for example, would not have been the same without Chatfield's support and meticulous staging of the event.

The essays on the farmworker movement allow us to understand many of the most interpreted historical episodes through the eyes and remembrances of someone who had the trust of the man who became the public face of the movement. Because memory is imperfect, surely Chatfield's accounts are open to debate, and yet the integrity for which he was celebrated by so many who knew him provides us near certainty that we are not being intentionally misled due to some personal agenda. On the contrary, Chatfield's writings are thoughtful and self-effacing, like the man who wrote them, and always alert to unavoidable contradictions that inhabited each occurrence. At those moments when he expresses strong opinions, those opinions ought not be taken as infallible but rather as the product of the lived experience in a context now many decades in the past.

The one constant across the farmworker essays in part 2 is Chatfield's unwavering dedication to the Mexican, Mexican American, and Filipino workers with whom he allied himself. His identification is notable at numerous points but especially in essay 7, where he refers to himself as a member of the ethnic group with which he had chosen to struggle: "In 1963 we were

Mexican American; it wasn't until a few years later that we became Chicanos, and then later still, we became Hispanics, and now some of us might be called Latinos." Here, the collective "we-in-struggle" gives birth to a no-less authentic identity than the one determined by one's birth or ethnicity.

A brief scene recounted by journalist Peter Matthiessen is particularly revealing on this score. Matthiessen writes:

> I had arrived in Delano late in the evening of the last night of July and was to meet Cesar Chavez for the first time the following morning in the office of his assistant, Leroy [sic] Chatfield. The whole staff had just returned from a retreat at St. Anthony's Mission, in the Diablo Range, "a holy place," Mr. Chatfield said, "where we tried to figure out how to make life miserable for rich people. . . . As Chatfield spoke of Chavez and the farm workers, his face was radiant; Mrs. Israel, struck by this, said "You really love these people, don't you, LeRoy?" [*Ann Israel, an organizer from the East Coast who had introduced Matthiessen to Chavez*]. It was a straight question, not a sentimental one, and it made him blink, but he did not back away from it. "Oh, yes," he said quietly. "I mean, you don't meet people like that . . ." His voice trailed off and he shrugged, at a loss, still smiling" (39).

One of the subjects not directly addressed in this book is what the historiography now identifies as the slow decline of the farmworker movement from its peak in the late 1960s to the transformation of the union/movement in the late 1970s, the fragmentation of the collective consensus that had attracted hundreds of volunteers over time, and the apparent changes in the leadership style of Chavez himself. When LeRoy and Bonnie Chatfield decided to leave the union in 1973, all of these changes were still rumbling thunderclaps in the distance—audible but not yet threatening.

Chatfield has written, "In August of 1973, I was not prescient enough to know that 'things were going to get a helluva lot worse.' If my friends and colleagues attributed this reasoning to me, I did not know of it" (FMDPd, December 23, 2004). What happened after has been the primary focus of recent revisionist histories, and in the essays included here the discerning reader will identify warning signs of what was to come. In any case, for this later period the Farmworker Movement Documentation Project (described below and in essay 35) is an invaluable resource for hearing the rising chorus of volunteer voices that began to express concern and often dismay about how the movement was drifting into turbulent waters. Many of the works in our suggested readings list also describe the period from the late 1970s until Chavez's passing in 1993.

ON LEADERS AND MOVEMENTS

On the reverse side of the United Farm Workers (UFW) union membership card designed for supporters in higher education was a quotation from the union's founder (see fig. 1).

For readers of this volume, two items in this quotation are of special interest. First, the idea that organizers, especially those in leadership roles, must make a long-term commitment to the struggle. Chatfield's essays contain numerous variations on the idea that "activism," if it is authentic, is never a casual activity. Rather, the "activist" must commit for "an awful long time." The second point raises one of the questions most closely linked to the unraveling of the UFW in the post-1975 period, which is, when is it time for the organizer/founder/leader to step aside so that younger leaders can take up the baton?

In the early twentieth century, the legendary organizer and intellectual W. E. B. Du Bois noted, "It's the same story with all organizations, as it is with some men. After they get to a certain age, they get out of touch with their surroundings, and if they can re-orientate themselves, all right, and if they can't they just die, even though they are living and walking around."[5]

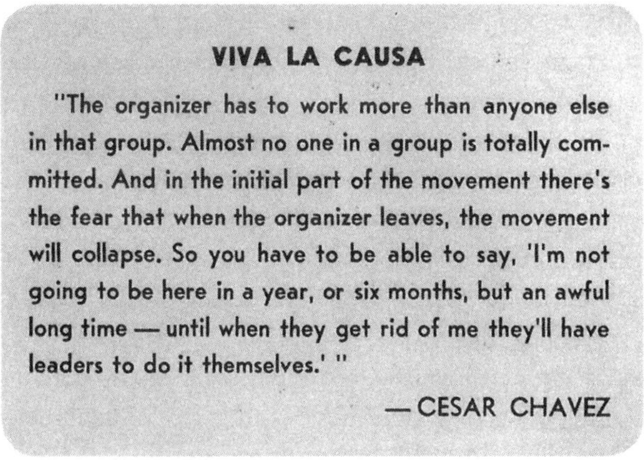

VIVA LA CAUSA

"The organizer has to work more than anyone else in that group. Almost no one in a group is totally committed. And in the initial part of the movement there's the fear that when the organizer leaves, the movement will collapse. So you have to be able to say, 'I'm not going to be here in a year, or six months, but an awful long time — until when they get rid of me they'll have leaders to do it themselves.' "

— CESAR CHAVEZ

FIGURE 1 UFW academic supporters' membership card (reverse side).

This complex issue arises at some point in all organizations but is especially urgent in grassroots movements for progressive change. How can we remain faithful to our founding values even as the objective conditions around us are in flux? This was the subject of fierce debate among UFW volunteers both during and after the peak of the farmworker movement. The phrase on the membership card above—"until when they get rid of me"—reveals Chavez's awareness that for an organization to stay strong, new leaders must emerge. His casual remark to Chatfield as early as 1968 that "sooner or later he [Chavez] was going to leave the union and he had decided that it was going to be sooner" (essay 18) surprises us because it shows that at some level Chavez was always already imagining when and how his departure would take place. And yet Chatfield's belief at the time—that the demands of leadership more than likely would never allow for Chavez to walk away—turned out to be accurate. A similar dynamic would take shape years later when Chatfield served as director of Loaves & Fishes, an organization devoted to the hungry and the homeless: when to stay, when to leave?

A related dilemma for present and future activists to ponder—beyond the eventual substitution of leaders, what if the transformed objective conditions require that the organization itself be displaced? Or, as longtime organizer and scholar Marshall Ganz put it, "For most people, social movements are just that—movements. . . . They are transitions, transformations, and they don't last forever, nor should they. The mistake may have been in trying to make it last forever, an abnormality when it comes to social movements."[6] In response to Ganz's comments, Chatfield proposed the following enigma: "That is the final and unexplainable paradox: carrying the movement to the human breaking point for 'most of us' [not in leadership] dramatically diminishes the capacity of the movement to live beyond the death or deposition of the founder; but compromising the idealistic principles on which the movement was built to accommodate 'most of us' defeats the goals, the aspirations, and yes, even the vision, of the founder" (FMDP "Social Movements and Most People," 2006).

Again, at some level Cesar Chavez was always well aware of this process. In 1976 in an interview with Tom Hayden, his remarks echoed Du Bois's insight and elaborated on the tension inherent in the movement/organization dynamic: "The other thing that takes place is that the founders of a movement are very idealistic because they had nothing but ideals to begin with. But when the leadership changes hands and the second wave comes in, that really is when the first big decision is made to become less a movement and more an organization. In our movement as long as the founders are active, we are going to have to try to keep the movement a movement. Once we leave, we'll see one of two things. We'll either become a stronger movement or just a run-of-the-mill organization."[7]

Because no individual or leadership group can control the flow of shifting contexts, both micro and macro, from around the time of this 1976 interview forward the farmworker movement would undergo a slow metamorphosis into a dramatically different entity than it had been less than a decade earlier—another sobering lesson for organizers that reappears throughout the pages that follow. In his introduction to the online group discussion with union veterans that he initiated, Chatfield offered the following reflections:

It should come as no surprise that in the development of any organization, a situation arises, a decision is made, and the result becomes a turning point in its history. Unfortunately, the turning point does not become evident until years later, when the time has long since passed to redo or undo what has already been done.

Some turning points may contribute greatly, if accidentally, to the successful outcomes of an organization, but there is little motivation to uncover and examine such points because it is generally assumed that the successes realized were the inevitable product of wise decision-making. There is little reason to question success, even if, truth be told, it was accidental or lucky.

But when a successful organization unexpectedly tacks off in a different direction or begins to stall or experiences a downturn in its fortunes, surely a turning point must have occurred. What happened to cause this change? Why did it occur? And when? What is to be gained by uncovering such a turning point? Even if it can be identified with some certainty, there is nothing to be done about it. The organization cannot rewind, erase, and redo this series of events. (FMDP, "A Turning Point," August 2010)

It was their good fortune, perhaps, that drew Bonnie and LeRoy away from their beloved union before it tacked off course and lost its direction. What followed for them were two periods of their shared pilgrimage, extending across many years, that are replete with commitments premised upon the core beliefs at work in earlier moments. Confirmed four times by the California State Senate during the first administration of Governor

Jerry Brown, Chatfield was named to the newly formed Agricultural Labor Relations Board (ALRB) in 1975. The board was poised to make major improvements to the existing conditions for farmworkers. It did not take long before emissaries from the Teamsters Union arrived at the ALRB office in Sacramento to rough up both Chatfield and the board chairman, Bishop Roger Mahony, telling them they should resign or bad things might happen to them. Both men received 24-hour police protection for several days.

A less dramatic appointment followed when Brown named Chatfield as director of the newly created California Conservation Corps (CCC). Inaugurated by Brown in 1976, the mission of the CCC was to "further the development and maintenance of the natural resources and environment of the State, and to provide the young men and women of the State meaningful, productive employment." Shortly after taking the reins of the CCC in 1977, Chatfield developed the organizational guidelines and established eighteen new field centers during his brief two-year tenure. Upon leaving state government, Chatfield in effect returned to his core intention of serving the poor and the unprotected, from the grassroots level. Now his commitment would be transferred to the homeless population, a demographic that had expanded dramatically during the two-term presidency of Ronald Reagan, grew under the rollback of social services during the Clinton era, and exploded by the end of the Obama administration. The transformation of the US economy to favor the wealthy and the attendant tearing apart of the social safety net meant that hunger and homelessness would increase in the richest nation in the world.

Like the writings generated by his earlier commitments, part 3 spans his time with the organization Loaves & Fishes and contains multiple lessons about how to organize disempowered communities. First, the logistics of providing the basic necessities for those who lack them; second, negotiating local bureaucracies that are not always supportive, from city governments to law enforcement; third, enlisting allies from a pool of organizations that might never have worked together; fourth, changing dominant negative stereotypes about the community one is serving. As the twenty-first century began, Chatfield, never one to back away from a fight against the mistreatment of those who were defenseless, had lost none of his spark. In 2002, one board member of Loaves & Fishes told a reporter this about Chatfield: "He is not a diplomat. . . . his idea is to create the confrontation and let other people be the diplomats. The farmworkers were successful not by being reasonable, they were successful by confronting the establishment with strikes and boycotts. This inevitably has shaped LeRoy's character and his approach to problems. He's almost itching for that still today."[8] Throughout these final essays, then, as in all of Chatfield's writings, the message he learned from Cesar Chavez is being passed on to those of us today—you will not have the power but you must have the commitment and you will always have the time. The fact that in 2018 Loaves & Fishes continues to serve the hungry and homeless in Sacramento is a testament to the original values upon which the organization was founded.

Finally, a few words about the Farmworker Movement Documentation Project, without which this book (nor many other recent books and documentaries) would not have been possible. As he explains in essay 35, Chatfield "retired" repeatedly from his work with the homeless population in Sacramento, which is to say, he never really withdrew from the work even though he initiated additional commitments. One of those new projects would be the gargantuan undertaking of creating an online repository of the history of the farmworker struggle in California from 1962 to 1993. When he was approached in late 2002 by a young researcher who was planning a book on Cesar Chavez, Chatfield dedicated several months to answering questions but soon realized his version of events was only one of many. What was needed, he thought, was input from as many other direct participants in the movement as possible; journalists, filmmakers, and scholars would then have a richer pool of materials from which to construct their interpretations. From May of 2003 to December of 2004, over 188 original essays by union volunteers had been submitted. A rich online discussion among those members would follow. Unfortunately, Paul Henggeler, the researcher whose initial inquiry had been one of the sparks for the idea for the archive (the primary catalyst being the recent publication of several revisionist histories of Chavez and the union), was unable to complete his project—he passed away in 2004. Chatfield's personal responses to Henggeler inform several of the essays in this collection.

Without any background in the technical aspects of creating a digitized archive, Chatfield collaborated with a young web designer, Jennifer Szabo, to produce one of the most complete and most accessible collections dedicated to a key moment in modern California history. To his role as one of the indispensable volunteers in the early years of the farmworker movement he added another essential contribution—a rich field of primary and secondary materials about that movement ready to be harvested by future students and historians.

On an institutional level, movements sometimes run out of steam, get co-opted and institutionalized. But movements leave behind an incredible infrastructure of talented individuals, organizational models, and institutional reforms. When many new movements develop, they often draw strength from the resources, songs, stories, lessons, and institutional allies of earlier movements.

Angie Fa FMDP, DECEMBER 14, 2004

In this brave new world of hi-tech consumerism, robust (and even toxic) forms of individualism, massive economic inequality, unregulated social media monopolies, niche blogs, troll farms, communities fragmented by internal divisions, and "post-truth" society, many of the values and actions described in the essays that follow will strike some readers as archaic residue from a bygone era. The personal sacrifice displayed by LeRoy Chatfield and his compatriots before, during, and after his time in the farmworker movement is surely being practiced in many places today, and yet because it is not a value celebrated by the culture as a whole, it remains largely unseen.

Eventually, and perhaps soon, history will demand that mass mobilizations for progressive change reemerge in the United States.[9] When such movements gain traction, the issues raised in this collection will resonate at a higher frequency—how can we maintain democratic structures in the organization, how much work can volunteers bear, who will be our allies, are charismatic leaders necessary or even desirable, when is it time for the organization's founders to cede authority to others, what are the best ways to work both the outside (grassroots resistance) and the inside (electoral politics, legislation, etc.), what if the founding vision of the movement becomes out of sync with a rapidly changing social landscape?

These are concerns that inform every step of LeRoy Chatfield's long pilgrimage of committed social activism, from the monastery to the schoolhouse to the fields of the Central Valley to the halls of Sacramento to urban streets where society's neglected men and women struggle to survive. The essays included here tell the story of one man's journey that in reality was the story of large groupings of people—students, farmworkers, the homeless—who needed vehicles of power in order to claim their economic and political rights. More important, they tell the story of a moral vision grounded in the notion that social justice was and is the natural right of every human being.

As Cesar Chavez said, "There's no trick to organizing, there's no shortcut:

a good organizer is someone willing to work long and hard. Just keep talking to people and they will respond" (Matthiessen, 284).

NOTES

1. "Quest for a Homeland," *Chicano! History of the Mexican American Civil Rights Movement*. Video. Austin, TX: Galán Incorporated, 1996.

2. Occasional endnotes located at the end of each essay refer the reader to books published by participants in the farmworker movement. With the exception of editorial inserts by Jorge Mariscal, the voices of nonparticipant scholars or journalists are not included in this volume; however, a list of suggested readings is included at the back of the book.

3. "Brother Misfit," *Syndic*, no. 15 (March 2017).

4. Oral history with Richard Ybarra. Ybarra also describes Chavez's advanced practice of yoga and his study of non-Western spirituality. https://libraries.ucsd .edu/farmworkermovement/media/oral_history/whowascesar/07% 20Spirituality1 .mp3.

5. Letter to Vada and John Somerville (January 31, 1935) in Meyer Weinberg, ed., *The World of W. E. B. Du Bois: A Quotation Sourcebook* (Amherst and Boston: University of Massachusetts Press, 1992), 244.

6. Ganz's remarks are from FMDPd, December 5, 2004. A few days later in the FMDPd, Ganz applies his insight specifically to the UFW in a more pointed manner: "Movements contribute what they have to contribute if they accomplish the changes for which people joined them—and it is all the large numbers of people that join that make it a movement. An isolated leadership cadre living in the hills may be a cult, a commune, a community, the remnant of a movement, or perhaps a shrine to a movement, but it is not a 'movement'" (December 14, 2004).

7. Tom Hayden, "Cesar Chavez and His Many-Layered Union," *Rolling Stone*, November 4, 1976. Chavez's response to Hayden's question is interesting, given the concerns expressed in several of the essays in this collection. Hayden asks, "How do you stay in touch with the workers and not become an administrator tied to a desk?" Chavez responds, "The problem is that administration is not the most important thing, but it's the most pressing thing. And then you start creating a world of your own detached from the reality of the workers. All of the bad decisions that I've made were because I didn't touch base with people."

8. Tom Hoeber, former publisher of the *California Journal*, quoted in Diana Griego Erwin, "Loaves & Fishes Fast," *Sacramento Bee*, March 19, 2002, B1.

9. The attempt by Reverend William Barber of North Carolina to revive Dr. King's idea for a Poor People's Campaign within the new context of 2018 is a hopeful example. As I write these words, the convulsive presidency of Donald Trump and its radical conservative agenda are generating mobilizations across the nation.

PART ONE
WITH THE
CHRISTIAN
BROTHERS

1   From Colusa

I was born in Arbuckle, but during my childhood years of the 1940s I was raised in Colusa, a rural community of barely 2,800 residents. The town is seated hard by the levees of the Sacramento River, sixty miles north of Sacramento. Starting at Bridge Street, the city streets run north, first to Tenth, and from the river, they run west—Main, Market, Jay, Oak, Clay, Parkhill, Webster, and Fremont. That's it, the urban square mile of my childhood world.

Colusa County, California, was built on native Patwin land (southern Wintu). The indigenous settlement Koru (with trilled *r*) along the Sacramento River became Colus in French and English corruptions; the variations Colusi and Coluse were used in the early US period. During the Mexican period, Governor Pío Pico sold the Rancho Colus land grant to one of the first recorded Anglos to settle in California, John Bidwell, who had arrived in 1841 at the age of twenty-one. Bidwell became a naturalized Mexican citizen in 1844 and began to accumulate his fortune when he discovered gold on his property shortly before the Gold Rush. He served as an officer in the US Army in the war against Mexico. In 1850, Bidwell sold Rancho Colus to Charles Semple, an attorney and farmer who had recently migrated from Kentucky. Since that time until today, the economy of the region has depended almost exclusively on agriculture.

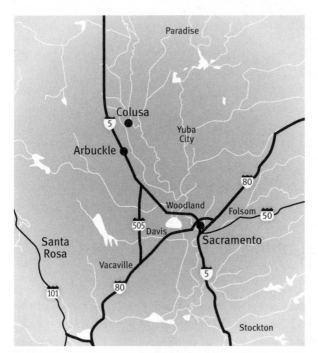

FIGURE 2
Born in Arbuckle
and raised in Colusa
(population 2,300),
LeRoy Chatfield
was educated at
various sites across
Northern California.
Courtesy of the us
Geological Survey.

FIGURE 3 Flooded rice fields near Colusa, with the Sutter Buttes—the world's smallest mountain range—in the background. Photo by Timothy Hearsum. Courtesy of Getty Images.

The birth of Colusa dates to 1850, the same year that California was incorporated as a state. Rice growing was introduced in 1912, and my uncle used to tell me that the United States produced more rice than China. This might have been something of a patriotic exaggeration, I don't know, but Colusa itself did grow enough rice by the 1940s to be ranked the number-one rice-producing county in the nation. It still is. On average, Colusa produces more than ten million sacks of rice a year, a half million tons or more, with an annual cash value of approximately $200 million. The federal government deems rice such a valuable commodity that in 2002, it paid $55 million in federal subsidies to nine hundred Colusa County rice growers, including some of my relatives.

If you can imagine two highways intersecting at midpoint, each one twenty miles long, one running east and west, the other north and south, flooded on both sides for five months of the year, you have the same view of the county that I had during my childhood. During the rice-growing season, the ten-mile drive from Colusa to Williams, where the highways described above intersect, seemed to me like driving through a vast lake on a narrow, elevated strip of asphalt. The terrain was flat, and without highlights to provide any dimension, it seemed eerie to me, like a watery wasteland.

The production of rice requires water, huge amounts of water, enough water to cover several hundred square miles of rice fields. For five months of the year, irrigators like Pop, my grandfather, flooded the rice fields. They regulated and controlled the water through a series of seemingly endless small, contoured levees called rice checks. Each check contained an irrigation box that permitted the irrigator to move the water and raise or lower it as the growing cycle required. Standing water in the rice fields meant extra-long days for the irrigators. From daylight to dark, they walked the levees with their long-handled shovels lying atop their shoulders, repairing levee breaks, regulating the water, and generally fussing over the rapidly growing crop.

My mother's family grew rice west of Williams, and the aforementioned Pop was a rice irrigator for a large ranch—but even though my childhood roots were in the rice fields, I knew that whatever the future held for Colusa, it did not include me.

My future was shaped by the convent school, my mother's devout practice of Catholicism, and my father's often-expressed wish that I should get an education and do better in life than he. I admired my father greatly and marveled at all the things he could repair and fix and figure out. But apparently, he did not attach much educational value to it. He hoped I would do better. I said I would.

In the 1940s, the devout practice of Catholicism in the rice town of Colusa meant attending Mass on Sundays and taking Communion if you had not broken the no-water-or-food-since-midnight rule; making a good confession every Saturday; serving the early weekday Mass for the parish priest; praying the rosary daily; not eating meat on Fridays; attending the convent school; observing the practice of Lent, including the weekly stations of the cross; and not entering a Protestant church, even for a social event. In fact, social relationships with non-Catholics were discouraged for fear they might lead to marriage with a non-Catholic, which was a cause of concern and very much frowned upon. Catholics were Catholics, and everyone else was something else, but each group was to be kept separate and apart.

Does this sound too simplistic and without nuance? I'm sure it does, but sixty years ago, in the rice community of Colusa, it seemed natural and commonplace—at least to me, the descendant of devout French Canadian Catholic ancestors.

I have no clear recollection that I was anxious to leave Colusa, only that I was destined to do so. I did well in the convent school and I wanted to attend a Catholic high school but the closest one was located in Sacramento.

FIGURE 4 **Marriage photo** of Raymond LeRoy Sterling Chatfield and Lucille Elizabeth LaGrande, 1933. Courtesy of the Chatfield family.

My father wanted me to get an education, and for some reason the small high school in Colusa was not what he meant. My mother was pleased because I could continue my Catholic education. All of the stars seemed aligned for the inevitable, so with great expectation and little fanfare they drove me to the Catholic boarding school one day early in September 1948.

That day was the last of Colusa for me. I came home a weekend or two a month, but I longed to return to school at the first opportunity; then in August 1949, I entered Catholic religious monastic life. My break with my childhood and with Colusa was complete and irrevocable. I never looked back.

I lived my childhood to the fullest. I was close to my uncles on the ranch, and I lived with my grandparents for a time. I was an avid reader, I enjoyed going to school, and I felt my parents wanted the best for me. Everyone needs to come from someplace and Colusa, the number-one rice-producing county in the United States, is a good someplace from which to come, but no return would be possible.

Now, writing as an old man, I am hesitant to ask myself if I fulfilled my father's wishes and whether I did more with my life than he did. I remind myself that to he who is given much, much more is expected in return. I was given much.

2   Boarding School, 1948

I graduated from Our Lady of Lourdes Catholic Elementary School in Colusa, California, a small rice town of 2,800 residents perched alongside the Sacramento River, sixty miles north of Sacramento. That such a small rural town would even have a Catholic school was quite remarkable, but those of us living there who were Catholic simply took its presence for granted.

My mother, a staunch Catholic, wanted me to attend a Catholic high school, and though the closest one available was in Sacramento, they provided a boarding department for out-of-town students. I too wanted to stay in Catholic school and had been encouraged by some of my teachers, Sisters of the Holy Cross, to enter junior seminary of the Fathers of the Holy Cross in Notre Dame, Indiana.

I decided to enroll at Christian Brothers High School in Sacramento and live in their boarding department, which was located on the campus. I was the first boarder to check in for the new school year—my first year of high school. My mother and father had driven me down Highway 99 from Colusa. I had one large suitcase that contained all the clothes and personal items I would need. The boarding department had sent us a list of what I should bring with me, and my mother had checked each item off the list as she packed it.

Brother Gilbert was the prefect of boarders. He was a big, broad-shouldered man who measured well over six feet tall and weighed 220 pounds or more. Sitting atop his huge frame was a smiling baby face with sparkling eyes. He spoke with an Irish accent, but a different one than the brogue of the priests I frequently heard in Colusa. His accent was East Coast—he was a Bostonian. I liked him immediately. Clothed in his flowing black robes and starched white collar, he exuded confidence and kindly authority but make no mistake—without doubt, Brother Gilbert was the man in charge. You could tell that just by looking at him.

"You are the first to arrive," he told my parents. We walked into the institutional-looking two-story building with high ceilings. From north to south, this wing of the high school was bisected down the middle by a wide hallway that fed the small dormitory rooms on both sides. The bathroom and shower facility rooms were located at midpoint. About halfway down, he opened a door and ushered us into a long, narrow room. It was wide enough to accommodate five metal beds with their headboards butted up against the south wall, leaving an informal hallway some four feet wide along the north wall. At the end of the room was a large window that began waist high and ran almost up to the high ceiling. In the corner next to the window was a bathroom-size sink with hot and cold running water. A mirror was affixed to the wall above the sink. The walls were bare. The only decoration was a large crucifix high on the wall above the middle bed.

"Well, LeRoy, because you are the first one here, you get to choose. Which bed do you want?" What bed did I want? I had no idea. I quickly looked down the room at the beds that were identical. Should I select the bed next to the window? A few seconds passed as my mother and father and Brother Gilbert waited expectantly. With a stab of desperation, I said the middle one. My non-Catholic father turned to Brother Gilbert and said, "He chose the one with the crucifix." Brother nodded and smiled in pleased agreement.

The Brothers of the Christian Schools, or De La Salle Christian Brothers, is a Catholic teaching institute founded in France in the late seventeenth century and officially recognized by the Vatican in 1725. Its original mission was the education of poor children. Members must take vows of poverty, chastity, and obedience. The institute established itself in Northern California in 1868, founding wineries, the proceeds from which maintained its schools and homes for retired brothers. The first Lasallian school in Sacramento, named St. Patrick's Institute, was opened in 1876. The school site eventually moved in 1924 and became Christian Brothers High School. A majority of graduates from the school entered military service in World War II; nine lost their lives.

I unpacked. There must have been bureaus in the room to accommodate five boarders but I don't remember them. I just can't remember them. (Why can I remember some details so well and others not at all?) Soon enough, I was finished. I walked with my parents out to the car, said goodbye with a hug from each, and they drove away. I was alone, the first boarder to arrive early in September 1948. I was fourteen years old. I don't remember crying, though I could have. I just remember being alone.

Surely, there must have been public detention centers for youthful offenders during the 1940s, but I don't remember any nor do I remember kids my age talking about them like I heard my own kids in the 1980s talk about juvenile hall or Boys' Ranch, a juvenile detention center serving the county of Sacramento. I found out soon enough that boarding schools filled a special niche in the juvenile court system of the 1940s.

I was the only boarder in my five-bed dormitory who was not the product of a broken home, that is, a home where only a single mother had the responsibility of raising the child. Either the husband was deceased or had drifted away or the parents were divorced. Strange as it might seem now, divorce was quite unusual during my childhood years, especially in rural areas of Northern California, and when it did occur it was talked about in hushed tones and certainly not in front of children.

In those cases where the single mother could not cope with raising the teenage child for financial and especially behavioral reasons, oftentimes the child would be named a ward of the court and was assigned to attend a boarding school. These institutions, especially those operated by Catholic religious orders, had earned the reputation of being strict with their charges, and the use of corporal punishment (about which I can personally attest) was not at all uncommon. Religious boarding schools believed in the principle of *in loco parentis*, especially when it came to discipline and respect for authority. My 1948 Sacramento boarding school had some tough kids present, and equally tough love methods were used to keep good order, maintain respect for authority, and promote good study habits. Frankly, I think they did a good job, and while I was not a problem child and was much too skinny and naive to be a tough kid, I thrived under this Catholic boarding school system of law and order.

I admired the work of Brother Gilbert, his fatherly concern for us

FIGURE 5 Brother Gilbert (Chatfield). After graduating from St. Mary's College of California with a degree in philosophy, he was assigned to teach high school in Bakersfield. Photographer unknown. Courtesy of the Chatfield family.

boarders, and his administration of law and order. So much so that at the end of the school year, I sought entrance into the order of the Christian Brothers and was accepted into their high school of monastic religious training in the Mount Veeder area, a few miles west of Napa. When I qualified to wear the religious robe, I was required to give up my family name and choose another. Quite naturally, I chose the name Brother Gilbert.

3   LeRoy, Merry Christmas!

My first Christmas away from home came in 1949, at age fifteen. In August, I had entered the Christian Brothers Junior Novitiate at Mont La Salle to begin a monastic religious high school training period that would eventually lead me to become a professed member of the Christian Brothers, a Catholic religious teaching order.

One of the purposes of the Juniorate was to wean teenagers away from parents, relatives, friends, and other worldly connections for the sake of devoting one's entire life to a religious vocation. That life included living in poverty, celibacy, and obedience. Among the methods used to create this separation was the rule that parents were permitted to visit only once a month on a designated Sunday afternoon. Another rule required that all mail, incoming and outgoing, was to be screened by the religious superior in charge of the Juniorate, and that Juniors were allowed to visit home only once a year during the first three weeks of August. Furthermore, religious trainees were not permitted to receive gifts from home; of course, this meant no Christmas presents.

The season of Christmas was celebrated at Mont La Salle with elaborate liturgy, including chapel decorations of fragrant evergreen boughs, full-sized trees, and thirty-six-inch wreaths punctuated by bright-red bows. Several dozen large, flaming-red poinsettias were arranged at various heights to create color accents on all sides of the altar, and dwarf-sized statues were used to create the traditional nativity scene built just beyond the altar rail and

FIGURE 6 Chatfield family at Christian Brothers Novitiate robing ceremony, 1952. *Front row (left to right)*: J. H. LaGrande, Adeline LaGrande, Lucille (LaGrande) Chatfield, Ray Chatfield. *Back row (left to right)*: Charles Chatfield, Brother Gilbert. Photographer unknown. Courtesy of the Chatfield family.

in front of the altar itself. The entire monastery chapel seemed to be transformed into a winter wonderland of greenery, decoration, music, and expectation. I had never experienced anything so colorful, dramatic, or exciting.

Certainly, I had celebrated Christmas with my parents and relatives, but with far less pageantry and decoration. I recall a small decorated Christmas tree, a few wrapped gifts on Christmas Eve, the Midnight Mass at Our Lady of Lourdes church, and then on Christmas Day the annual dinner/family reunion held at the home ranch of my grandparents. Whatever else Christmas was, it was first and foremost about family gatherings.

The religious family at Mont La Salle was composed of three groups. The largest was made up of approximately fifty high school teenagers and four faculty members, the next was composed of a couple of dozen post–high school religious trainees called novices, and lastly there was a small community of retired Christian Brothers whom we called ancients. All lived and operated their programs in separate sections of the same monastery complex, but all shared the church-sized, centrally located monastery chapel.

Christmas Eve arrived at Mont La Salle. The Midnight Mass was celebrated with traditional Christmas hymns, Palestrina, and Gregorian chants, with colored spotlights focused on the crèche. Candles and votive lights flickered everywhere, and the Liturgy of the High Mass was sung by the celebrant. The entire chapel was filled with the fragrance of the fresh evergreen trees and the clouds of liturgical incense that floated up to the vaults of the high ceilings. It was such a festive and religious experience that visitors from the surrounding area of Napa filled up the usually vacant pews at the rear of the church. The monastery celebration of the annual Christmas Midnight Mass was an unpublicized Renaissance event reserved for those who care about such pageantry.

After the celebration of the High Mass, the Juniors assembled in their recreation room; by this time, it was almost 2 a.m. Pitchers of hot chocolate were brought from the kitchen, poured into cups, and distributed. Drinking the chocolate, we stood around chatting in informal groups, waiting to be told to go to our dormitory beds to get some sleep before the Christmas morning liturgy the next day.

There was a stir in the room, but before I could figure out what had happened the director, generally aloof and unapproachable, came right up and stood in front of me and with a sort of smile. He said, "LeRoy, Merry Christmas!" and handed me an unwrapped gift. Half-dazed and drowsy from lack of sleep—and a little intimidated—I said, "thank you" as he moved on to the next person. I looked at my present: it was a Pendleton shirt. For my first Christmas away from home, this was the Christmas present from my newly adopted monastic religious family.

More than any other event, I think, this Christmas gift of a Pendleton shirt severed forever my family ties to childhood. Never again would I spend Christmas Eve with them or open their few presents, nor would I be present at the Christmas Day family reunion at the ranch. In fact, I believe the Pendleton shirt colored any future celebration of a family Christmas Eve I might ever enjoy.

4   Observe, Judge, Act

Fifty-six years ago, I was recruited by a very young and pious Christian Brother to become a member of his Catholic Social Action cell. Even at the tender age of fourteen, I knew he was pious because he wore a black skullcap that he constantly repositioned on the top of his head. Apparently, it had to sit just so.

Parenthetically, my young recruiter was also the same person who left religious life years later to become a raging public alcoholic and who was eventually killed in a fiery automobile crash while driving under the influence. I don't believe there is any relationship between the before and after of this man's life, but it does give me pause as I reflect about this accidental pairing of youthful religious idealism and late-middle-age adult despair.

As I remember it, there were six cell members, all of us the same age. We met once a month in the evening in one of the small parlors used by the religious order to receive visitors. For some reason, these meetings, and even the very existence of our cell, seemed secretive and clandestine. This was due, I think, to the palpable intensity generated by our cell leader, and the fact that he spoke deliberately in breathless and hushed tones. At our first meeting, he made it clear that he had handpicked each one of us for cell membership. He had chosen us, we were special, and therefore different—better, I presumed—than the other students in the high school. Why we were thought to be better, I did not know, save for the fact that we had been chosen.

Chatfield graduated from St. Mary's College in 1956 with a bachelor's degree in philosophy. Because the Christian Brothers expected brothers to continue their education, he enrolled in summer sessions at Stanford's Graduate School of Education. While at Stanford, he lived at the Catholic Retreat Center in Menlo Park, whose director, Father Eugene Boyle, was among the best-known activist priests of the 1960s. Father Boyle advocated for civil rights for African Americans and gay and lesbian people; when he provided space in San Francisco's Sacred Heart Church for the breakfast program of the Black Panther Party, he became a target of the FBI's notorious COINTELPRO. He was also one of most prominent clergymen to support the farmworker movement. Father Boyle passed in 2016 at the age of ninety-four.

Many years later, during my first week at Stanford University, I was made to feel this way by professors who reminded the class that we had been chosen to attend the university, not the other way around. We were chosen because we were exceptional students and, therefore, the usual grading standards that applied to other universities were not applicable to us. Mere attendance at class, we were told, was the only requirement for satisfactorily completing the course. Neither as a Stanford student nor as a cell member did I completely embrace the principle that a chosen person is a better person but some of that mindset rubbed off on me, I'm sure.

I cannot recall the agenda of the social action meetings except that we recited in unison a special prayer, which was followed by a presentation given by our cell leader about the need to participate in Catholic Social Action. After his short exhortation, he attempted to lead us in discussion. I say *attempt* because my recollection is that we were so young and naive that we did not know what he was talking about or what kind of participation he expected of us. If he knew, either he couldn't explain it to us or it passed right over the tops of our heads. Saying the prayer in unison and listening to him speak was adequate participation, it seemed.

But clear as crystal now at age seventy, I remember the three principles of Catholic Social Action expounded by this young idealist during our cell meetings: Observe. Judge. Act. If we wanted to be members in good standing with Catholic Social Action, we were duty bound to observe, judge, and act.

Observe what? Judge how? Do what? Certainly, this religious brother, as young and inexperienced as he was, must have explained the use of these principles but I cannot say for sure. I can only speculate that we cell members were to observe the conduct and behavior of other students, judge whether it was right or (presumably) wrong, and then take action to change it. At age fourteen and newly arrived from a small rural town that was surrounded by rice fields, I felt ill equipped to accept the responsibility of changing either my freshman classmates or, God forbid, sophomores.

I faithfully attended all the cell meetings, said the prayer in unison, tried to understand the exhortations of our leader, and eventually the school year came to a close. The following year I entered the religious order of the Christian Brothers and began to make my way through their rigorous monastic religious training program. Just like the rest, I applied myself, I took direction from my superiors, I grew up, I became a high school teacher, and I became a social justice activist. But I tell you that NOTHING in my life since age fourteen has served me better or landed me in more hot water than those damn principles of *observe, judge, act*.

In this period, as the Cold War began, the term Catholic Social Action did not figure prominently in the US Catholic hierarchy, although the National Catholic Welfare Council had included a social teaching component since the early twentieth century. Of course, social justice activism had long been a concern of numerous individual priests and nuns, especially with regard to trade-labor organizing. The Catholic Worker Movement was created by Dorothy Day and Peter Maurin in the 1930s, but Day in particular encountered opposition from church officials during the Cold War period. Chatfield's sense of his being recruited for a clandestine activity may have been related to an emerging climate in which church authorities were wary of any activity that might feed the climate of anticommunism and red baiting. In 1958, however, the church organized the National Catholic Social Action Conference and priests like Monsignor George G. Higgins soon became known as "labor priests." By 1963, when Chatfield attended the National Catholic Social Action Convention in Boston, where he was exposed to Daniel Berrigan and other activist priests, Catholic Social Action departments existed in almost every diocese in the United States.

5 Are You Democrat or Republican?

Are you Democrat or Republican? This was the question posed to me in 1955 by Brother Matthew, a history professor at St. Mary's College who also served as the campus registrar of voters. I knew this was an important question that must be answered but I never had occasion to think much about it. Was I Democrat or Republican? Or something else?

My mother was a Republican, that's for sure. In fact, all my relatives who lived on the ranch in Colusa County were Republicans, but I never heard them talk politics. My father was a Democrat. My uncle Jerome, who was a mechanic at the Buick garage, was a Republican and he and my dad used to argue politics when we visited. I loved to hear them argue back and forth and while I was too young to understand a lot of what they were talking about, I do remember my father getting very worked up on behalf of the common man. My father once assured me that one day, Harry S. Truman would be considered one of the best presidents our country ever had. It didn't occur to me to ask him why, but then this was my dad speaking.

Brother Matthew was a busy man and acted a bit officious; I could sense he was growing impatient waiting for my answer to his important question. Are you Democrat or Republican?

I said, "My father is a Democrat." "Fine," he said, "I'll register you as a Democrat."

I could tell he was pleased.

FIGURE 8 Brother Gilbert with parents at a "Thank You" dinner sponsored by Garces High School students' families, 1964. Photographer unknown. Courtesy of the Chatfield family.

If I have ever voted for a Republican, I do not remember doing so. I think it has something to do with the common man my father was so concerned about.

6 My Journal
Mexico City (Excerpts)

How can I now, looking back thirty-four years, remember the circumstances surrounding my decision to study Spanish in Mexico City during the summer of 1961? I cannot be sure.

I had spent the previous summer of 1960 studying Spanish at the Monterey Institute for Foreign Studies, and later that year I remember applying to the International Institute of Educational Studies for a yearlong grant to study the Mexican school system.

I was twenty-six years old and teaching English at Sacred Heart High School in San Francisco when I decided that I wanted to learn a foreign language and live abroad, maybe as a missionary or just as a graduate student. And yet I knew that because I had no seniority in the Christian Brothers, my chances of being approved for such a study program were minimal. At the same time, I felt that I could package myself in such a way to convince an appropriate organization to give me a scholarship to do just that.

I confided in no one. I filled out the lengthy application forms, wrote the supporting essays, and filed them, supremely confident that I would be accepted for a fellowship grant. And I was accepted, all expenses paid. When I announced this to my superiors, they were nonplussed. I came to them with a financial bird in the hand—a year's study and research in Mexico, all expenses paid. But in their eyes, I did not yet have enough seniority to qualify for advanced study, and I was carrying a full teaching load at Sacred Heart in addition to my extracurricular activities with the students. What were they to do?

As sure as I was of obtaining the fellowship, I was equally sure that I would not be given permission to take advantage of it. But I could sense that my superiors did not want to refuse me outright. After all, I was probably the only brother in the Province that year to qualify for an all-expenses-paid grant for anything. What to do? How to handle this situation? I forget the nuances of the negotiations, but my recollection is that I offered (or perhaps they offered) to exchange this wonderful educational opportunity for a summer of study in Mexico City living in community with the Christian Brothers. A deal was struck and the California Province paid all my expenses for the summer of 1961 in Mexico City.

I can't say what prompted my desire to become a global person. After all, I had never been out of California except when I lived with my parents for a few months in Parker, Arizona, while my father harvested crops at the Japanese concentration camp in Poston. Once or twice I had crossed the Nevada state line to see what a gambling casino looked like. Whatever the driving force, I was determined to break the bonds of being just an American. I wanted to have a foreign cultural experience.

It is interesting that Brother Gilbert's testing of the limits of hierarchy and collective restrictions on the individual in order to venture into the larger world came during the papacy of John XXIII, who was elected in October of 1958. John XXIII, the son of poor farmworkers, was the first pope since the mid-nineteenth century to venture outside of Vatican City. In January of 1959, the pope announced the convening of the Second Vatican Council, which he opened on October 11, 1962, with the speech Gaudet Mater Ecclesia (Mother Church Rejoices). In that speech he declared: "In the present historical moment, Providence is leading us to a new order of human relations that, by the work of humankind itself but also by forces that are beyond human intention, will lead to the fulfillment of higher and unexpected designs." Although he did not live to see the Council's work realized, his framing of the deliberations would have a lasting impact on the church, igniting a new commitment to social activism and so-called liberation theology in Latin America and around the world.

Now, re-reading my journal thirty-four years later, I am struck by my self-confidence and fearlessness in the face of the complete unknown. I did not know a single person in Mexico City; I had only a letter of introduction from Brother Robert of Mary to his "friend," the Master of Novices in Mexico City. I had never taken a long airplane flight before. I had to dress in civilian clothes instead of a religious habit for the first time in nine years and I was not fluent in the language of the country that I wanted to visit. What on earth was I thinking?

With the benefit of hindsight, I believe this decision to seek out a foreign experience was simply my first effort to break the artificial boundaries of religious life, at least as defined by the Christian Brothers. And I was clever enough to manipulate the brothers into granting me legitimate approval to break away, at least for a summer, from the external constraints of my chosen lifestyle.

Somehow, I knew they could not leave me empty handed when I offered them an all-expenses paid fellowship financed by an educational foundation. After all, I had been honored as one of their own—a Christian Brother. How could they not respect the independent judgment of their peers about my worthiness—and by extension their own? I knew they could and would not grant me permission to accept this honor, but I also knew they had to make a counterproposal.

Four years later, I left the Christian Brothers in October of 1965 to join the farmworker movement. I now believe that I took my first step to strike out on my own in 1961. I had willingly, even eagerly, embraced the monastic discipline since 1949 when I entered the Christian Brothers. Now, twelve years later, I began to loosen the bonds. A flood of memories overwhelms me during the process of reading, typing, and editing this Mexico City journal.

Without doubt, the most human experience I had during that summer was my camaraderie with the kitchen sisters. They adopted me as one their own. They looked after me, talked Spanish to me, cooked for me, and nursed me when I was ill. I had never experienced such feminine caregiving. They made me their king for a summer and showered me with affection. I did not expect it, I did not ask for it, but I loved it.

When I left to return to the United States, they presented me with a simple handkerchief with all their names sewn into the fabric. It was such a fitting gift. I kept it as a long-forgotten treasure until just a year or two ago, when I took it out from the box in my dresser to examine it. I could no longer make out their names, or perhaps I had just forgotten them over these past decades. I threw it out.

FIGURE 9

Brother Gilbert with domestic sisters at Colegio Simón Bolívar in Mexico City, 1961. Photographer unknown. Courtesy of the Chatfield family.

I remember the pageantry and the ritual of the bullfights. For some reason, I did not memorialize these adventures in my journal. In all, I attended three or four fights. I still tingle with the feelings of the expectation and the thrill of the crowds as the matador plied his deadly trade. The music, the liturgy, and the ritual of the event were very moving. I felt that something far more important was at stake than simply the killing of a wounded and raging bull.

And the poverty—I had never imagined such poverty. I still remember the young boy sweeping up the rice with his hands on the sidewalk in front of the church after a wedding—food for home. Or looking through the marvelous wrought iron gates of the hacienda (now a resort) and seeing women and children in abject poverty looking back at me. They were not begging but staring in wonderment about our mutual fate in life. This Mexican poverty was such a shock for a religious brother like myself, who had taken a vow of poverty and yet possessed everything I had ever wanted. This poverty seared my conscience and I have never forgotten it.

And finally, I remember the greatest meal I ever had. After we crossed the border at Mexicali on our reentry into the United States, we stopped at a diner and I had the biggest, and the best, milkshake of my entire life.

June 15, 1961

Departure as planned, more or less. And so it is with all plans, more or less. My first Spanish word, *quince*. That is my seat number. When the stewardess gave me an English newspaper I bravely said, "En español." She answered in Spanish that she didn't have one right then. Already a failure. Oh well.

There is something nonchalant—and proudly so—about being a world traveler, especially a loner like myself. You casually take everything in stride, watching the others around you scurrying, complaining, edging for first place, and fanning themselves, or whatever. But we professional travelers just watch the world go by, aloof and undisturbed.

LA international airport was confusion supreme. No one seemed to know where to go or where to sit. One PanAm clerk checking in Mexico City passengers knew absolutely no Spanish and very little about his job. Perhaps he was hired just for the day.

Ordered a bourbon and ice on the plane. I have an idea the steward is accepting only American money. "That will be 80 cents," he said in perfect English. I will break through the dollar barrier here pretty soon, I guess. My change was two pesos. I feel more Mexican already.

Just caught bits and pieces of a conversation comparing Los Angeles, San Francisco, and Chicago to Mexico City. The United States was the loser. Singing, dancing, gayety, and nightclubs took it on the chin. It seemed to me (remember this was all in Spanish) that Los Angeles took it the worst. Except for the beaches in San Francisco, "frio y sucio."

June 16, 1961

This morning I tore myself away from the security of the Continental Hilton and walked out into Mexico City. To Sanborns for breakfast. All world travelers meet at Sanborns. I had bacon, eggs, and coffee. Then I walked at a leisurely pace toward the Zócalo. There was a church at Madero and Isabel la Católica so I stopped to attend Mass. The name of the church is La Profesa Católica [also known as El Templo de San Felipe Neri]. While Mass was being said, workmen were high aloft making repairs. There were very few people at this 9:00 a.m. Mass. No Communion given that I could see. A collection was taken up during the service.

I walked through a rain shower to the Zócalo, where a solemn High Mass was underway in the Cathedral. There is a large organ here and a choir of young boys, or so it sounds to me. And here too, in the nooks and crannies of the church, repair work is ongoing. Sawing, scraping, chiseling, and nailing. The work will probably take several generations to complete but the sooner we get started, the sooner we will finish seems to be the prevailing attitude. The architecture of both churches is Roman with the use of much wood for decorative purposes, along with gold-colored altars and pillars. During the Offertory, the organist played a selection from Bach. It sounded somewhat muddled but the baroque classical sound was very pleasing and reassuring to me. The choir just filed out close by where I am sitting, jotting down these notes. All are clad in white and red leggings but as boys will, pushing, shoving, grinning, and whispering. I ventured a "Qué tal" to one but he said "no." I wonder what he meant by that. Many women in the Cathedral walk from statue to statue.

At La Profesa I saw an old man, his sombrero at his side, dressed in a ragged and dirty fashion, weeping at a shrine of Our Lady. Here at the Cathedral, priests sit in the open confessional waiting for someone to come up and make their confession. And does it really matter whether others, who are standing around, hear you or not? After all, did we not offend them too? I notice that many of the men here use such tokens of worship as the Sign of the Cross and money for prayer offerings, but it is the women who actually kneel down and say prayers. This is probably a very hasty conclusion but it seems so to me.

My visit to the top of the Latin American Tower last night was most disheartening. Some of the ice breaks around the world traveler, I guess. But consider this: alone in a strange country and trapped as a victim in a commercial enterprise. How that irritates me. People running around waiting on you, taking advantage of you, liking you for money. And the irony of the situation is that all of it is being done in perfect English. I have been here eighteen hours and have not needed to speak Spanish at all. Just money, just being a tourist. It is not their fault entirely, it is ours too. We have reaped what we have sown. But I do not believe this is the real Mexico, the real people, or the real country.

June 19, 1961

Adventure. So many exciting things happened today that it is difficult to get them all down. I was so tired last night and getting up at 4:30 a.m. is so dreadful that I slept straight through (pillow and mattress of straw notwithstanding) the religious exercises. After breakfast I kicked around for a while and finally settled down in the common room to write a few postcards. The common room here is no larger than the size of two small bedrooms at Sacred Heart High School in San Francisco. Just as I was getting settled, one of the domestic sisters came in to clean up the chapel that adjoins the common room. Her name is Plácida Ortiz. She was assigned for two and one-half years at a Christian Brothers School in Minnesota and speaks English well enough to get along. We talked. She worked and then we talked some more, all in Spanish.

After she left I decided to visit one of the primary classes. My choice was sexto C. The brother teaching the class gave a lesson reviewing verbs—for my benefit, I suspect—but I was grateful because it proved to be helpful. Then to prayers, to eat, and to the schoolyard to talk with the boys until about 2:30. School starts here at 8:00 a.m. and lasts until 11:30 a.m. It takes up again at 2:30 p.m. and lasts until 4:40 p.m. There is one recess in the morning and one in the afternoon. These hours might seem long, but you would be surprised how relaxing it is to teach school under these circumstances. "Leisurely" is the only word I can think of right now to describe it. At 2:30 p.m. when the boys went back to class, I thought it best to walk outside and find a place to buy stamps. I stopped in the kitchen first to get a drink of water. And the floodgates opened! I asked one sister whom I saw working in the dining room for a glass of water and off she ran but came back with another sister and then another and yet another and so we started to talk. The superior herself came and what a good time we had. They trying to make me understand and I trying like the devil to do so, if only for their sakes. After they finished working, they took me to their motherhouse that was just around the corner at Calle Asturias #28. I was shown the whole place from top to bottom and met all the sisters. I left them about 4:30 p.m. and came back through the yard to the common room but I was waylaid by some of the students who wanted to talk some more. If I could keep up this talking for a week or two, I would soon be a native speaker. But it is very tiring to think in English, translate what you want to say into the few words of Spanish you know how to say, and then translate their responses back into English.

But more about those sisters. About fifteen years ago, Brother Antonio Maria, the assistant at that time, founded their order. They are domestic sisters and their work is to help the work of the brothers by cooking, doing the laundry, and the cleaning. A girl enters at the age of sixteen, has one-half year of postulancy, a year of novitiate, and then a year (or perhaps more) of scholasticate. Until now, they are able to take only annual vows because Rome has not as yet officially approved them. They are called Sisters of the Christian Schools of St. John Baptist de la Salle. Young and bouncy and work like slaves, believe me. The brothers donated their motherhouse and, according to the architectural custom here in Mexico, it is built from the outside in. The front walls are three stories high. The first floor contains the parlors and the sewing room. The second and third floors are for the novices and postulants. The spacious gardens are filled with flowers and caged birds. There are a parrot and two shaggy brown dogs the size of small horses. Their open kitchen reminded me of a sort of washhouse that I have seen on a ranch somewhere. There are three dining rooms that open out onto the backyard. Some of these openings are natural but others are more like windows without panes or doorways without doors.

These sisters of mine are poor indeed but very happy too. And they chatter like the birds in the garden. During my tour I tried to avoid being stepped on by the animals they call dogs but those little nuns just ordered those brutes around with a word or two. The weak shall confound the strong. The superior's name is Salud del Niño Jesus, which means Health of the Baby Jesus—a beautiful name.

June 20, 1961

Took a nap after breakfast this morning only to be rudely awakened by a revolution, or so it sounded. It was only the band called La Banda Guerra practicing outside my window three stories down below in the playground. It was a stirring march the drummers were beating out. So much so that I got up to watch them. Read the paper. Wrote two postcards. Watched the semester exams in calisthenics from the balcony. Every boy who did not have a uniform consisting of a blue T-shirt, white pants, and tennis shoes had to sit on the benches at the side of the yard and received an automatic failure. During the recess I stayed up on the balcony because I had learned that if I went out into the yard among the boys, I would get mobbed. These kids just love affection and want to be near the brothers. I have seen them run from afar just to shake hands with a brother or to hold his hand while they are walking from one place to another. In fact, when they come up to me they shake my hand, say good morning or good afternoon, depending upon the time of day, and when they are ready to leave, shake my hand again and say, "con su permiso" or "buenos," and off they go. If I ask a boy

FIGURE 10 *Nuestra Señora Virgen de Guadalupe*. Basilica, Mexico City. Public domain.

his name he says, for example Carlos Ortiz, "a sus órdenes" (at your service) or Roberto Romero "para servirle" (at your service). If they are nothing else, they are politeness personified. This salutation would be very strange for American boys, wouldn't you say?

At 11:00 a.m., I went to the kitchen and that was my undoing. The sisters were waiting for me, sat me down with a cup of coffee and some pears, and away we went. Talk, talk, and talk. Some would leave but would soon return and listen or talk some more. And we all laughed and had a grand time. The cook's name is Sister Basilia Pérez. Another is named Marta Eugenia. They are going to ask the superior general when she returns if I can teach them English at the convent. And wouldn't that be fun. Two brothers, exiled from Cuba, were here today and their Spanish was very poor, or so it seemed to me. They spoke so fast, they chopped off all their endings. It isn't as musical sounding to me as the Spanish I hear in Mexico City. They told me that unless Castro is overthrown in six months, all of South America would be lost to communism.

July 15, 1961

Thirty days ago, I arrived here, in the land of la Virgen. And today I am in her house here at Guadalupe. Are there ten thousand flowers or one hundred thousand? Pilgrims in an out with candles, on their knees, some well dressed, some poor and some very, very, poor. And la Virgen? Looking out from her shrine of gold and silver and more gold again, she is beautiful. But these precious metals do not compare with her simplicity. Her delicate choice of colors and dress. Just fabulous. Have just finished High Mass and at least two other Masses are now in progress and in yet another adjacent chapel, lined with gold, Communion is distributed. The Bishop sits in the chantry behind the altar as his choir sings. A Mexican peasant kneels next to me dressed in sandals, white shirt, and hat; he is clutching five pesos in his hand to purchase a candle and make his offering.

Some five years after this moment, Chatfield would commit himself to the farmworker movement in California, a movement that adopted la Virgen de Guadalupe as its iconic standard-bearer.

The woman on the sidewalk, perhaps thirty years old, a mile away from the Basilica, is moving step by step on her knees supported on either side by servants or friends and accompanied by a man laying out serapes in front of her. Another man is just starting his journey.

July 22, 1961

I am reading *The Diary of Anne Frank* in Spanish. It still holds me spellbound. Her acute observations of self-certainty strike a familiar chord.

July 30, 1961

With every ill wind blows some good. Trapped in this paradise with English, we left this morning to hunt for a church for Fathers Kohles and Poget to say their Masses. That took us to Xox, a pueblo of ten thousand souls surrounding a very old church that was small, clean, and garishly decorated with statues, crucifixes, animals, fresh flowers, lighted candles, and artificial flowers.

This village, seemingly without any role, surrounded by mud and rock walls, full of small, squat adobe huts, sported a plaza in front of the church complete with a basketball court. Most of the villagers were barefoot or wore poorly made sandals. What is the future for these people and this village?

Is this not the Mexican problem? Just because these inhabitants might not now know the difference, it won't be long before their self-contained life of birth, marriage, and death will no longer be enough to offset the influences and the lure of the cities. In their desire to break with the past they will dismiss the role of the church that not only does not preach social justice but also is the symbol of the status quo and the establishment. Just as an adolescent must rebel against authority, I believe that these villagers must someday strike out against their impoverished conditions.

PART TWO
WITH THE FARMWORKERS

7   Bakersfield to Boston
to Delano, 1963

Forty-one years ago, I traveled from Bakersfield to Boston to attend the National Catholic Social Action Convention. While attending one of the sessions, I heard a panel speaker, Father Phil Berrigan (if I am not mistaken), mention that a man by the name of Cesar Chavez was organizing farmworkers in Delano, California. I sat there dumbfounded. I had traveled three thousand miles to learn that something as important as organizing farmworkers was taking place just thirty miles from where I lived and worked.

When I returned to Bakersfield in September, I tried to get in touch with Cesar Chavez, but he was not listed in the phone book and none of my circle of activists—fellow high school teachers and community leaders—had heard of him. I tracked down the convention panelist and asked him how to get in touch with this Cesar Chavez. All he could tell me was that Chavez had a brother by the name of Richard who lived in Delano and maybe he could assist me. Sensing my skepticism, he reassured me that Chavez was organizing farmworkers in the fields in the Delano area. Indeed, there was a Richard Chavez listed in the Delano telephone directory. I called him and he said he would relay my message to his brother. Several weeks passed and Cesar Chavez finally called back. I introduced myself, told him I was interested in his work, that I would like to learn more, and could I come and meet him?

Chavez was soft spoken and sounded a little cautious. He asked me some questions about my interest and how I knew about him, but he finally invited me to come visit and gave me directions. That is how I found my way to 102 Albany Street, the headquarters of the National Farm Workers Association (NFWA) in Delano, California.

The building was located on the last southwest corner of Delano. There were open lands to the west and to the south. They were desolate-looking fields, as I remember them, with little agricultural value because of the lack of irrigation water on the west side of Highway 99. The association head-quarters was a converted church building that Chavez had painted and remodeled on the inside so that when you walked in the front door, his office was behind a counter on the left and straight ahead was another counter made to look like a bank teller's window. Behind that counter were an all-purpose work area and a small closet-like office that in a few years would become the offices of *El Malcriado*, Cesar's organizing newspaper— his pride and joy! There was a toilet at the rear of the building and another storeroom, as I recall. Aside from the building on this very small lot, not a piece of landscaping could be found. It was quite barren. I had never realized how desolate the Central Valley could be until I found the west side of Highway 99.

Chavez was very friendly and greeted me. We talked for a long time; he told me about his organizing work. He had moved to Delano because he had a brother living there who was a carpenter. His wife, Helen, had a sister and many relatives and friends there. This would give them and their eight children the support base they needed. And besides, it was all he could afford. He knew that if he were going to do this kind of work, he would earn almost nothing, so with many relatives in the area he figured his family would not starve. He was building what he called the National Farm Workers Association. He did not dare call it a union because the powerful agricultural interests, with their control of the surrounding towns—McFarland, Richgrove, Earlimart, Shafter, Wasco, and Corcoran—would run him out of the area. His cover was that he was a well-meaning Mexican American do-gooder who was helping his own people. (I'm pretty sure that my memory is correct about this: in 1963 we were Mexican American; it wasn't until a few years later that we became Chicanos, and then later still, we became Hispanics, and now some of us might be called Latinos. Though it is possible at that point in 1963, we were still just Mexicans.)

Who was eligible to join the National Farm Workers Association? The basic requirement was that you had to be a farmworker. This was later amended to include such fellow travelers as myself. And what benefits did farmworkers receive as a result of their membership? There were four, I think. First, you received a wallet-sized card that certified you were a member in good standing. This card had a red band at the top with a white thunderbird eagle, and it was signed by Cesar E. Chavez, General Director, and Anthony Orendain, Secretary-Treasurer. Second, you paid monthly dues that I believe were $3.50 a month. Third, you received a small death benefit when you died, perhaps as much as $500. This would ensure that your burial expenses would not be a burden to your family. And fourth, the most important of all, you were invested in the dream that someday, perhaps not in your lifetime but in the lifetime of your children, you would have a union strong enough to negotiate with the growers for better wages; access to bathrooms in the fields; drinking water available on the job; rest breaks; an end to stoop labor with the short-handled hoe; and medical, pension, and unemployment benefits. (You must remember that since the 1930s, farmworkers were specifically excluded from all labor legislation, including coverage under the National Labor Relations Act, the labor law that protected all other workers in the United States.)

I told Chavez that as a teacher I thought education was the answer to

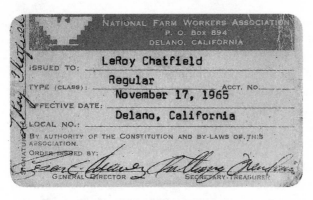

FIGURE 12 LeRoy Chatfield National Farm Worker
Association membership card. Courtesy of LeRoy Chatfield.

improving the lives of farmworkers. He disagreed. He said that he himself
had attended twenty-eight elementary schools because he had to work in
the fields and follow the harvest of the crops to help support the family.
Farmworker families, he said, had to have some stability before their children could take advantage of education. He maintained that a farmworker
union was the first step in this process. In truth, this corresponded with my
own teaching experience in San Francisco, where I had taught for many
years. Most of my students did come from families whose fathers were
members of unions—longshoremen, building trades, teamsters, retail clerks,
and firefighters.

I asked him why he didn't have a telephone in his office. First of all, he
said, he couldn't afford it, and secondly, who would call him? Farmworkers
didn't have telephones either. If someone wanted to speak to him, they
would find him. After all, hadn't I found him, and wasn't I here in his office
talking with him? Thus began my ten-year friendship with Cesar Chavez
and his farmworker movement.

In his series of responses to questions from scholar Paul Henggeler from
2002 to 2003, Chatfield recalled:

> When I met Cesar in 1963, two years before the table grape strike, I was
> a member of the Christian Brothers, a three-hundred-year-old Roman
> Catholic religious order of French origin, dedicated to teaching poor kids.
> Unfortunately, the Christian Brothers had long since abandoned their
> commitment to the poor by the time I entered the order in 1949, but it was

still part of their historical mission statement. Cesar asked me personally to leave my career in the Christian Brothers to join him. For nearly ten years, Cesar was my best friend. I could talk to him about anything: personal family matters, movement strategy, staff evaluations and gossip, Oakland Raider football, election politics, religious politics, union politics, nonviolence, etc. Several times, especially in the early years, Cesar's wife, Helen, would call to ask me to speak to Cesar about this or that because "he will listen to you." I also think Cesar needed someone to talk with, someone who would respect the confidence of the conversation, no matter how far out it might sound to others. Cesar himself was religious, and very Catholic. He had been much influenced by a few Catholic priests from the San Francisco Archdiocese during his Community Service Organization (CSO) years working with Mexican American communities. These priests were part of what was called the "Mission Band," and they preached the social justice teachings of the Catholic Church. In effect, they provided the religious and theological context for the community-based work that Cesar was doing with Mexican Americans. I believe one of the reasons that Cesar and I worked so well together was because we shared the same religious references. (LC/PH)

8 Brother Gilbert's Appeal Letter, 1965

My dear friends,

This is rather a difficult letter to write but one that I feel obligated to send because of your interest and kindness to me in the past.

Very simply put: I am withdrawing (voluntarily) from the Christian Brothers in order to work full time for the National Farm Workers Association—a grassroots movement begun in Delano, California, by Cesar Chavez to organize farmworker families in California. For my non-Catholic friends: my withdrawing from the Christian Brothers does not mean that I have to leave or that I intend to leave the Catholic Church. I will once again assume the position proper to that of a "layman," i.e., a member of the church but without the religious vows of poverty, chastity, and obedience.

My reasons for such a decision are really not very profound or complex. I just feel that I can no longer work on behalf of social justice at the level of abstraction that my life as a religious teaching brother seems to indicate. Then too, my ever-increasing involvement and identification with the poor only continues to widen the gap between my obedience to religious authority and my own understanding of what my life as a Christian must entail. Actually, the decision to make a decision was probably the most difficult part.

I must emphasize that it is not with an attitude of bitterness or hostility that I leave the Brothers. Quite the contrary! I will always be most grateful to them for the opportunities that I had to work with young men and women—that experience alone has been worth a lifetime to me. Then too, many of my closest friends are Brothers and will continue to remain so. In short, whatever "levels of consciousness" I have attained is due in large measure to my having been a Christian Brother.

As I have indicated, I will be working for the NFWA at a salary of $20 a month. I will serve as the Director of Co-op Development. Our idea is to build a complex of cooperatives (clinic, pharmacy, credit union, garage, etc.) somewhere in the valley—but this complex would be owned and controlled by farmworkers themselves. Since almost all of these families make less than $3,000 a year, this idea presents some unique difficulties that must be overcome. My job—as I see it—is to attempt to organize these co-ops by setting up their overall economic and legal structures and to recruit professional men and women (doctors, lawyers, pharmacists, accountants, teachers, etc.) who will give us one or two years of their lives to work for the poor through the co-op at prices that farmworkers can honestly afford to pay. We look upon this as a prerequisite for serious grassroots organizing.

I estimate that it will take two years to organize such a co-op—granting of course that it can be done! Since at the age of thirty-one I begin from "scratch" without financial resources, I will have to live in a kind of voluntary poverty for the next two years at least. By voluntary poverty I mean that I will have to live on $100 a month and buy (and support) a Volkswagen. Since the NFWA can only afford to salary me at $20 a month at this time, I am going to have to be dependent upon friends who believe in me enough to pledge, let's say, $5 a month for a year to support my efforts at organizing.

Honestly! This is not a letter of appeal. God knows you have received enough of them from me in the past. I don't want you to do anything for me or for the cause I believe in unless you really want to. I realize that what I propose to do will strike some of you as "crazy" or "naive" or "nuts" and maybe in two years' time I will agree with you. But right now I am convinced that Cesar Chavez and the NFWA represents a true anti-poverty program that respects the dignity and integrity of the people involved.

For those of you who want to know what you can do, consider the following:

1. Keep me free to organize by contributing small amounts each month for my support.
2. Make a small contribution toward the purchase and support of a VW.
3. Let me know if I am welcome to stay with you for a day or two when I am in your area. Believe me, I won't overstay.

4. Put me in contact with professional persons or persons with specialized talents who might want to work in a co-op situation at the grassroots level. Warning: This work will entail a kind of voluntary poverty and the living conditions will be very basic.
5. Arrange for me to speak to potentially interested groups about the NFWA and our co-op movement.
6. Refer me to existing co-ops that you are personally acquainted with so that I can visit and learn more about them.

Thank you, thank you, for all you have done for me in the past. I hope that you will look with understanding on what I feel that I have to do to close one chapter in my life and begin another.

Love,
LeRoy Chatfield
(Formerly: Brother Gilbert, FSC)

Two months after the farmworkers declared a strike against table grape growers, Chatfield began his decade-long commitment to the movement. His first assignment was not what he expected:

Shortly after my Delano visit, Cesar called me in Los Angeles and asked if I would come to Delano to work with him in the farmworker strike. His telephone call made a profound impression on me, I decided to leave USC and resign from the Christian Brothers in order to work with him. Much to my surprise he asked me not to involve myself directly with the grape strike but to raise funds to begin a farmworker cooperative. The NFWA already had its own credit union, of which Cesar was very proud. He positively glowed when he talked about it, but he also envisioned a cooperative gas station where farmworkers could purchase gasoline less expensively, and service and repair their cars with tools and expertise provided by the cooperative. He explained to me the importance of the automobile to the economic well-being of a farmworker family, and how beneficial it would be for union members to have such a cooperative. He was also mindful that such a cooperative would be yet another "organizing benefit" to attract nonunion farmworkers. He did not tell me what to do or how to do it; he set no timetable or deadlines; I was completely on my own. However, the goal was clear: raise funds to organize a farmworker gas station cooperative. Cesar did not expect me to know anything about cooperatives, and I did not, but he did expect me to find out what I needed to know, and then make it happen. (LC/PH)

The genealogy of the farmworker movement was long and complex. One of the volunteers who arrived in Delano the summer before the strike was Doug Adair, who later recalled:

There were many, many old timers in Delano in 1965, including virtually all the Filipinos, who had been through struggles in the '30s and '40s and '50s, and the generation of Cesar and Gil Padilla and Tony Orendain and the Hernandezes was very aware of the failures, as well as successes. They had been children but had family who had participated. Fina Hernandez told stories of the Cotton Pickers' encampment at Corcoran, 30,000 workers on strike [in 1933], a peasants' armed militia guarding the stockade, closed at night to protect against the night riders.

The other roots of the movement were in Mexico, and I remember Tony, especially, but others, too, who had a deep knowledge of the Mexican Revolution, and its successes and failures. I would guess that if there had been a poll of the workers voting to strike in Delano on September 16, 1965, an overwhelming majority would have endorsed Zapata's vision, that the land, like the air and the water, belonged to the people.

The ideology I picked up in Peoples' Cafe was that society was based on the workers who planted the seeds and pruned the vines and harvested the fruit, that bringing justice and respect to that labor was the priority of our struggle, and we judged folks, movements, and systems on how they fared in that struggle. (FMDP, December 4, 2004)

The growers have the money but . . .
the farmworkers have the time.
Cesar Chavez

9   The Delano Grape Strike

From 1962 to 1993, more than 2,200 people—all ages, all walks of life, and from all parts of North America—signed up as full-time volunteers to help Cesar Chavez and his farmworker movement. Tens of thousands of part-time volunteers in US and Canadian cities participated in Chavez's grape boycott by picketing supermarkets that sold California grapes, attending marches and demonstrations to publicize the boycott, raising funds to support his movement, and most importantly not purchasing California table grapes.

What kind of person, what kind of cause, could be so compelling as to attract thousands of volunteers and boycott supporters?

After I met Cesar Chavez in 1963, I became one of those full-time volunteers, who walked away from a religious vocation and an eight-year high school teaching career, left my place of residence, and relocated to Delano, California, to join Chavez and his farmworker movement.

THE CAUSE

By the 1960s, the plight of California farmworkers had been well documented: there was Carey McWilliams's book *Factories in the Fields* (1939), Dorothea Lange's work as a photojournalist during the Great Depression for the Farm Security Administration (1935–1940), and John Steinbeck's best-selling novel *The Grapes of Wrath* (1939), followed by director John

Ford's Academy Award–winning movie based on Steinbeck's novel that starred Henry Fonda (1940). Moreover, Edward R. Murrow's Peabody Award–winning national television documentary *Harvest of Shame* (1960) about the plight of US farmworkers was viewed by millions of Americans, and Dr. Ernesto Galarza published his comprehensive study *Merchants of Labor: The Mexican Bracero Story* (1964) about the US emergency wartime use of 4.6 million Mexican citizens to provide cheap field labor to US agribusiness from 1942 to 1964.

Much was known about the plight and suffering of farmworkers—pitifully low wages, a cruel piece-rate wage system designed to push and maximize worker production, hours of nonstop back-breaking stoop labor, no access to drinking water or toilets, no paid work breaks, the financial necessity of having to bring children to work in the fields to earn additional money for the family, and living six months of the year as migrant workers as they worked their way north following the crop harvest seasons. They lived in farm labor camps in one-room shacks with no running water, one electric outlet in the ceiling for a light bulb, a gas line hookup for a two-burner stove, a few water spigots located in the camp for fresh water, and a dozen stall showers and outhouses to serve the toilet needs for several hundred people.

With such god-awful working conditions and pitiful wages provided to so many millions of farmworkers for more than half a century, why could not something more humane have been done to "better" their wages and working conditions? What most Americans, like myself, did not know in the 1960s was that, indeed, "something had been done" to ensure that farmworkers could *not* "better" themselves.

In 1935, Congress passed the National Labor Relations Act—federal legislation that guaranteed the right of US workers to organize into unions and bargain collectively with their employers about wages and working conditions. After signing the National Labor Relations Act, President Franklin Roosevelt is quoted as saying, "If I went to work in a factory, the first thing I'd do is join a union!"

The shocking irony of President Roosevelt's pro-union statement was that this new federal law he had just signed specifically excluded millions of farmworkers (read: Filipinos, Mexican Americans, and African Americans) and domestic workers (read: Filipinos, Mexican Americans, and African Americans). With a stroke of Roosevelt's pen, the nation's farmworkers were relegated to second-class citizenship and became forever an underclass of cheap and exploited immigrant labor. Farmworkers were powerless to

FIGURE 13 Huelga flag flying at the NFWA headquarters at the corner of Albany Street and First Avenue, Delano, California. Photo by Mark Jonathan Harris. Courtesy of Mark Jonathan Harris.

negotiate with their agribusiness employers and their employment status was reduced to little more than that of a tool for the agricultural industry to use or dispose of as they saw fit. Farmworkers in the United States were barely a cut above slaves or indentured workers. They were powerless.

Powerless, that is, until Cesar Chavez arrived on the scene in 1962 and began his National Farm Workers Association in Delano, California, at 102 Albany Street, which was located on the last southwest corner of Delano in a small, converted church building.

FAILED UNION ATTEMPTS TO ORGANIZE

Despite being excluded from federal legislation that protected the rights of US workers to organize into unions, there were many attempts in the 1950s and early '60s by organized labor to unionize California farmworkers. The primary catalyst for these organizing efforts was the use of harvest-time strikes to increase wages and establish a union, but each and every organizing effort was systematically crushed by agribusiness that used its powerful influence in the rural communities where its farms were located.

The police and sheriff departments were quick to arrest strikers and union organizers for any alleged violations of the law, corporate lawyers petitioned the local courts to grant injunctions against picketing and other strike activities, district attorneys were quick to file charges with the court about alleged violations of these highly restrictive and probably unconstitutional injunctions, and judges wasted little time making their rulings— guilty as charged—and sentencing the violators to jail. Likewise, the local community newspaper fanned the fears of violence and civil disorder by raising the specter of the presence of "outside agitators" and "communists" as the cause of the labor unrest in the community. If the police and the courts were not enough to break the farmworkers' strike, the corporate growers would bus in strikebreakers from as far away as the Mexican border to work the harvest. This was the final blow. Yet another chapter was written in the agonizing history of failed attempts to organize farmworkers into a union.

THE COMMUNITY ORGANIZER

In 1962, when Cesar Chavez arrived in Delano to begin his crusade to organize farmworkers, he came with a plan. First of all, he did not believe farmworkers were powerless; they just had a different kind of power than their employers. He often said: "There are two kinds of currencies: time and money. The growers have the money but they do not have the time. Farmworkers have the time but they do not have the money. Each side uses its own currency."

One time during my early years working with Chavez, I asked, "Cesar, how long do you think it will be before we win a contract in the table grapes?" He was silent for a minute, then said, "I had planned on it being about twenty years." I never again asked him that question. We did not have the money but we had the time.

Chavez came to Delano not to organize workers to call a strike at harvest time with the hope of securing a union contract, but rather to organize farmworkers and their families into a community organization, which he called the National Farm Workers Association. "LeRoy," he would say, "if I called the NFWA a union, the growers would run me out of town. We are a service agency to help farmworkers with their day-to-day problems—getting a driver's license, a meeting with the social worker at the welfare department, filling out and filing their annual tax forms, translating and explaining letters received from a government agency and writing an answer back for them, helping them to mediate a student issue with a school administrator, or any other issue they needed assistance with."

In addition to his NFWA Service Center, his wife, Helen Chavez, administered the state-approved farmworker credit union she and Cesar had organized. Members of the NFWA also received a $500 death-benefit insurance policy to ensure that a family member could be given a proper funeral and burial service. But to receive these services and other benefits of the NFWA, farmworkers had to be members in good standing, which meant their dues of $3.50 a month needed to be paid up. The NFWA created by Chavez was a membership organization for farmworkers, not a charity. This fledgling farmworker community organization became the base to build enough power to challenge their agribusiness employers, to demand they recognize their union, and to bargain collectively about wages and working conditions. Yes, it meant the grower employers would have to share their power. A tall order, and a mountain to climb, but this was the goal set by Cesar Estrada Chavez, and he would commit his life to achieve it.

FILIPINO FARMWORKERS

Despite the fact that I had been raised as a child in a very small rural community in Northern California and that my mother's family was heavily engaged in rice production—or even the fact that my father for a time managed a rice ranch for an absentee San Francisco investor and at another time owned his own crop-harvesting business—I did not know much about the role of farm labor in large-scale California agriculture. The only contact I had with farmworkers was the handful of young braceros—government contract workers imported from Mexico during World II and the postwar era—who lived in a bunkhouse on the ranch my father managed. They were nice guys, full of energy, and they loved kids.

When I came to Delano, California, in 1965 to join the farmworker movement, I soon learned the shocking history of Filipino farmworkers, best summarized by *New York Times* reporter Jason DeParle: "They are among the last of the 'manongs,' the approximately 100,000 Filipino men who flocked to America in the years before the Depression seeking education and wealth but finding instead impoverished lives of stoop labor and racial codes that forbade them to own land or marry."[1]

Forbidden to marry. Without doubt, this has to be one of the saddest chapters in the long and cruel history of California agribusiness's recruiting and using cheap immigrant labor. Forbidden to be husbands, forbidden to be fathers of a family, forbidden to enjoy the love and respect of their grandchildren. They were free to work in the fields, to enjoy a life of bachelorhood and profound loneliness.

Forbidden to own land. You are not from here; you cannot stay here; you must leave here when your harvest job is finished; you are not welcome to stay here. You must come back next year to work in the fields.

On occasion, when I brought up the subject of the subjugation of the Filipinos, Chavez—a husband and father of eight children—would tear up and was barely able to keep his composure. He vowed that someday his farmworker movement would build a retirement center where the elderly "Filipino brothers" could live out their days in peace and tranquility. True to his word, the Agbayani Retirement Village was dedicated on the union's Forty Acres in Delano in 1974.

The key to the survival of Filipino farmworkers in California was cooperative living and working together to lower the cost of their living expenses. According to their own personal likes and dislikes, they formed their own migrant worker crews and selected their own crew chiefs they wanted to work for. They traveled and worked together as an organized unit following the California harvests and pruning seasons. They owned and maintained automobiles together and lived in remote employer-owned labor-camp shacks, separate and apart from the local communities where the farms were located. They shared the costs of maintaining a common kitchen facility in the labor camp and in the case of Delano, they were welcome at the Filipino Community Hall for social events, meetings, and entertainment. Because they worked in preorganized crews together for years at a time, they developed special expertise and efficiencies that matched up well with the cruel and competitive piece-rate wage system—the faster you work, the more you earn. Filipino farmworker crews were especially known throughout the California table grape industry for the quality of their table grape field pack.

Every payday, Filipino farmworkers religiously sent money back home to family members to support living parents and to pay for the education of nephews and nieces. For example, Philip Vera Cruz, a farmworker friend and colleague of mine during my years with Cesar Chavez and his movement, told me he sent back enough money to pay for an entire law library for one of his nephews who was opening a law practice. "LeRoy, it cost me a lot of money, but I think it was worth it." All totaled, the amount of remittance money sent back home by Filipino farmworkers is measured in the billions of dollars.

The last thing in the world Cesar Chavez wanted in 1965 was a harvest strike in the Delano table grape harvest. He was only in his third year of building the community-based National Farm Workers Association and he was not ready to confront California agribusiness with a strike for union recognition. These strikes are horribly expensive to maintain—strikers had to be fed and housed, minimal strike benefits had to be paid, picket lines had to be manned, union staff supported, and strike headquarters rented, not to mention the transportation, legal, and myriad other costs to be met. The NFWA in 1965 simply did not have the financial resources to stay the course long enough to achieve union recognition from agribusiness employers and an agreement to bargain collectively about wages and working conditions. Anyone could predict the outcome—simply another failed attempt in the long history of California's failed attempts to organize farmworkers.

Wildcat harvest-day strikes are different and sometimes can be successful because union recognition is not the issue—the only issue is the per-hour wage and the per-box bonus the employer is willing to pay. Sometimes a wildcat strike lasting a few days at the beginning of the table grape harvest will bump up the per-hour wage and the per-box bonus rate, especially if the retail markets are favorable—but oftentimes the wildcat demands were not met, leaving the workers with little choice but to eat it or leave the harvest area and look for work elsewhere.

In 1965, after a ten-day harvest strike in the Coachella Valley—including incidents of the type of violence generally associated with labor strikes—the growers agreed to raise the hourly rate for picking and packing table grapes from $1.20 to $1.40 an hour and raise the per-box bonus to 25 cents, up from 10 cents. The growers would not agree to union recognition or sign a union contract, and the organizers of the strike, the Agricultural Workers Organizing Committee (AWOC, AFL-CIO), paid for the property damage caused by the strike.

Because of the affiliation with the AFL-CIO and its vast bureaucracy, AWOC's ability to act was limited. Chatfield recalls an incident that was illustrative of the problem:

Cesar Chavez and I were present at a meeting in Stockton, California, with Al Green, the regional director of AWOC, and Larry Itliong, the AWOC strike director, along with a handful of other AFL-CIO organizing staff members. Ostensibly, the purpose of the meeting was to better coordinate the strike tactics used by the NFWA and the AWOC in the Delano grape strike, and to work out strategy differences between the two groups. Cesar and I barely said a word. After the introductions were made, Larry continued his strident advocacy for the use of tougher strike tactics in the Delano grape strike, but seconds later, the AFL-CIO attorney shut Larry up, and began to lecture him about federal labor law, the threat of employer injunctions and lawsuits, and the legal risks that might be incurred by AFL-CIO-affiliated unions. . . . he ordered Larry around as if he were a rebellious teenager and spoke to him in the most condescending manner possible. Larry said nothing. The labor attorney summed up his final orders to AWOC and hung up. The meeting was over. (FMDP, 2009)

Chavez would never allow himself to be treated in such a manner, and he and his associates would refuse to accept the kind of limitations imposed by the AFL-CIO upon the mainly Filipino AWOC leadership.

After the Coachella Valley harvest, the Bakersfield and Delano table grape harvest would be next in line. The Filipino farmworkers, again led by AWOC, were expecting the $1.40 per hour and the 25 cents per-box bonus. Instead the growers offered only $1.20 per hour and 10 cents a box. The Filipino farmworkers were outraged. They demanded the wages the Coachella growers had paid or they would strike. The Delano table grape growers did not bother to respond to their demands, would not even accept the registered letters from the union that represented the Filipino farmworkers. The Delano growers were their own worst enemy, and their attitude about Filipino farmworkers—and all farmworkers for that matter—perfectly captured the state of farm labor relations in the 1960s: arrogant and dismissive. "Boy, we do the talking, you do the listening, take it or leave it, we do not negotiate!"

Farmworkers who pick and field-pack table grapes work on their knees in the dirt for hours at a stretch in sweltering heat that can reach one hundred degrees. No fresh water or toilet facilities were provided and there was no protection from pesticide or fertilizer residues that might be left on the vines or from the wasps that make nests there. If workers took a lunch or rest break or had to walk deep into the field to find privacy to relieve themselves, they were financially penalized because they were not paid for that time—only for the grapes they packed that day.

The Delano Grape Strike began at 3 a.m. on September 8, 1965. This date marks the beginning of a political transformation for the state of California that continues even today. Who knew? Chavez was right: We do not have the money but we have the time.

Fifty-two years later as I sit here thinking and writing about the start of the Delano Grape strike, a watershed event in the history of California, I am struck by how petty and insignificant the issue was. Think about it: asking 10 cents more an hour than the then-current California minimum wage of $1.30, and asking for a 25 cent bonus for every field-packed box ready for market—both wage requests exactly the same as was granted the previous month in Coachella Valley in the same industry and by many of the same growers. It does not make any sense, but it shows again that California agribusiness growers were answerable to no one and certainly not to uneducated, "second-class" immigrant and migrant workers. The growers had the power—common good, social justice, all men are created equal be damned! Their only defining issue was that of farmworker servitude.

Grapes are California's second-largest agriculture industry—$3 billion dollars and counting. It covers more than 478,000 acres and employs more than 50,000 farmworkers. To create a visual of how large the table grape industry in California is, consider this: If you stacked the field-packed boxes of table grapes harvested in 1965 twelve high, you could build a seven-foot-tall wall from Delano to Boston, a distance of 3,000 miles. Or consider this: To haul the cases of wine produced by California grapes, the number of truck trailers needed would stretch from San Diego, California, to New Orleans, Louisiana, a distance of 1,800 miles.

The size of this California industry was huge, its financial resources staggering, and its political influence without equal—and it had a fifty-year unblemished record of crushing any efforts to organize farmworkers. The fact that Cesar Chavez could even imagine, let alone actually decide, to devote his life to organizing farmworkers into a union that could achieve recognition from employers and bargain collectively about wages and working conditions was mind boggling, even death defying.

The labor-strike drama had begun: the Filipino farmworkers, under the leadership of Larry Itliong of AWOC, called a harvest-time wage strike against the Delano-area table grape growers and set up picket lines at the entrances to the farms, where many of workers already lived in the growers' farm labor camps. But now the question became not only how will the growers respond? but perhaps more importantly, what will Cesar Chavez and his

National Farm Workers Association do? His membership was overwhelmingly Mexican American. They too worked the table grapes, but for the most part lived in Delano on the west side of the railroad tracks—where poor people lived—or in the small towns and hamlets surrounding Delano that are populated mostly by farmworkers. If the NFWA did not honor the harvest strike, it was doomed to failure.

Again, the last thing Cesar Chavez wanted in 1965 was a harvest strike of the Delano table grapes. His community-based organization, the NFWA, was not ready, and did not have the resources to strike for union recognition; perhaps it would never be ready, but certainly not in September 1965. The sheer size of the grape-strike area itself was not manageable. The vineyards were located in California's Central Valley and extended from Earlimart in the north to Arvin in the south—a distance of sixty miles—and the east to west measurement of the strike area was approximately five miles. All totaled, the Filipino farmworkers grape-harvest strike would be played out over a three-hundred-square-mile area involving thirty-one agribusiness employers.

Compare this strike area to that of a more traditional American strike. A United Auto Workers strike against the largest West Coast Ford automobile plant in San José, California, had covered thirty-two acres, was fenced and gated, and involved five thousand workers. That's right! There is no comparison! Mission impossible!

Chavez had no intention of crossing the AWOC picket lines but he needed time to think though his options and develop a plan before he made a final decision about how to proceed. Larry Itliong called Chavez to ask him if the NFWA would join the strike. Chavez replied that before he could make that decision he would have to call a meeting of his NFWA membership at the end of the week and put the question to them—whether to join the strike, or not. Chavez then requested a meeting with Al Green, the AFL-CIO director of AWOC, whose office was located in Modesto, 170 miles north of Delano. He needed to hear firsthand how Green viewed the strike relationship between the two unions. The meeting took place at the Stardust Motel in Delano. They agreed that each union would retain its own identity and both organizations would work together in a cooperative and collaborative manner. Such an arrangement was acceptable to Chavez, but he made it clear the NFWA would strike for union recognition, not just a harvest-wage increase. The goal was a union contract.

Chavez explained the strike conditions for the NFWA: The Delano Grape

Strike would not be a harvest-wage strike. It would be a strike for union recognition by the grape growers and a signed union contract that covered wages, benefits, and working conditions. In other words: even if the growers agreed to pay the $1.40 an hour wage and the 25 cents per box bonus, the farmworkers—AWOC & NFWA—would not end the strike until the growers accepted the union as the bargaining agent for the workers and bargained with them to create a mutually acceptable union contract.

The strike would be waged under the conditions and principles of non-violence. Violence directed against employers or farm employees or their property would not be tolerated and that would include any violence against strikebreakers who would be imported by the grower to work the harvest.

AWOC and NFWA would remain separate entities but would agree to collaborate together in planning strategy and picketing the grape fields, and they would share facilities as needed for feeding strikers, meetings, storage, etc.

ORGANIZING RESOURCES

Cesar Chavez was a trained organizer. From 1952 to 1962 he worked as a Mexican American civil rights activist employed by the Community Service Organization (CSO) to organize CSO chapters throughout the state of California to promote citizenship and voting and to defend against discrimination of working-class people in housing, employment, and education. He was so successful that in 1958 he was promoted to the position of National CSO Director.

In 1965, Cesar Chavez did not believe he was ready to challenge the California grape industry, but given the Filipino grape strike in Delano, what choice did he have? Even though he did not have the financial resources and material support at hand, as a creative and gifted organizer, he knew where to find the resources he needed and how to mobilize them. Making something out of nothing was right up his alley. Chavez once told me, "LeRoy, the lack of money can never be used an excuse for not organizing. There is always a way!"

The NFWA rented the Arroyo Camp located across from the Delano city dump as its strike headquarters. It contained a few acres, an old farm labor camp kitchen facility, a World War II Quonset hut for storage and an old mobile home—10 feet wide by 50 feet wide, which would house a primitive medical clinic staffed by a farmworker volunteer nurse. (If memory serves,

I think the farmworker strikers had installed a gravity-fed gasoline line from a large fuel tank positioned seven or eight feet high off the ground so they could gas up the autos of the strike captains whenever needed.)

Women who knew how to cook for large gatherings were recruited from the NFWA membership to cook the main meal of the day for the patrolling strike crews who manned the picket lines wherever strikebreaking harvest workers ("scabs") were found. They also fed the volunteer staff who worked in the strike office handling paperwork, answering the phone, greeting supporters who came to donate food and money, as well as the volunteer organizers who plotted the strategy for waging war with the California grape industry. The strike kitchen had counter seating for perhaps two dozen people so it took two to three hours to get everyone fed. Counting the prep time and the cleanup, the kitchen volunteers worked nine-hour days—day after day, after day, after day, after day for as long as the strike continued. You have heard the expression "An army marches on its stomach." Well, so does a strike army.

You will not be surprised when I tell you that academics and historians do not write books about "those who do the work" but only about those who have the titles. Too bad! Because those who work in the kitchen, in the back office, in the commissary storehouse, picking up the litter, sweeping the floors, and cleaning the toilets are the very ones who make the history books possible.

THE FARMWORKER PICKET LINE

Strikes begin with a bang! High energy, adrenaline flowing, spirits high, catchy slogans shouted to show confidence and to predict a speedy victory. That is how I felt as a thirty-one-year-old high school teacher driving from Los Angeles to participate in my very first labor strike and my first picket line ever! I had taken part in civil rights marches in Bakersfield and Washington, DC, with the NAACP, and in a farm-labor rent strike march in Visalia, but I knew this would be much different . . . and it was.

Cesar Chavez had called me a few days earlier to ask if I could collect some food and bring it to Delano for the farmworker strikers and their families. It was the second week of the strike, he said, and they really needed help. I was living in Los Angeles at the brothers' residence at Cathedral High School, which is next door to Dodger Stadium, so I asked some of the teachers I knew pretty well if they would make an appeal for food from their students and their parents. Just as I expected, the response was good: my car was loaded down with food donations and I was on my way to Delano!

I arrived early in the morning at the strike headquarters, unloaded the food, and located Cesar. We visited, caught up a bit, and then he asked me if I would be able to go to the picket line and help out. I was eager to go and he gave me the directions. Driving east on the county road through miles of vineyards was somewhat of an eerie experience: with vines standing six or seven feet tall and four or five feet wide on both sides of the narrow two-lane road, it felt like driving through a very thick forest with no horizon visible—just large masses of lush grape vines dripping with large clumps of green grapes waiting for the required sugar content to be harvested. I found the farmworker picket line and pulled off the road onto the dirt strip next to the vineyard. Here I go! I was excited! I was on the front lines of the farmworker movement!

Most union picket lines I was familiar with took place in large cities at job sites or in front of retail stores. The unions sponsoring this type of picketing have long been established and are protected by federal legislation dating back to 1935. The picket line usually consisted of five or six union retirees carrying a sign with the name of the union and the word *strike* or *unfair* lettered on it. Mostly in silence, the picketers would walk slowly round and round in an elliptical circle for a few hours and then stand close by an entrance until it is time to leave. This kind of informational picket line was used to publicly record the fact that a strike or an unfair labor practice existed at the location and needs to be resolved.

Another kind of union picketing, which also took place in large cities, was more taunting and raucous, with loud shouting or chanting, and because of the presence of several dozen or more union members massed in a line in front of an entrance to a hotel, for example, it was meant to intimidate potential customers or cause a sudden interruption of business as usual. Either the hotel was nonunion and the picketing union was ratcheting up public pressure on the employer to recognize the union and sign a union contract, or if it was union already, then there was a serious labor dispute about wages and working conditions that needed to be resolved. This kind of intimidating picketing would come and go and generally last for an hour or two until the police arrived to investigate the civil disorder.

The farmworker picket line I joined did not take place in a city or even close to one, but was located miles away in that part of the Central Valley where vast acreage was devoted to the production of table grapes for supermarket consumers or wine grapes for the wine industry. The only communication available was by a two-way radio system and even that could be problematic.

The Delano Grape Strikers I met lived in small rural towns or hamlets where there were no strangers and "everyone knows everyone else." They came from Richgrove (population 1,000), Earlimart (population 2,900), McFarland (population 3,700), or from "the other side of tracks" in Delano, where mostly all the farmworkers lived (total city population 12,000).

With the strike now in its third week, the growers retaliated by recruiting strikebreakers to take the jobs and harvest the grapes. Many scabs were known to the strikers on the picket line: perhaps they were friends or extended family members or neighbors. Others were total strangers because they had been recruited from hundreds of miles away by the grower-hired labor contractors who transported them to the fields to pick the grapes and break the strike. In fairness to these outside strikebreakers, they were never told they would be used as scabs. Only after they were transported to the grape field and saw the picket lines did they understand how they were being used. Their options—work and get paid or walk out and find their own way home—made for a difficult decision but one they had to make. Some walked away, but because of money, many stayed.

The emotions of the farmworker strikers on my picket line were razor sharp and sky high. Strikers were waving the red-and-black strike flags with the word HUELGA (Spanish for *strike*) emblazoned on them and yelling out to the scabs who were within earshot, trying to explain to them there was a strike at this field, that they were being used by the grower to break the strike, that they should come out and join the picket line. No response. Again, over and over, pleading and then begging them to stop work and honor the strike. No response. More yelling out to explain how a farmworker union would benefit all farmworkers, even them—better wages, better working conditions. No response. Then another striker, this time a woman speaking into a bullhorn, took over and yelled out her questions: "Brother, why are you betraying us? Why are you siding with the grower? Why can't you stand up for yourself and act like a man? For the sake of your wife and children, why don't you come out on strike and join with us? Act like a man!" No response. The crew of scabs moved farther into the field, hoping to escape the magnified sound of the bullhorn and the shouting of the strikers.

Several hours passed and not one of the scabs walked off the job in support of the union. The mood of the strikers, especially the women, had changed and in their frustration they took turns on the bullhorn, calling the scabs names and shaming them. I was amazed how creative these women were. They could really bring it! The emotions ran high because the stakes were high. These strikers made the decision to leave their job in order to fight for the right to have a union and be treated as human beings and not as some kind of farm tool that could be tossed out when no longer useful. They were sacrificing all they had to try to create a better future for their children and their grandchildren.

But that day on the picket line, they were not earning any money to feed and support their families. They were surviving on donations of food—like the car full of food I brought from the parents and students of Cathedral High School in Los Angeles who wanted to support the Delano farmworkers strike. These strikers were eating one meal a day in the strike kitchen. They had bills to pay with no money coming in except what their extended family members were chipping in to help them stay on strike. They had good reason to be discouraged and upset about their future but there was no turning back at that point. Tomorrow would be better. Some of these scabs would not show up tomorrow and those who did, they would wear them down. They would never give up until they had a union contract. I was exhausted. Picketing is hard work. My voice was hoarse, but I was ready for more. These farmworker strikers were not giving up and I wasn't either!

PICKET LINE TEACHERS

This was life as I had never seen or experienced it. These workers, under the leadership and example of Cesar and Helen Chavez, were willing to sacrifice everything they had for the right to have a union—their own farmworker union. They were determined to overcome their lives of enforced servitude by accomplishing what other union members in the United States had already accomplished—the right to bargain with their employer about wages and working conditions and to be treated like human beings.

I was a longtime member of a Catholic religious order, then a high school teacher and administrator, who was committed to live and teach Gospel values: love your neighbor; respect the life and dignity of each person; treat every person justly, as you would want to be treated; feed the hungry and shelter the homeless; everyone is born a child of God; whatever you do for the least of my brothers and sisters, you have done for me. But as much as I tried to put into practice what I was teaching, it seemed abstract and theoretical. I had never before found myself standing side by side with working men and women who were willing to sacrifice everything for the sake of improving the lives of others. I felt privileged—maybe not quite worthy—to be in such strong company. I was an experienced teacher but those striking farmworkers on that picket line were teaching me how to live for others. It is no exaggeration that fifty-two years later, on my eighty-third birthday [in 2017], I can write these words: those Filipino and Latino striking farmworkers changed the entire course of my life. I am indebted to them, and I have never forgotten what they taught me.

FROM THE KNOWN TO THE UNKNOWN

My carful of donated food was certainly not the first food donation brought to the striking farmworkers in the early weeks of the Delano Grape Strike, and what I brought was barely a drop in their ocean of need. Cesar Chavez was a tireless master organizer. "LeRoy," he said, "you always start with the known, which then leads you to the unknown, and you work from there."

The closest "known" to Chavez was Helen's extended family living in Delano and his own large extended family living in San José and East Los Angeles. Without a doubt, they were the first responders to send food to the Quonset hut at the strike camp now designated as the NFWA commissary. Appealing for food to feed hungry families is like no other appeal you can make—its importance resonates with each person because hungry people have to eat. Until that need is met, nothing else matters. These strikers have to eat every day as long as the strike continues. No matter the cost, no matter the amount of time it takes, these hungry families need to be fed.

The CSO network, another "known," was extensive. The ten years Chavez spent as an organizer for the CSO took him to every Mexican community of any size in the state of California. When Chavez left the CSO in 1962, there were thirty-two chapters and ten thousand paid members, and because he organized the vast majority of those chapters he knew them all—and believe me, they knew him.

A few Mexican American leaders in local unions were yet another "known." Organized labor in the 1960s was booming—the United Auto Workers (UAW) with the automobile plants in San José and Los Angeles and the new aerospace industries in Southern California, and the unions for the rubber workers, steelworkers, laborers, meat cutters, and butchers, concentrated in Los Angeles County.

Mexican American workers in great numbers were being organized into these AFL-CIO unions and some were beginning to rise to the level of elected local presidents. They knew of Chavez from his organizing work with the CSO and were keenly aware of how difficult it was to organize any union from scratch, but especially in the Central Valley in the areas of Fresno, Bakersfield, and Modesto.

Another "known" was what I call the "labor priests" in the Catholic Archdiocese of San Francisco. Officially, they were named the Spanish Mission Band. In the 1950s, these four young priests wanted to work full time in Oakland and San José parishes where there were large populations of Spanish-speaking Catholics. I call them labor priests because they were much influenced by papal encyclicals spelling out the Catholic teaching regarding social justice, a just wage, and the right of workers to organize into unions and bargain with their employers. Chavez became good friends with these priests and was greatly influenced by them. They in turn championed and supported his work of organizing Latinos and were ecstatic when he made his decision to devote his life to organizing farmworkers into a union. Through these labor priests, Chavez was connected to other Catholic priests who were predisposed to support his work of organizing farmworkers and did so for many years.

Perhaps the best-known labor priest was Monsignor George G. Higgins mentioned in essay 4 above. The so-called Spanish Mission Band (originally known as the Spanish-Speaking Band), founded in 1950 and operating out of the San Francisco archdiocese, exercised a tremendous influence on Chavez. They included Father Donald McDonnell, who was directing the Rural Life Conference when he met Chavez in San José and took him on as a lay assistant; Father Thomas McCullough; Father John Duggan; and Father John Garcia. The impact of the earliest encyclicals on the rights of labor, e.g. *Rerum novarum* (1891) and *Quadragesimo anno* (1931), together with Pope John XXIII's *Mater et magister* (1961), the Vatican II reforms, and Dorothy Day's Catholic Worker group, cannot be overstated. Under pressure exerted on bishops by corporate growers, the Mission Band lost official recognition in 1964 but individual priests carried on with their efforts on behalf of farmworkers and other laborers.

To organize the financial resources to wage the Delano Grape Strike, Chavez began to work the phone, calling everyone he knew who might respond quickly to his appeal for food for the strikers and their families. As with his own call to me, his voice was low-key, calm, and confident. He was brief and to the point—after all, he was speaking to someone he knew and who knew him. "We are on strike against the growers—can you collect food for the strikers and their families and bring it to Delano? We need help!"

FOOD FUND-RAISING

Chavez knew the strongest and most effective fund-raising appeal he could make was to personally ask someone he knew to collect food for hungry families who are on strike. People who are motivated to collect food for families on strike will also donate money when they deliver it. And he was right. There was a trickle of food and money in the first three or four weeks, then a steady stream, and by Christmas it was a veritable flood. Farmworker supporters in food caravans were coming weekly, visiting the NFWA strike camp to unload the food and then attending the full-house, standing-room-only, Friday-night strike meeting at the Filipino Community Hall. During the meeting, Chavez would introduce the leader of the food caravan, ask him or her to say a few words, and then receive whatever financial donation they brought with them. The striking farmworkers expressed their appreciation with thunderous applause!

Chavez, ever the creative and knowledgeable organizer, knew that the people who delivered the food would meet the Delano Grape Strikers and hear their stories about why they went on strike; they would see firsthand how determined the strikers were to sacrifice and struggle for a farmworker union to better their lives and to be treated as human beings by the growers. These personal interactions created a long-term bond between the visiting food donors and the striking farmworkers, which would continue to pay dividends far into the future—and did it ever.

CALIFORNIA MIGRANT MINISTRY

For more than four years, quietly and without fanfare, Chavez had nurtured another network of supporters to build a farmworker union, and now was the time to ask for their help. His final call to the "known" would be to a young Presbyterian minister, Chris Hartmire, who was the director of the California Migrant Ministry (CMM). From as far back as 1920, the CMM had been ministering to the needs of farmworkers and their families: setting up recreational camps for young children during the harvest season, teaching English, providing remedial education and personal hygiene classes, sponsoring day-care centers, and even maintaining emergency food lockers to feed desperate families. All these services were meant to make the lives of farmworkers more tolerable and, if possible, help them to assimilate into the larger society so they would not have to work in the fields.

One cannot fault these charitable services, and without doubt, many farmworker families benefited, especially the children. One of my best friends and colleagues of long standing was born and raised in a farm labor camp in Corcoran and to this day recalls the kindness of a migrant minister to the children in the camp. I'll never forget what he said. "The minister rounded us kids up and took us swimming in the blazing-hot afternoons. He was such a nice guy. We had so much fun."

By the late 1950s, the leadership of the CMM decided the time had come to change the course of their mission. Whatever the reasons, farmworkers had been consigned by society to live a life of servitude and no amount of charitable work was going to change that reality. To break the cycle of their impoverishment, farmworkers themselves needed to create their own self-help organizations to change their destiny. The ministry did not have the answers to how this could be done, but in 1961 they hired Chris Hartmire as their new director to find a new and more effective way to support farmworkers.

This decision to rethink and retool the CMM's assistance to farmworkers was quite remarkable for a faith-based religious organization and rarely happens with religious institutions. The leadership must have been so frustrated and aggrieved about the unchanging enslavement conditions endured by farmworkers; they knew there must be another way to help and there was.

In 1961, Chris Hartmire met with Cesar Chavez, the CSO director, and with Chavez's mentor, Fred Ross, who was one of the original founders of the CSO. They introduced him to the model of building a community-based organization that would be strong enough to bring about changes in employment and education opportunities, affordable housing, neighborhood improvements, and more respectful treatment by city government officials, including the police. In other words, the community organization created enough political power to improve the lives of all its members and the community at large. Reading these words on paper make it sound like it is easy to organize a community self-help organization. Why did it take so long? The reality is much different. Organizing is tireless and detailed evening and weekend work—door-to-door visits, house meetings, explaining, teaching, answering questions, setting the example, following up and reminding people, civic confrontation, and public demonstrations. It is hard, hard work, difficult on your family, and doesn't pay very well.

PROTESTANT CHURCHES IN ACTION

Chris Hartmire had anticipated Chavez's call asking for help with the Delano Grape Strike and was already hard at work mobilizing a response from the California Council of Churches (ccc) and their parent church body, the National Council of Churches (ncc), which was headquartered in New York City. Protestant church leaders wanted the facts, they had questions, they needed answers, and whatever help they could give would have to be done through various church committees tasked to handle these kinds of requests.

Hartmire, a Princeton graduate in engineering, worked for three years for the Naval Civil Engineering Corps at the Philadelphia Naval Shipyard before entering Union Theological Seminary in New York City to become an ordained Presbyterian minister. Because of his background and training, he was perfectly suited to be an effective communicator of facts and answers to questions and was also adept at navigating the various Protestant church bureaucracies.

From his third-floor office, close to downtown Los Angeles, he wrote and published an ongoing series of mimeographed newsletter briefs about the Delano Grape Strike: "A Chronological Fact Sheet," "Questions & Answers," and "How You Can Help." These publications were mailed out on a regular basis to all church ministers and their social action committees who were enrolled in the ccc and in the ncc, as well as to dozens of church ministers who had already been actively supporting the cmm. As Hartmire expected, the response of the Protestant ministers was solid and timely and it would grow significantly as word got out about the strike.

As important as the contribution of food and money by Protestant churches to the farmworker strikers was, even more important was the fact that by working with the cmm, these state and national church leaders were able to build a public relations firewall that prevented the antistrike propaganda generated by the Delano growers from gaining even a toehold of credibility with California print and television media. As Hartmire noted in his historical account of the farmworker movement,

It was hard to portray Cesar Chavez as a communist if churches and church leaders were supporting him.

It was hard to claim "there is no strike" when church leaders kept coming to see the strike and then went home to report on it.

It was hard to claim "our workers are happy and the so-called strikers are outsiders" when church people came and talked to farmworkers on the picket lines and heard their stories

The civil rights movement made it hard for the growers and local clergy to claim, "these Migrant Ministry people are outsiders; we live here! We know the true situations." In that era, many church leaders had been to the South; because of those experiences, that had discarded the belief that "local white people know best." (Oral history with Chris Hartmire, FMDP, October 6, 2004)

THE PROMISE OF THE 1960S

Such a confluence of national and international support generated for the striking farmworkers, developed in months—not years—showed the promise of the 1960s. Manifest change in the United States was everywhere to be seen and felt: the influence of the Beat Generation on American culture and politics; President John Kennedy's creation of the Peace Corps; the social impact of the new birth control pill; the civil rights Freedom Riders from the North integrating restaurant lunch counters in the South; the founding of Students for a Democratic Society (SDS) and the publication of its *Port Huron Statement*; the Student Nonviolent Coordinating Committee (SNCC) voter registration drive in Mississippi; the release of Bob Dylan's first album; the free speech movement at the University of California, Berkeley; the 1967 Summer of Love in San Francisco; the Woodstock Festival in 1969; and the Chicano Movement in cities across the Southwest. All of these things influenced and brought support to Cesar Chavez and his farmworker movement. Change was in the air and young people especially felt called to save the world. What an experience it was!

What Cesar Chavez had not foreseen, I think, was the unannounced arrival in Delano of volunteers—not just university students and recent graduates but lawyers, nurses, doctors, photographers, filmmakers, graphic artists, carpenters, auto mechanics, and many others. These volunteers wanted to join the cause of the striking farmworkers and provide whatever skills and talents they possessed. There was only a trickle of volunteers in the early months but as word got out about the farmworker strike—especially in the publications of SNCC, SDS, and the CMM, and by the national television coverage of the three-hundred-mile March to Sacramento by the striking farmworkers in the spring of 1966—dozens of volunteers arrived in Delano to join the farmworker movement. By the time the strike had been won in July 1970, with union recognition achieved and a collective bargaining agreement signed, Cesar Chavez had a sizable volunteer army at his disposal.

I too felt the lure in the 1960s to seek social change. Even though I had an established religious vocation and a teaching career, I was attracted to causes of social justice and perhaps subconsciously was even looking to join one. I had become a friend of SNCC to support their voter registration work in Mississippi, and I was connected to the members of the Catholic Worker Movement in Oakland, especially Ammon Hennacy, who founded a House of Hospitality in Salt Lake City.

I had participated in civil rights marches sponsored by the NAACP in Washington, DC, and Bakersfield, and, with state senator Walter Stiern, I had publicly campaigned in Bakersfield for the Rumford Fair Housing Act (which, of course, was soundly defeated). On my own initiative, with my high school students, I began a Saturday School program for poor farmworker kids who lived in the Cottonwood Road area of Bakersfield. Using teachers and students I recruited from San Francisco and Sacramento, I sponsored a full-blown summer school program serving farmworker children in Delano and Bakersfield.

The Catholic Worker Movement, founded in New York City by Dorothy Day and Peter Maurin in 1932, began with a newspaper and "Houses of Hospitality" as vehicles for furthering pacifism and enacting Catholic social teachings. Ammon Hennacy (1893–1970) was a Christian anarchist born in Ohio who engaged in a series of radical actions across the Midwest, including refusing to serve in World War I, for which he spent two years in prison. After working intermittently as a migrant field worker, he moved to New York in 1953 to work on the *Catholic Worker* newspaper. He often used fasting as a mode of protest. By the early 1960s, he had moved to Utah to found with Mary Lathrop a House of Hospitality for the homeless. California state senator Walter Stiern (1914–1987) was one of the creators of California's three-tiered system of higher education. In 1963, the California legislature passed the Rumford Fair Housing Act, outlawing discrimination in housing. In an attempt to nullify the act, conservative groups drafted Proposition 14, which voters passed in 1964.

The California Supreme Court ruled Proposition 14 unconstitutional under the protections of the Fourteenth Amendment. It was finally repealed by a ballot initiative in 1974.

What was there about Cesar Chavez that would motivate me to change the entire course of my life and join with him and his cause to organize farmworkers?

VOLUNTARY POVERTY

Without a doubt, what motivated me the most was the decision of Chavez and his wife, Helen, to live in voluntary poverty in order to devote their entire lives to improving the lives of farmworkers and affirming their status as human beings. At this time in my life, I was a member of a Catholic religious teaching order and I lived with a vow of poverty. I did not own anything, but I paid for nothing. I was provided with everything I needed. You cannot compare my poverty to the at-risk poverty embraced by Cesar and Helen Chavez and their eight children. There was no comparison.

Giving up the pursuit of material goods for the sake of helping others is a profound commitment and attracts other activists. First and foremost, this is what attracted me. I was not joining with a leader who organized and spoke to me about helping others but at the same time was also seeking to enrich himself. This kind of authentic and selfless leadership is rarely found and I was fortunate enough to have found it.

My friendship and work with Chavez lasted from 1963 to 1973. I was present prior to the Delano Grape Strike; on the picket line after it started; raising funds for the farmworker movement on university campuses in Northern and Southern California; present at the March to Sacramento, Cesar's twenty-five-day fast for nonviolence, and the funeral of Robert Kennedy; working on the consumer boycott in Los Angeles; present at the signing of the union contracts with the Delano growers; managing the day-to-day union operations when Cesar traveled a month at a time stoking the consumer boycott of grapes in the major cities of the United States and Canada; present at his 1972 fast in Phoenix; and present to manage the 1972 California "No on 22" campaign to defeat the grower initiative that would have prevented the unionization of farmworkers.

Because of my long-term involvement and close association with Chavez, it was only natural that those who were not present—documentary film-makers, historians, writers, and others—would want to interview me years after Chavez's death in 1993. Perhaps I have given as many as a fifteen such interviews, some of them lasting for many hours. What puzzled me about these interviews is why all the interviewers showed such little interest in Chavez's commitment to a life of voluntary poverty in order to help uplift the lives of farmworkers. I tried to impress upon them how important this was, because not only did it completely free him up to serve others, but it also greatly impressed the farmworkers he was organizing into a union.

The workers viewed Chavez, a former farmworker, as a person who was sacrificing his life for them. He was a leader they could trust and one who lived even more poorly than they did. I also tried to explain to the interviewers how much Chavez's life of voluntary poverty impressed an outsider like me, along with many other volunteers. His personal example challenged me to leave everything I had behind and to join with him in his movement to help farmworkers. I am still puzzled why these "chroniclers" were reluctant to discuss this or even ask follow-up questions, as they did with almost every other subject they asked me about and were interested in. They changed the subject and pushed on to their next question.

I do not understand their lack of interest in the power of voluntary poverty, but let me leave you with this thought: Francis of Assisi lived eight hundred years ago and today he is remembered and revered because he lived a life of voluntary poverty to help the indigent poor—the very reason why in the year 2013 the new pope took the name Francis as his own.

INDIGENOUS LEADER

Another important reason I decided to volunteer with Chavez was because he was an authentic indigenous leader. He was raised as a farmworker and knew firsthand their servitude because he had lived it himself. As a child growing up, he attended twenty-eight elementary schools before dropping out of junior high school to work full time in the fields. At eighteen, he joined the navy and left his farmworker life behind. But he never forgot the exploitation he and his family members had endured.

The first time I met Cesar, we talked for a couple of hours. I was very impressed and he gave me much to think about. One piece of advice I remember well and has served me in good stead: "Don't romanticize the poor;

if some of them had the power, they would be worse than the growers." On my drive back to Bakersfield I made up my mind: I had met my authentic indigenous leader who was living and working with the poor.

PERSONALITY OF CESAR CHAVEZ

Long after the death of Cesar Chavez, I had occasion to talk with a former farmworker movement volunteer who is now a longtime friend of mine. I had recruited her at some point in the 1960s; she now lives in Milwaukee. She told me a story that captures the personality of Cesar Chavez.

Chavez had come to Milwaukee to promote his union's lettuce boycott. As part of a multiday visit, a local farmworker support group had planned a large fund-raising dinner event at a Catholic parish hall. My friend attended with one of her children because she wanted to introduce him to Cesar. The hall was jam-packed so she waited until the close of the event. She could not find Chavez until she made her way to the rear of the hall where the kitchen was located, and there he was helping the (mostly women) volunteers wash the dishes and fold and stack the chairs to be stored in the equipment room.

FIGURE 14 Cesar Chavez in NFWA office, with posters of Robert Kennedy and Mahatma Gandhi. Photo by Arthur Schatz. Courtesy of Getty Images.

She waited and then approached him to re-introduce herself. Despite the intervening years, he recognized her immediately, gave her a warm embrace, asked about her family, and was visibly pleased to meet her son.

"That is so Cesar," I told her. He was more comfortable back in the kitchen being helpful to the working ladies than he was sitting at the head table with the city's political, labor, and religious leaders. He felt more at home with those who did the work and less so with those who carried the titles. One on one, Cesar was a master listener. He paid close attention to what you were saying; his eyes did not glance away while you were speaking, so he never gave the impression he might have other, more important things that were waiting for him to do. No, you had his complete attention. His responses were soft spoken, thoughtful, confident, and always caring. During my ten years of friendship and work with him, I never heard him shout orders or boss people around. I never saw him lose patience or speak sharply to a volunteer or a striker. He was low-key, confident, and never seemed to be rattled. He provided answers full of common sense based upon decades of working with people and institutions and understanding how they operate.

NONVIOLENCE

Martin Luther King Jr. was the embodiment of nonviolence for me. I admired his work in Alabama seeking to integrate the bus system and his campaign to register African Americans and force the state to permit them to vote. Members of his Southern Leadership Conference were harassed, beaten, attacked by police dogs, and sprayed with fire hoses, and King himself was jailed in Birmingham for eleven days. Chavez, of course, was well aware of King's nonviolent resistance campaign and the civil rights movement in the South. In fact, Marshall Ganz, who organized the three-hundred-mile March to Sacramento, was a SNCC veteran from the Mississippi Summer Project for voter registration; he later joined the farm-worker movement as a full-time volunteer. But Chavez looked to Mahatma Gandhi for his inspiration and understanding about the use of nonviolent resistance to achieve political and social change. In fact, I think it is fair to say he was a student of Gandhi.

Chavez was firmly committed to using nonviolent resistance to wage the Delano Grape Strike and often stated the strike could not be won by using violence. In fact, during one the darkest and most frustrating periods of the strike when there was some braggart-type talk about the need to use violence to win and some evidence that vines had been damaged, Chavez called a mandatory strike meeting to announce he was going to suspend the strike and undertake a personal fast until the strikers renewed their commitment to nonviolence. Chavez fasted for twenty-five days before the strike continued. Chavez understood that violence begets violence and, in the end, farmworkers will be the victims, and he was unwilling to live with that result.

NOTE

1. "Last of the Manongs: Aging Voices of a Farm-Labor Fight Find an Audience," *New York Times*, May 11, 1993.

10   Farmworker Volunteers

The first thing that must be understood about being a volunteer in Cesar Chavez's farmworker movement is that there was no money to be made. All volunteers were paid a subsistence stipend, the famous "five dollars a week" salary. Of course, it cost the movement much more than the five-dollars-a-week spending money. There was room and board, approved preexisting loan payments (typical examples might be a car loan and insurance, student loan payments, a home mortgage, etc.), house utilities, grocery allowances for families, transportation costs, and so forth. But all of this was union approved and tailored to meet the individual needs of the volunteer and their family, if applicable. There was always financial tension between the union and the volunteer. On the union side, it was too much money, and on the volunteer side, it was never enough money.

This financial arrangement alone ensured that most volunteers would not overstay their usefulness. And volunteers without family obligations were much less expensive because young unattached adults could live in boycott or field office communities or in the dorm rooms of the La Paz union headquarters and eat their meals in a communal kitchen. Those volunteers who were assigned to the boycott cities had more access to additional living support than those working in Delano or later at the La Paz headquarters, for the simple reason that they could appeal to churches and unions for additional resources.

As the years of the movement wore on, there was a concerted effort made by the farmworker staff to lobby for a modest but more traditional type of salary program, but Cesar would not hear of it. This was yet another example, I believe, of his determination to build a movement, not a union, even if it meant losing good people because of their need for more financial stability and their desire to be less dependent on having to individually plead their case for additional funds.

The tension caused by two seemingly distinct organizational goals—building and sustaining a "movement" and building and sustaining a labor union— would be in play from the earliest days of the NFWA until Chavez's death in 1993. In retrospect, the fragile synthesis of the two approaches, at least in the union's first decade, may have been the farmworkers' greatest achievement. The cross-fertilization between the farmworkers' actions and the incipient Chicano Movement and other youth-driven mobilizations made the separation of the two approaches virtually impossible. Mike Miller, SNCC liaison to the UFWOC and coordinator for the first grape boycott, recalls: "Those of us who got involved with NFWA learned about the difference between the 'migrant stream' strategy of AWOC and the 'shoestring communities' approach of NFWA. We further learned about Chavez's ideas of a 'community union,' and the importance he gave to mutual aid activities" (FMDP, 2006).

Many of the original volunteers came from the striking workers themselves. Some were single and others were married with small children. Their first assignments were such usual strike activities as picketing, union meetings, rallies, and marches. But within a few years, as the boycott operations expanded, many were asked to leave Delano and accept assignments in boycott cities across the United States and Canada. Some of the married strikers left their wives and children at home with members of their extended families when they went out on the boycott, while others took the whole family.

Most of the volunteers from the cities who joined the farmworker movement were young and unattached. Some stayed for a few months, others for several years (65 percent of the volunteers stayed five years or less; 45 percent stayed three years or less). The hours and days and months of unrelenting work (and relocations at a minute's notice) were so demanding that a kind of burnout was always close at hand. It was just a matter of time before volunteers moved on to resume more normal lives that would include college and/or graduate school education, marriage, child-rearing, and professional careers. In short, they felt the need to free themselves to plan for their own future. Because of the relatively short time span of their involvement, volunteers rarely overstayed their welcome.

The story of one volunteer sheds light on one of the many avenues that made up the recruitment process:

> Little coincidences lead to lifetime consequences. I was a 23-year-old English teacher at St. Paul's High School in San Francisco's Mission District, and I loved my job. . . . Sister Michael David, head of the English department and my teaching mentor, told me about a summer teaching project in Bakersfield. She had served on several high school evaluation committees with Brother Gilbert (BG), formerly in San Francisco, but now vice principal of the Christian Brothers' Garces High School in Bakersfield. BG had organized Saturday schools for farmworker children in the area, using high school students as the children's teachers. It was a novel concept at the time. The summer project was an expansion of the program. It would run for eight weeks and serve many more farmworker children in "Negro" and "Mexican" areas. BG was recruiting student teachers from several Catholic high schools throughout the state, as well as master teachers to direct. The second weekend in May, I drove to Bakersfield to meet BG and get more information. . . . BG had met a Mexican-American organizer, formerly with the Community Services Organization in San José and Los Angeles and now trying to build a farmworker organization in Delano. It was called the National Farm Workers Association. Cesar Chavez had asked BG if they could have a summer project for their kids. With BG and some other teachers, I drove 32 miles north on Highway 99, turned west on Garces Highway and went to Cesar's "office." My idea of offices was the San Francisco buildings in the Financial District. Cesar was soft spoken and articulate, answering what were probably very naive questions. My first meeting was absolutely inauspicious. (Bonnie Burns Chatfield, FMDP, 2004)

Many married volunteers joined the farmworker movement under the auspices of the National Farm Worker Ministry, and while no special accommodations or distinctions were made in terms of the kinds of union assignments they received or in the work expectations imposed upon them, they were provided with slightly more financial security and with much less dependence upon Cesar's budget constraints.

For those union-supported married volunteers who were assigned to the

FIGURE 15 Volunteers arrive for Delano Strike Summer, organized by Reverend Jim Drake, 1966. Photo by Jon Lewis. Courtesy of FMDP/Yale Collection of Western Americana at the Beinecke Rare Book & Manuscript Library.

La Paz headquarters, it didn't take long before the reality of the cultlike atmosphere of Cesar's movement wore down one spouse or the other. It sometimes became necessary to create more personal space by taking an assignment away from La Paz until the need to return to a more normal life became obvious and necessary. But if that option wasn't available, then married (and unmarried) volunteers would tough it out for as long as they could; sometimes that period would be measured in years.

Older volunteers who came later in life frequently came with a specified length already in mind, generally one or two years, and many of them were associated with the National Farm Worker Ministry, which offered some outside organizational support services. Some were priests and nuns, who at their own request were assigned to the farmworker movement by their diocese or religious orders and were supported by them.

But the individual case of every farmworker volunteer was different, and there were notable exceptions to the general categories of volunteers that I have identified. In fact, some volunteers, both from within the strike itself and from the outside, adapted to the demands of the movement so well and manifested such great motivation that as the success of the farmworker movement grew, they were appointed to positions of responsibility; some were eventually elected to the union's board of directors. These volunteers seemed destined to make the farmworker movement their life's career, and a few have done just that.

So then, what was the problem?

The problems were no different from any other organization, except that in Cesar's movement it was a closely held and supercharged occupation. It was a cause, after all. People were called to undertake this all-consuming work and felt privileged to be associated with its leader, a person who was known worldwide for his dedication, leadership, and moral stature. Volunteers, more or less, depending on their status within the farmworker movement, shared in the glow of his celebrity status.

But in the final analysis, Cesar understood the cause of the farmworker movement to be a way of life, a life that not only included organizing farmworkers into a union, but that would also emulate and support his vision. And while key leadership staff tolerated his demand for total commitment for the sake of unionizing farmworkers, they were much less enamored of his vision. Ultimately, the need for a personal life and individual status clashed with Cesar's priority of building and maintaining a strike-force community. But no compromise was forthcoming. Cesar was the founder, it was his vision, and he had the final say. As a result, the stage was set for a few board members and key staff to be summarily forced out and, I'm sad to report, vilified. For the sake of his vision, everyone was expendable.

Today, more than twenty-five years later, I still sense from some of these long-term, dedicated, and gifted former volunteers a sense of loss. They talk about the loss of opportunity for farmworkers, snatching defeat from the jaws of victory, inflexibility and stubbornness, lack of union democracy, the refusal to incorporate and assimilate nascent farmworker unions, and unwillingness to compromise. At the same time, after so many years of personal service, they find it difficult to publicly express their feelings concerning their forced departure, and it is this stubborn silence that engenders their personal bitterness and feelings of loss.

It isn't a question of whether Cesar was right or wrong in defending his vision. As long as I knew him, he never pretended that it was otherwise or held out any other promise. He possessed a vision of what the farmworker movement should be, and when he felt it was threatened, he brooked no opposition or interference, whether from family, friends, board members, or supporters. True enough, he expanded his vision over the course of years, but it was always his vision, and everyone knew it.

Chatfield would reflect years later:

> The tension between normal living and movement volunteering can only be managed for a time, and even that is determined by such individual variables as: age, single or married, career level, personal financial resources, etc. . . . Each of us came to the movement with a burning desire to help. We did whatever was asked; we went wherever we were told, sometimes on a minute's notice; we worked very long days for months on end without time off or vacation; we worked for the love of a cause, not for money; we were separated for long periods of time from our spouses and children; and so forth. These are only a few examples of the unrelenting, and insatiable demands that the farmworker movement made upon each of us, and we responded with a heartfelt yes. . . . Intense, day after day, months at a time, I don't see how the volunteers did it; I don't understand how I did it. But then victory was in the air, you could feel it, and besides, there was no such thing as a defeat, because the seeds of victory were always "sown" in a temporary setback. Nothing was impossible, everything was possible, and God was on our side. (FMDP, December 2004)[1]

1. Marshall Ganz provides context for the surge of student activism in California in the 1960s:

> Student leaders organized a statewide conference on farmworker poverty and formed a Student Committee for Agricultural Labor (SCAL) at UC Berkeley and one at Stanford. By June 1965, nine student groups inspired by the 1964 Mississippi Summer Project, which had brought several hundred northern students south to organize black voters, launched their own summer projects in the San Joaquin Valley. UC Berkeley SCAL members worked in the fields and assisted local farm worker organizers. UCLA tutors served in a Kern County labor camp near Arvin. The Student Medical Conference Migrant Programs of USC and the Los Angeles College School of Nursing were active in five counties. The Sacramento State College Agriculture Committee took part in community organizing programs in eight counties. The Berkeley YMCA led a summer tutorial project near Yuba City. The American Friends Service Committee hosted a tutorial project in the Linell labor camp in Tulare County. The Garces High School Catholic Student Project, led by LeRoy Chatfield, ran tutorial projects in Kern County. (*Why David Sometimes Wins: Leadership, Organization, and Strategy in the California Farm Worker Movement* [Oxford: Oxford University Press, 2009], 108)

FIGURE 16 DiGiorgio Boycott solidarity in San Francisco. Several unions supported the action, which included a speech by Cesar Chavez at City Hall. The California SNCC newspaper, the *Movement*, edited by Terry Cannon, published a special supplement on the boycott. Cannon also served as the media coordinator for the 1966 March to Sacramento. Photo by Jon Lewis. Courtesy of FMDP/ Yale Collection of Western Americana at the Beinecke Rare Book & Manuscript Library.

11   Stop the Grapes

The call came to me in San Francisco: "The grapes are being trucked from Delano to the San Francisco docks. Stop them from being loaded onto the ship." That was it. The rest was up to me.

I was a volunteer organizer for Cesar Chavez, assigned to the San Francisco Bay Area, to support the farmworkers' grape boycott. Using my contacts with the longshoremen's union, I was able to confirm that grapes were to be loaded the next morning at San Francisco pier number such and such; also, the growers had obtained a restraining order prohibiting picketing at the dock. Without a picket line, the longshoremen's union had no excuse not to load the grapes onto the ship. But my informant also told me that the picketers had the right to read the injunction before the police gave the order to stop picketing and disperse. A group of us, a dozen or more, showed up early the next morning to set up the picket line, read the injunction, and disperse when ordered to do so.

We arrived at what seemed like a Hollywood stage set—eight refrigerated trucks were lined up on the dock waiting for the pier to open so they could drop their loads shipside, dock workers were milling around outside the pier gate waiting to see what was going to happen, a high-priced San Francisco attorney had arrived with dozens of injunctions stuffed into his bulging briefcase, the police were at the ready, and we stood across the street from the pier next to the railroad tracks. And then it was as if someone shouted, "Camera, action!" The drama began.

One young woman from our group crossed the street, holding a picket sign aloft. She walked to the main pier doors and began to walk back and forth in front of the entrance. The attorney served her with the injunction, and as she read it word for word she kept the picket sign high above her head. When she finished reading every word of the multipage legal document, the police ordered her to disperse. As she crossed the street to join the other demonstrators, she handed the picket sign to the next person and the cycle repeated itself many times. For their part, the members of the longshoremen's union were satisfied that as long as the picket sign was in front of the entrance, their lives might be endangered if they crossed it.

After two hours of this street theater, the growers' attorney gave up and left. The longshoremen went to work loading the rest of the cargo onto the ship, the idling refrigerated grape trucks remained outside waiting for another day, and we went out for a glorious breakfast.

Throughout his first full year on the NFWA staff, Chatfield was involved in a series of diverse activities up and down the state: picket lines at Bay Area docks, the *peregrinación* (pilgrimage) from Delano to Sacramento, the merger with AWOC, and fund-raising in Los Angeles:

> In 1966, I recruited Doug Weston of the Troubadour Club in Los Angeles to produce two sold-out back-to-back Joan Baez concerts at the Santa Monica Civic Auditorium and raised $60,000 for the farmworker movement. In addition, and in about the same time period, I organized a $100-a-person garden party event in Beverly Hills, which netted perhaps $15,000 for the farmworkers. These monies were slated to be used to organize farmworker cooperatives, an assignment I had been given by Cesar when I arrived in Delano in October of 1965 to begin my full-time work for the National Farm Workers Association. The Joan Baez concert and the garden party events were the culmination of my fund-raising efforts during my first year of service to the farmworker movement. (LC/PH)

Joan Baez performed the concerts in December of 1966, the same year she marched with Dr. King in Mississippi and participated in anti–Vietnam War demonstrations in Europe.

12   Pushing the Buttons

During the 1960s, I developed tactics that made politicians feel so uncomfortable they would frequently reverse themselves in order to accommodate newly discovered realities. Or, in the case of corporations, the long-sought-after meeting that had always been denied—"We are not involved"—suddenly became possible and even a priority.

I attribute the development of this tactical sixth sense to my love of high school geometry. I poured over geometric relationships seeking the size of angles, the length of the sides of rectangles or triangles, etc. I would carry these problems with me for days at a time. I massaged the different variables during my daily shower period, during the silent evening meal, during my twilight sleep zone, and then picked them up again at the 6 a.m. morning bell. I exhausted all the options and possibilities within my power, and when I finally found the correct relationship, the answer would bring an afterglow of satisfaction.

I gradually came to realize that decision-making is a matter of understanding and laying out one's options. I used this approach when I counseled high school seniors. First, I helped them articulate the predicament with which they were struggling; second, I explored with them the various decisions that could be made to deal with it. Even when life's decisions, big or small, are seen as unpleasant or unpalatable or cannot yet be faced for fear of the unknown, it can be a reassuring and freeing experience to realize there is a way forward. One is not paralyzed.

FIGURE 17 Chatfield speaking at a Los Angeles demonstration against collusion between the Teamsters Union and the American Farm Bureau, 1971. Photo by Glen Pearcy. Courtesy of Susan Due Pearcy/Glen Pearcy Collection, American Folklife Center, Library of Congress.

From time to time, I see a woman, now seventy years old, who left her husband thirty years ago because, she said, I was the first person to explain to her that her previously held position—not to decide—was truly a decision. So if in reality she made the decision not to decide, then she was free enough and capable of making another decision—that is, to decide. Non-action is as much of a decision as action.

Whether my love of geometric relationships gave rise to my tactical sense of how to manipulate politicians and organizations is probably beside the point. The fact is that I have demonstrated many times over the years my ability to bring about maximum pressure because I can find the correct buttons to push.

I remember the case of the liberal state senator who refused our request to publicly call for an investigation of the misuse of police power against striking farmworkers. In our view, his public statement was deemed essential because if he spoke out publicly, the media would take it seriously. But if we, a ragtag group of activists, raised the issue, it would be considered self-serving and easily ignored. I pleaded with him. He said no. His office said no. He made it very clear that he had helped us on many occasions, but this time it was final, his answer was no—and stop bothering me.

I asked five people, farmworker staff and supporters, some of whom spoke only a few words of English, to visit his Los Angeles office and wait there until he agreed to meet with them. I knew, of course, that state senators are rarely in their district offices because their daily work keeps them in the state capital. They only return to their district for speech-making and ribbon-cutting events. I instructed the volunteers to carry with them thermos bottles, blankets or sleeping bags, and a picnic cooler filled with food and drinks. They were not to agree to any meeting with an aide or office receptionist. They would say instead that they would wait until the senator had time to meet with them.

Less than two hours later, I received a call from the senator's office in Sacramento asking me what it was I wanted the senator to do. I spelled out the items I thought should be in a press release, and I stressed how important it was to raise the issue in the media. Less than an hour later, I heard the senator quoted extensively on the two Los Angeles twenty-four-hour news radio stations. He spoke forcefully: he said it was vitally important that government agencies investigate these allegations raised by the striking farmworkers, and that he himself would be monitoring the situation, etc. He could not have been more helpful. I ask myself, how could this brief, nondescript "sit-in" bring a powerful senator to reverse himself and come out swinging for the rights of farmworkers when he had sworn he would not do so? It must be the geometry of the situation that changed the relationship.

In the early 1970s, as a result of an off-the-record conversation I had with the president of Chiquita Banana at a meeting arranged by the produce buyer for Mayfair Markets, the United Fruit Company became so concerned about whether I could prevent their offshore banana boats from being unloaded in California ports that they flew two senior labor negotiators from Boston to meet with me as the first step in opening labor negotiations affecting their produce operations in the Salinas Valley. Farmworker union contracts followed soon after.

In 1968, Marshall Ganz and I were able to transform the five floors of the Kern County Courthouse into a hushed, reverent, and cathedral-like atmosphere by lining all the corridors of the building with thousands of praying farmworkers—men, women, and children. Cesar Chavez, our founder and leader, who was in the middle of his public fast for nonviolence, had been hauled into superior court to answer allegations made by the growers about union violence. The presiding judge rejected the growers' attorney's argument that the courthouse building be cleared because the presence of thousands of farmworkers would certainly intimidate the court. The judge then ordered the hearing to be continued after Cesar had finished and recovered from his fast.

There are buttons to push in every politician or organization, public or private, in order to bring proper attention to the issue at hand. The tactical problem is to uncover the whereabouts of these buttons and to push them effectively. One must examine and understand relationships that already exist in order to connect with the persons who have the power to make decisions. These decisions will rarely be made out of compassion or concern, but will be made primarily out of self-interest.

Pushing the buttons is not much different, it seems to me, from understanding geometric relationships in order to find the answers to the questions at the end of the chapter.

Marshall Ganz was a principal actor in the history of the farmworker movement. Chatfield and Ganz had met in Bakersfield, where Chatfield was teaching at Garces High School and Ganz was a student at Bakersfield High School. After attending Harvard for three years, Ganz traveled to Mississippi and became a SNCC field secretary. In 1965, Ganz met Cesar Chavez and soon after became a SNCC-paid organizer working for the NFWA. He would go on to become one of the indispensable players in the farmworker struggle. In 2004, Chatfield remembered him as "Marshall Ganz, one of the most gifted union organizers ever to walk the agricultural fields of California." It should be noted that Ganz met another key participant in the early years of the farmworker movement—Jessica Govea—through a Friends of SNCC chapter in Bakersfield organized by Brother Gilbert (Chatfield) and Ganz. Both Govea and Ganz left the union in early 1981. In 2004, Ganz wrote the following to Chatfield: "I often marveled at your talent for matching people with tasks, asked you about how you did it, and tried to emulate it in my own work. I always had the greatest respect for the way you managed your people and I think you may be being too hard on yourself as you look back. Although, to be sure, many of us behaved in ways that we would later look back on, wonder what we were thinking about, and, hopefully, learn from" (FMDPd, December 6, 2004).

13   Strike Violence vs. Nonviolence

From the first day I met Cesar Chavez in 1963, he advocated nonviolence as the means to build his union, despite the fact that the US labor movement was built through the use of violence by both employers and workers. For one thing, I think Chavez believed it was the right thing to do, but, perhaps even more important, he believed it was the only strategic way to protect striking farmworkers from the violence that would certainly be visited upon them by law enforcement personnel and grower-sponsored thugs. He also reasoned that the use of nonviolence would encourage the support of religious people and church bodies for his farmworker movement, and that could be critical to the survival of his fledgling organization.

Still, during my ten-year involvement with the movement, I heard many rumors about the use of violence in the Delano Grape Strike. At the time, based on the rumors I heard and the strikers and volunteers from whom I heard these rumors, I concluded that 33 percent were based on wishful thinking, 33 percent stemmed from bravado expressed after a few beers, and 33 percent were real. Now, thirty years later, as a result of organizing the Farmworker Movement Documentation Project, wherein I collected two hundred essays written by the volunteers and strikers who built the movement—and having participated in an exceptionally frank and emotionally charged eight-month online discussion with more than three hundred volunteers and strikers, and having communicated privately for three years with hundreds of strikers and volunteers—I can say with utmost confidence that the percentages should be 45 percent wishful thinking, 45 percent bravado, and 10 percent real.

The question is, what is the definition of violence in the context of a farmworker movement strike? For example, the purpose of the picket line itself was to intimidate strikebreakers from going to work and breaking the strike. Is that violence? Certainly, local judges agreed with the growers who came before them and made the picket-line-violence argument; growers were granted injunctions to prohibit picketing altogether or to limit it to such a degree that it could not be effective.

What about the farmworker union–sponsored marches, candlelight vigils, and processions in neighborhoods where labor contractors lived and strike-breakers were housed? I expect that the labor contractors or the strikebreakers who were the targets of these neighborhood demonstrations considered them to be intimidating and even violent, and perhaps they feared for their families, their homes, and their automobiles. Is that violence? Local law enforcement considered these confrontations violent and did everything they could to prevent them, including arresting some of the strikers on occasion.

And what about the Anglo volunteers who posed as process servers and walked into the fields armed with a legal summons to be served to the crew foreman in the presence of his crew, for the purpose of intimidating workers who feared they would also be served with a legal summons and be forced to make a court appearance? Was the use of these trumped-up legal tactics a form of violence?

When the union newspaper, *El Malcriado*, published photographs of strikebreaking labor contractors and wrote unflattering articles about them, which were then distributed throughout valley towns where the workers lived, is that to be considered violence? Certainly, the hope was that these contractors would be so intimidated that they would work elsewhere or at the very least be ostracized by their friends and neighbors.

In the very early months of the strike, union members followed strike-breakers home after they left the fields, in order to discover their addresses, license plate numbers, and the names of any neighbors friendly to the union who might put pressure on them to work elsewhere. The union hoped that even the act of tailing strikebreakers would provide enough intimidation to cause them to stop breaking the strike. Is this violence?

Without a doubt, there was some overt personal property damage directed against the vehicles used by strikebreakers, e.g., holes punched into radiators and/or tires slashed. The purpose, of course, was to intimidate these strikebreakers and to send a message throughout the community that automobiles owned by strikebreakers might suffer a similar fate.

On dozens of occasions, union organizers followed the commercial trucks that transported the harvested grapes hundreds of miles to either Los Angeles or San Francisco in an effort to intimidate the drivers and to find out where the grapes were being delivered so that picket lines might be set up at produce terminals. How intimidated did the truckers feel when they were followed by strangers for such great distances? Is this a form of union violence?

There were reports, especially during the first year of the strike, that hundreds of vines had been cut with a chain saw, dozens of irrigation pumps disabled, and a couple of ancient packing sheds near railroad sidings burned to the ground. These are obvious cases of property damage directed against an employer for the purposes of intimidation. But without minimizing it, they represented run-of-the-mill property violence that might be found in a major labor dispute anywhere.

I believe this to be true: every farmworker striker and volunteer experimented at some point with "violence" or at least considered the possibility of using it if they thought it might force the growers to recognize the union. How could it be otherwise, especially in the United States, where the labor movement has resorted to violence or counterviolence to press its demands? In the case of California agriculture, these struck table grape growers had near-absolute power. They were beholden to no one. They controlled the courts and law enforcement agencies, they imported thousands of strikebreakers hundreds of miles by bus from the Mexican border, and for decades they ran roughshod over the rights of workers to organize and bargain collectively.

After the first harvest season of the Delano Grape Strike in 1965, it was clear to the union and the striking farmworkers that the grape strike could not be won in the fields. The situation was hopeless.

As Chatfield notes above, the difficulty of winning the grape strike by traditional methods became clear early on. The move to boycott all California table grapes instead of targeting individual growers instilled new energy into the movement as boycott centers opened up in cities across the country. For Chavez, the boycott itself was a manifestation of nonviolence: "To us the boycott of grapes was the most near-perfect of nonviolent struggles because nonviolence also requires mass involvement. The boycott demonstrated to the whole country, the whole world, what people can do by nonviolent action. Nonviolence in the abstract is a very difficult thing to comprehend or explain. I'd read a lot, but all of it was in the abstract. It's difficult to carry the message to people who aren't involved. Nonviolence must be explained in context" (Levy, 269).

And yet in the face of this hopelessness, Cesar Chavez advocated that nonviolence was the only way to win the strike and secure union recognition. Was he aware that many strikers (and AFL-CIO establishment union leaders) rejected the strategy of nonviolence as a viable option to win union recognition? Yes, and he was not only aware of the mounting calls for violence, but he also chose to confront them. He undertook a twenty-five-day fast to force his followers to make a decision—do it my way or leave the movement. Was he personally conflicted about the need to use or not use violence to win union recognition? Of course he was. Had he himself experimented with the use of violence? I believe he had. But in the final analysis, and very early in his movement, he made the personal decision that violence was not a viable route to win union recognition. Did his decision about the use of nonviolence mean that his followers would never again perpetrate violence? No, of course not. But they would know full well that it violated Chavez's irrevocable commitment to nonviolence.

What were the results of his commitment? Correct me if I am mistaken, but during the thirty-one-year period of his movement, not a single grower or family member was killed or injured, their homes were not burned, and their automobiles were not vandalized. The same is true for every agribusiness supervisor, local law enforcement officer, and farm labor contractor. No farmworker striker or organizer was ever convicted of doing bodily harm to a strikebreaker. Only one farmworker organizer was ever convicted of causing property damage. On the other side of the ledger, three farmworkers were slain during strike activity, and a company truck driving through a picket line killed one young farmworker volunteer. During this thirty-one-year period, there were hundreds of strikes and thousands of strikebreakers and striking farmworkers. All of this is an amazing tribute to the leadership of Cesar Chavez.

On balance, I conclude that Cesar Chavez and his movement were extremely successful in preaching and practicing nonviolence to accomplish their goals. Unfortunately, the same cannot be said about agricultural employers.

14   The Fast

Prior to Cesar's fast for nonviolence, there were certainly instances of property destruction. I assumed they had some relationship to the table grape strike, despite the union's public commitment to nonviolence. I heard talk of vines being cut (perhaps one hundred to two hundred), about some attempts to shoot out the refrigeration units on piggyback trailers carried by train through the Tehachapi Mountains, about holes that had been punched into the radiators of the cars of strikebreakers, and of course I knew about the two local packing sheds on the railroad siding that burned down, because I saw the smoldering ashes left behind. I never heard about any damage to irrigation pumps, but it would not surprise me if that did happen. I never heard any of this talk in Cesar's presence. It was something whispered about. Some of it I believed to be true, and some of it I believed to be bravado, depending upon who was doing the talking.

A month or two after I heard this whisper talk of property violence, Cesar and I took a drive out into the countryside and he told me in confidence that he was going to undertake a fast after the manner of Gandhi. He told me he was worried about physically being able to fast for any length of time because he had experimented with fasting for a few days in the previous weeks and he didn't think he could do it.

Cesar Chavez told journalist Jacques Levy:

> We had to stop long enough to take account of what we were doing. So I
> stopped eating. It was a Thursday. Then I didn't eat on Friday or Saturday
> or Sunday. LeRoy Chatfield, a former Christian Brother, who was, I guess,
> the only one who knew I was fasting, started coming with me and helping
> me through the first few days. He would drive me home and pick me up
> and hear about all the pains I had and all the nightmares about food. . . .
> After four days, I called a meeting of all the strikers and the staff at Filipino
> Hall to announce what I was doing. (Levy, 272)

Chatfield provides additional details: "I had been given advance notice by
Cesar personally—he wanted me to drive him out to the vineyard areas outside of Delano so we could talk (I thought it was just to get a break from the
office so he could relax a bit) about what he had planned to do. What I did not
know in advance was when he planned to do it" (Personal correspondence).

Within a few days, we were called into Filipino Hall for a special meeting, wherein Cesar announced there was a split in the union leadership over
his commitment to use nonviolence to win the strike—but his mind was
made up. The leadership, the volunteers, the strikers, and that day's visitors to
the strike had to choose between his commitment to nonviolence and those
who were advocating the use of violence. For his part, he said, he was going
to walk to Forty Acres, undertake a fast, and live there until the issue was
settled once and for all. He walked off the stage and left the hall by himself.
Then Helen Chavez said she was leaving to go with Cesar.

Confusion reigned at the meeting. Tony Orendain, Fred Hirsch, and
some others seemed furious and defiant, and began muttering about Cesar's
remarks; others defended Cesar, and some didn't know what was happening
or what to make of this drama. Everyone present certainly understood that
Cesar had drawn a line in the dirt, and the leadership would have to choose
up sides.

I stood up to announce that as long as Cesar was on Forty Acres it would
be considered sacred ground, and that I did not want anyone driving their
cars onto the property. They should park outside along the roadways and
walk onto the property. Then I left and caught up with Cesar, but by that
time he had almost reached the property. Many others came soon after—
they parked on the roadway and walked onto the property—and we began
the process of converting the newly built adobe building (planned to be

The first NFWA building built on the union's Forty Acres property in Delano. A filling station that was designed to sell "Huelga" brand gas never opened but later was repurposed to house Chavez during the twenty-five-day fast in 1968. A Mass was celebrated there every evening. Photo by James Rosenthal. Courtesy of Heritage Documentation Programs, Historic American Buildings Survey, National Park Service.

used someday as a co-op gas station for farmworkers) into a sleeping area for Cesar (one very small room) and a chapel (a large room) that might hold fifty people or more for the daily Mass that would surely be celebrated there. A group of Filipina women strikers painted the windows of the chapel room with religious and union symbols to simulate the look of stained glass windows.

The 1968 fast immediately became the subject of fierce debate within the organization. Some of Chavez's most ardent supporters opposed the fast, with some Catholic priests objecting to what they viewed as a misappropriation of a religious activity for political motives. Chatfield recalls:

> After he left the meeting and began to walk to the 40 Acres a couple of miles away, the meeting erupted in confusion and some people spoke out against what Cesar was doing and others tried to defend it. But there was no order to the discussion, people on all sides were confused and frustrated but I knew the reality was this: Cesar had made up his mind what he was going to do and all the rest of us had to make up our own mind about what we were going to do. In my own case, I understood the religious role

of fasting from having extensively read *The Lives of the Saints* and realized how fasting can inspire others. In fact, instinctively I admired the concept and was not at all put off by it." (Personal correspondence)

Marion Moses kept notes during this period and shared them with reporter Peter Matthiessen:

The masses were beautiful [celebrated by Father Mark Day]. On the first night LeRoy and Bonnie [Chatfield] made an offering of a picture of JFK, and Tony Mendez gave a crucifix. About 100 people came to the first mass and probably 200 will come tonight. It really looks good—the huge banner of the Union is against the wall, and the offerings the people make are attached to the banner: pictures of Christ from Mexico, two crucifixes, a large picture of Our Lady of Guadalupe—the whole wall is covered with offerings. There is a permanent altar there (a card table) with votive lights, almost like a shrine. It's impossible to describe the spirit of what is happening. (Quoted in Matthiessen, 182)

Years later, the analysis of another dedicated supporter was more ambivalent:

Looking back, I see the fast of 1968 as having an unhealthy impact on him psychologically, as well as physically. When he informed the staff of his decision to go to the Forty Acres and fast, he described it as a very personal journey, and asked that we continue our work, and NOT follow him. But the nightly masses were orchestrated so that people were literally worshipping at his feet. And he emerged from the fast physically frail, receiving visitors from his bed. For months, access was controlled by Marion Moses and LeRoy, limited to a few minutes, hushed voices, and our issues, personal or departmental, seemed pretty puny to bother him with. I think the fast had tremendous positive impacts, but it also had a down side. (Doug Adair, FMDPd, December 29, 2004)

Attorney Jerry Cohen told author Jacques Levy, "It was ironic. People who were supposed to be good organizers were so blinded by their intolerance of the religious aspects that they could not see what a great organizing tool the fast was, and that, in a way, it was there for everybody to make of it what they could" (Levy, 283). Apparently, Saul Alinsky himself, when he heard about the fast, was opposed to it and only relented in his opposition when Fred Ross Sr. explained the positive impact the fast was having.

15   Kern County
        Courthouse Cathedral

Cesar Chavez was in the second week of his fast for nonviolence and living at Forty Acres. Farmworkers were coming from miles around to visit Cesar, attend the daily Mass in the evening, and move into the tent city we had set up. Just as we had transformed the newly constructed co-op gas station building into a chapel, we were building a twenty-four-hour-a-day farmworker city.

Perhaps that is how the idea came up. We would transform the Kern County Courthouse into a farmworker cathedral so that the playing field of justice would be more level when Cesar had to make his court appearance to answer charges filed by the growers claiming that he was fomenting violence.

In those days, we were young, and working around the clock meant nothing. Marshall Ganz took the lead in organizing thousands of farmworkers to descend on the multistory courthouse building several hours before Cesar Chavez arrived. Marshall and I led the unending column of workers into the building when it opened, and we lined the corridors on all the floors. A hushed and profound silence settled over the courthouse as the workers began to softly pray the rosary and other religious devotions. All was ready, and as we escorted Cesar into the building to walk the silent corridors to the designated courtroom, not a word—not even a ¡viva!— was uttered.

For the first time in its short history, the farmworker movement had officially arrived in Bakersfield, the county seat of California agribusiness.

FIGURE 19 Chavez, weakened by fasting, departs the Kern County Courthouse, assisted by the union's general counsel, Jerry Cohen, and LeRoy Chatfield, 1968. © 1976 George Ballis. Courtesy of Take Stock/The Image Works.

The growers' attorney was furious and represented to the presiding judge that the presence of the praying farmworkers was intimidating.

"Mr. Quinlan," the judge replied, "if I order this courthouse cleared, it will just be another example of gringo justice. I don't consider this to be intimidation." The day's hearing was canceled. The farmworkers filed out as silently as they had entered. It took nearly an hour to vacate the newly consecrated cathedral building.

Jerry Cohen, the general counsel for the farmworker union, has said many times that because of this farmworker demonstration, he never again felt the oppressiveness of the Kern County justice system when he entered the courtroom to represent the legal rights of farmworkers.

Jerry Cohen recalled:

> On the thirteenth day of the fast Cesar was hauled into Kern County Superior Court, charged with contempt of the Giumarra anti-picketing injunction. Three thousand farm workers stood outside the building and lined the halls of the courthouse in a silent prayer vigil. Giumarra's attorney Bill

Quinlan argued to Presiding Judge Walter Osborne in chambers that the workers should be removed. I made the constitutional arguments that they should be allowed to stay, but the pressure of the fast and the presence of the workers and not the constitutional arguments won the day. Judge Osborne said, "Look, Bill, if I kick these workers out of this building, it will be one more example of goddamn gringo justice." (FMDP, "Gringo Justice," February 2008)

Jerome "Jerry" Cohen grew up in Washington, DC, attended Amherst College, and earned his law degree at UC Berkeley's Boalt Hall, where he was active in the free speech and antiwar movements. While working for the California Rural Legal Assistance program, he met Cesar Chavez, and at the age of twenty-six he became general counsel to the United Farm Workers union, where he worked from 1967 to 1979: "Cesar said that if I wanted to help the Union, I should come to work for the Union because of the constraints on the federal program. I told him that having just graduated from law school I didn't know much. He lied and said he didn't know anything either and that we would learn it together. The next day we met in the office of his administrative assistant, LeRoy Chatfield, and worked out the details of my new job" ("Gringo Justice"). Years later, Chatfield wrote: "Jerry Cohen, the very young attorney who defended the rights of the farmworker movement aggressively and intelligently—and with great passion! He sued the bastards at every turn, pursuing them even to the California and U.S. Supreme Courts" (LC/PH).

16   Bobby

The Kennedy family, beginning with President Kennedy, was absolutely revered by the farmworker community, Cesar in particular. In Cesar's mind, the Kennedys were fundamentally committed to helping the poor and the downtrodden. His respectful and positive attitude toward the Kennedys stood in stark contrast to his generally negative and wary attitude toward other politicians. For some reason, the Kennedys, especially Bobby Kennedy, were not considered "politicians," but ruling-class torchbearers for social justice.

Another common bond, perhaps more subliminal than overt, between farmworkers and the Kennedy family was Catholicism. The overwhelming majority of farmworkers were Catholic. A Kennedy coming to Mass with Cesar to celebrate the end of the fast would be a shared religious experience with a common denominator understood and appreciated by all present.

We in the union leadership all understood the need to attract a major celebrity, not only to help make the Mass and rally a huge success, but to imbed Cesar's fast for nonviolence into the history of the farm labor movement. Without doubt, Robert Kennedy was our first choice, but at the time it seemed like such a long shot; yet I don't have any recollection of a backup plan to invite another celebrity if the Kennedy plan fell through. A major logistical problem with any planning was that Cesar would make no commitment to me or anyone else when he would stop fasting. Everything was day to day until the end of the third week, when I really pressed him

FIGURE 20 Bobby, Teddy, and Jack Kennedy. The older brother, the first
Catholic president, was revered by the farmworkers. The two younger brothers
supported the farmworkers' union in important ways. Photo by Cecil Stoughton.
Courtesy of the National Archives.

and threatened to set a specific day myself. He responded by saying, "You won't be able to get the people until Sunday." That is how the date was set.

It is my recollection that Jim Drake was the person from the union side who made the contact with Kennedy and secured his commitment to come. I have the distinct impression that it was Jim who drove him to the Mass and drove him away at the end of the rally. I myself was not involved in any of the Kennedy arrangements, but rather served as Cesar's planning liaison with the Mass and rally events themselves.

At the urging of his contacts in the United Auto Workers, Robert Kennedy had visited Delano somewhat reluctantly in 1966 as a member of a US Senate sub-committee delegation holding hearings on migratory labor. By the time of the 1968 visit, Kennedy had been following the farmworker movement through his aide Peter Edelman, who was in touch with union staff. Dolores Huerta, who was directing boycott efforts in New York, recalls that she too was in touch with Kennedy operatives: "We went down to see his assistant in New

York and asked him to ask Kennedy to come. Carter Burden's [RFK legislative assistant] reaction was, 'I don't think he should go. I think it's terrible to use a religious ceremony like a mass for that purpose'" (Levy, 285).

Nevertheless, by the time Kennedy arrived in Delano to witness the end of the fast, he was an enthusiastic supporter, proclaiming at the rally that Chavez was "one of the heroic figures of our time" and telling the workers that in the distant future, "though you may be old and bent from many years of labor, no man will stand taller than you when you say, 'I marched with Cesar.'" After the assassination of RFK, Chavez, accompanied by Chatfield, traveled to New York, where he stood watch at the foot of the casket for one hour as an honorary pallbearer the night before the funeral. The next day, Chavez and Chatfield were both surprised to hear people booing President Johnson as he entered St. Patrick's Cathedral.[1]

Bobby Kennedy's participation in the Mass and rally, along with an estimated eight thousand farmworkers, brought the national media spotlight to the farmworker movement as never before. The impact was huge: Cesar's national status was elevated yet again. His fast for nonviolence became the cornerstone for his movement and silenced his critics. More important, farmworkers throughout California and Arizona experienced and appreciated firsthand the power demonstrated by their union—it was so powerful that even the Kennedy family responded.

Not surprisingly, it turned out that Kennedy's appearance with Cesar jumpstarted his as-yet-unannounced presidential campaign. Cesar and the farmworker movement were big news every day in California, and with just one farmworker appearance Bobby Kennedy captured the liberal heart of the state's Democratic voters. In the June 1968 California presidential primary, the farmworker movement closed down almost its entire operation for three weeks in order to "get out the vote" for Bobby Kennedy—all purchased and paid for with just one appearance. Amazing.

Bonnie Burns Chatfield elaborates:

In April, Cesar ended his fast at Memorial Park in Delano with Senator Robert F. Kennedy in attendance. The mass was a spectacle of spectacles— only the Vatican could compete. LeRoy's religious background served him well. The crowd (thousands) was high with celebratory joy. As RFK was preparing to leave the park, shaking hands, patting shoulders, inching his

FIGURE 21 Dolores Huerta and Chatfield greet Senator Robert Kennedy at Memorial Park in Delano to take part in the religious ceremony ending the 1968 fast. Two months later, Kennedy would be assassinated. Courtesy of Walter P. Reuther Library, Archives of Labor and Urban Affairs, Wayne State University.

way through an adoring crowd, he spontaneously jumped to the hood of a car and asked, "Should I run for president?" The affirmation was deafening. He announced his candidacy a few days later.

In late May, LeRoy went to East Los Angeles to organize the get-out-the-vote (GOTV) campaign for RFK. The first of June, I met my mother in Modesto so she could take our daughter Clare to San Francisco for a long weekend. Then I was off to East L.A. as well. I have rarely, if ever, worked as hard as I did those next several days. I walked door-to-door, finding voters to serve as precinct captains for our massive GOTV on Election Day and making sure that every registered voter knew where to go on Tuesday.

Every house had a picture of JFK and a statue or picture of the Virgin Mary. I was often invited in for food or drink, but rarely accepted because I had too much territory to canvas. Every voter was for RFK. I just had to make sure that on Election Day, they got to the polls. I walked, usually alone, from 8 in the morning until 8 in the evening. But I recruited many local Chicanos to help me. They were as energetic and excited as I was. We knew we were going to win. (FMDP, 2004)[2]

The afterglow of Cesar's twenty-five-day fast, and Bobby Kennedy's trip to Delano to join Cesar when it ended, lasted for many, many, years. In part, this was due to Bobby's assassination only a few months later, but it was mostly due to the historic public fast that Cesar undertook for the sake of nonviolence—a first in the history of this country, I would say.

The assassinations of King and Kennedy brought home to all of us in the farmworker movement the sobering reality that Cesar might also be a target for assassination, if not now, perhaps someday in the future—but what to do about it?

My 1968 journal clearly shows the baby steps we tried to take in order to provide some security for Cesar. But you cannot provide security without paying for it, deciding what kind of security is needed, and securing the cooperation of the person being secured. In the beginning, Cesar would not authorize money to be spent for his security. We tried as best we could to override his financial veto. We ourselves could not decide what kind of security made sense, and Cesar was personally very uncooperative.

As my journal states, we had a minor scare while Cesar was in the hospital in San José. Ultimately, some of the older Filipino strikers were dispatched to the hospital to keep watch outside the room, but this was only a temporary arrangement. Cesar was embarrassed about it because it made him feel like a big shot. All of us felt the responsibility to do something to protect Cesar, and with Cesar still away from Delano, several union leadership meetings were held about it. There was much weeping and gnashing of teeth, but none of us really knew what to do or how to pay for it without Cesar's approval.

I have a recollection that at some point during this time, the issue of assassination came up with Cesar present at a union leadership meeting. He simply stated that he had already thought out his position and was at peace with the fact that an attempt could well be made on his life. But he simply had to ignore it and go on.

1. In his interview for the RFK archives, Peter Edelman recalled:

And then sometime in February I got a call from, I suppose it was Jim Drake or Jerry Cohen, those were the two people that I usually dealt with, saying that Cesar had gone on this fast and it was then about the sixth or seventh day and no one . . . it hadn't drawn any attention. And they just wanted the Senator to know that he had done that and also to know that they were worried about Cesar and they were not sure just what his intentions were and wanted to alert us because they felt they might want to come back to us in a week or so after that, because they were worried that perhaps the only way they could get Cesar to go off the fast would be if the Senator would ask him, come out there personally and ask him. So I went to him and he was deeply moved by it, really, you know, I think grasped immediately that Cesar was doing something that was just very meaningful. It was a, you know, a tremendous gesture on behalf of nonviolence and one that was a physical risk to himself. And he [RFK] asked me every day, you know, Have you . . . How is he today? Have you called out there? Do they want us to do something? What can I do? . . . and it was on that private plane flight from Los Angeles to Delano that I first knew for sure that he was going to run for president because he said explicitly, I am going to run. Now I have to figure out how to get McCarthy out of it. The Delano thing was very beautiful, lot of people there and marvelous kind of pageantry about it and a joyous occasion and very moving and Cesar was helped in and of course they broke bread together. They sat next to each other and broke bread together and Kennedy delivered a very moving speech which was largely his, just his own extemporaneous thing based on some drafts that he'd been given and so on. (Peter B. Edelman Oral History Interview—RFK #1, 7/15/1969, JFK Library, https://www.jfklibrary.org/asset-viewer/archives/RFKOH/Edel man%2C%20Peter%20B/RFKOH-PBE-01/RFKOH-PBE-01)

2. In a 1969 interview, Kennedy campaign coordinator Walter Sheridan recalled: "Cesar Chavez had twenty sound cars manned with his people speaking in Spanish on election day, which made a big difference. . . . Originally, they were going to put twenty cars in the Mexican community and twenty in the black community. We got the twenty for the Mexican community through Bert Corona." Walter Sheridan Oral History Interview—RFK#2, 8/13/1969, JFK Library, https: //www.jfklibrary.org/Asset-Viewer/Archives/RFKOH-WS-02. aspx.

17   On Movement Leaders

January 20, 1969—Richard Nixon was inaugurated that day. Say it isn't so. Just didn't seem possible. What a feeling of ennui overcomes me when I think about it.

As a person grows older—or perhaps it is because I have seen power at work and what prompts it to work—he loses his respect and fear for authority. How I used to be in awe of the pope, for example, until I realized what forces were at work to make him pope and why he said certain things and in a certain way. The personality of a man like John or Robert Kennedy can command respect and command authority even while those around him are still aware of the "humanness" of his position.

Something like that occurred to me a few days ago. Reading a few excerpts from Gandhi made me glow all over. What he said was great and it should have been said and its purpose was a kind of propaganda calculated to appeal to my idealism and to win me over to the justice of his cause. Cesar was frequently the same way. He would teach and preach and really turn people on, but he knew well enough that it is the ideal he was expounding and something not attainable, even for himself. I wonder if Jesus was the same way? I'm sure he was.

I realized too—and vividly—that Jesus never wrote anything himself. That the writers of the Gospels could be as "free" and as "loose" as they wished about what Jesus said and did. I can imagine some of us who will be

FIGURE 22 Chatfield explains the new Robert F. Kennedy Farm Workers Medical Plan to union members. Cesar Chavez translates to Spanish. Photo by Nick Jones. Courtesy of Nick Jones.

writing about Cesar someday will overstate that which was appealing to us and that which we want to drive home to others.

I also realized that movements have to have leaders and be embodied in personalities. In some of the student movements, there is a deliberate attempt to keep the leadership anonymous and in the background. While a certain kind of self-effacement and humility is powerful, people must have a person to identify with and relate to. They will idolize and "blow up" that person, but they need someone. And he has, therefore, to be willing to meet the press and give his views and explain what's happening. Events and acts do not magnetize and lead people. A person creating events and acting can.

In 2004, Chatfield reflected on recruiting young people, and returned to the issue of leaders:

I was a true believer in Cesar Chavez and his farmworker movement, and thirty-five years ago I could not believe there was anything more important in life, especially in the life of a college-age student, than the cause of the farmworkers. Do I believe that now, at age 70? No, I don't, but that is due in large part to the fact that I am no longer a true believer in anyone, or in any cause, and never will be again. Years after my farmworker experience, when I had several opportunities to build other organizations, I studiously avoided many of the "true believer" characteristics I had embraced so easily during my farmworker movement years. I don't know if it made my later work any better, but I felt better about myself and about the relationships I had with the people with whom I worked. Perhaps, I felt more human, I don't know. (FMDPd, December 6, 2004)

18   My Journal
Delano (Excerpts)

May 22, 1993

I have no clear recollection of having kept a journal during 1968 and 1969 but I did. I found it because Cesar Chavez died and was buried last month.

After I returned to Sacramento from the funeral, I kept thinking about a farmworker poster that I had seen at La Paz because it reminded me of a photograph that Cesar had taken of Sarah, my second daughter, when he was recuperating in the Tucson area after his Arizona fast in 1972. I rummaged around in the den closet, flipping through some of our family photo albums but then it occurred to me the picture was oversized and it wouldn't have fit in one these albums. Then I remembered having seen some old photos in one of the desk drawers a few months ago—or was it years? There, at the very bottom of the third drawer, I found a folder entitled "Personal Memorabilia." There was no picture of Sarah, but I found my journal.

It isn't surprising to me that I kept a journal in 1968, because I kept one in my senior year of high school (Mont La Salle, 1952) and again when I taught at Sacred Heart High School (San Francisco, 1960), and again during my summer sojourn in Mexico City (1961). As a senior high school English teacher, I required my students to keep weekly journals, which I collected and graded, if you can believe that. I was such an advocate about the need for students to write journals, it is surprising and disappointing, I might add, that over the years I did not practice more of what I had preached.

But there it was—written in long hand and unread for twenty-four years. The file also contained some photos of Cesar that have never been published, a few newspaper clippings from my farmworker days, and my "Open Letter" (1965) to friends explaining my resignation from the Christian Brothers in order to work with Cesar and his farmworker movement. But the most important document, and the most personal, was a touching letter sent to me by my wife, Bonnie, in 1968 when I was away from home tending to Cesar's medical care and therapy for his lower back pain.

Cesar's sudden death, my week at La Paz to help with the funeral arrangements, and now these relics from my years with the farmworker movement—quite overwhelming!

It will be easier to understand some of my comments and concerns of that time and place if you keep in mind that a major war, i.e., the grape boycott, was being waged in large cities of the United States and Canada. Farmworker board members, leaders, and organizers had been out of Delano for many months or more taking the fight for union recognition to the supermarkets and wholesalers. Such union players as Gilbert Padilla, Fred Ross, Eliseo Medina, Marshall Ganz, Marcos Muñoz, Richard Chavez, Chris Hartmire (CMM), Joe Serda, Dolores Huerta, Marion Moses, Julio Hernandez, Jessica Govea, et. al., were all out on the grape boycott, leaving behind a skeleton crew back home to carry on the strike, raise the money, provide the legal defense, and run the union bureaucracy.

The journal records that in the month of August alone, I received 1,350 newspaper clippings having to do with the union and the boycott. I am confident in remembering that the farmworker movement had a major full-time boycott presence in twenty-five cities.

You should also have in mind that Cesar had completed his first fast, twenty-five days in length, which he called his "fast for nonviolence." Senator Robert Kennedy, who had come to Delano, accompanied by many thousands of farmworkers and supporters, to be with Cesar Chavez when he broke his fast, all but announced his candidacy for presidency from the top of a car in Delano's Memorial Park after the event. A few months later, he was assassinated at the Ambassador Hotel in Los Angeles while many of us who had worked on his campaign in East Los Angeles were celebrating his primary victory. Martin Luther King Jr. had been assassinated earlier that same year.

And during this time, the United Farm Workers Organizing Committee had farmworker union contracts with the DiGiorgio Corporation and some of California's largest wineries: Christian Brothers, Paul Masson, Almaden, Gallo, Perelli-Minetti, Franzia, and Schenley Industries.

It is fair to say that by mid-1968, Cesar Chavez was already a national/international news celebrity. The grape boycott was constantly in the newspapers, on radio and TV, and the press, especially AP and UPI, were in close touch—sometimes daily—with the union in Delano asking for comment and background information as the controversy developed and boiled over between the growers and the union.

My Chavez-assigned mission when I had arrived in Delano in 1965 to work full time was to develop the co-op movement to provide consumer services for farmworkers and their families. A credit union had already been established—operated with meticulous care by Helen Chavez—and I proceeded to organize and build a co-op gas station, open a farmworkers' one-stop social services center, raise and administer funds for staff and legal support, and purchase and develop the first union headquarters in Delano (Forty Acres). Several years later came the purchase of La Paz in the Tehachapi Mountains for the location of the United Farm Workers national center. I also administered the on-again, off-again farmworker union medical clinic in Delano.[1]

This led to the development of the Farm Workers Medical Plan, which we later named the Robert F. Kennedy Farm Workers Medical Plan. This is one of the very few tangible and hopefully lasting contributions I might have made to the farmworker movement. As it turns out, twenty-five years ago, we were on the cutting edge of healthcare reform by putting our meager ten-cents-an-hour employer health and welfare contribution called for under the union contract into a self-insured preventative medical plan that stressed outpatient care, full maternity care, medications, short-term hospitalization, and term insurance. This happened because Cesar Chavez was determined that we would not give the money over to insurance companies to provide the usual union-type health plans, with all their emphasis on long-term hospitalization and medical benefits available primarily through inpatient care.

You ask, how much was my life influenced by Cesar Chavez? Let me give you some practical examples. It was because of Cesar that I left religious life. Because of him, I met Bonnie and got married in June 1966.

Bonnie Burns Chatfield, who had become a volunteer in 1965 (see essay 10), remembers:

FIGURE 23 Bonnie Luise Burns and LeRoy Joseph Chatfield on their wedding day in San Francisco, June 18, 1966. Photographer unknown. Courtesy of the Chatfield family.

LeRoy and I were married in June at St. Cecilia's Church in San Francisco. Jack Doyle, then a Paulist priest who had worked on the summer project in Delano, officiated. I was a traditional bride, and we celebrated a traditional wedding and reception but had only a two-day honeymoon in Bolinas at the Kincaids' cottage. The Kincaids were San Francisco liberals and farm-worker supporters and contributors. We moved to Los Angeles, where we would live until November. Our small office was west of the San Diego Freeway on Olympic Blvd. It was the first official NFWA office in Los Ange-les. (FMDP, 2004)

We had four daughters born in the farmworker movement—Clare and Sarah in a Bakersfield hospital, Kate at the UCLA Medical Center, and Amy at the community hospital in Tehachapi.

It was because of Cesar that after we were married we lived in a trailer park in Torrance; in a mobile home in an open field next to a farm labor camp in Delano; in a custom farmhouse next to the rose fields between McFarland and Delano; in a Delano tract home across from the high school ball field (two separate times); in a one-room apartment in Silver Lake (Los Angeles); in a custom-built home in the Hollywood Hills; in the black ghetto of central Los Angeles, in a two-story Berkeley-type house that had been closed up for up for more than ten years; in a parsonage under the LAX flight pattern; in a two-room house in Guadalupe, Arizona; and in a three-room, five-hundred-square-foot duplex at La Paz with four small children. That's eleven moves in seven years and I might have missed a few.

Bonnie Burns Chatfield provides details of their time in South Central LA:

The large, two-story, brown-shingled home on South Harvard Street with a wide front porch became our home. It would serve as the Los Angeles boycott house for many years. South Harvard, parallel to Western and Normandy, was just north of Pico, and very close to USC and the Migrant Ministry office on Olympic Blvd. We were the only white family on the block. The whole area was Black, not yet transitioned to Korean. The front door didn't lock from the outside. I left strollers, tricycles, and other toys on the front porch. I walked from my car, often at night, after attending a meeting, by myself. I was perfectly safe. . . . The house was owned by the American Friends Service Committee, which had inherited the property years before. . . . Cesar and Dolores, and several others from Delano, were among our first overnight guests. . . . We had a piano in the house. Dolores played. Cesar taught me how to make nopales with chili sauce. During that year on South Harvard, I would cook many, many meals for our boycotters, as well as guests. I thought nothing of whipping up some kind of meal for ten or twelve people. . . . In addition to leafleting and talking to people at Ralph's, I spent time meeting with church groups and other potential supporters in our continual quest for assistance, volunteers, and of course, money. (FMDP, 2004)

Cesar never wanted to have employees in the union, only volunteers. He had seen too many examples from other organizations (not only unions) of how employees became interested only in the "job" and not the cause. His solution was to give every volunteer five dollars a week in spending money, provide them with room and board, and pay their necessary bills (car payment, college loan, house payment, utilities, etc.). Not only did this approach save a lot of precious money, but it was also a daily reminder to the staff person of why they were part of the movement. It also ensured that the less committed left sooner rather than too late. This approach also honed the survival skills of staff workers who were assigned to boycott cities. They were expected to "live off the land." Housing, food, automobiles, office space, medical care—everything had to be hustled.

There were exceptions made to this policy, but as few as possible. I was one, so were Fred Ross, Jerry Cohen, the other attorneys, and a few others. Some staff members were assigned to the union but were on other organizations' payrolls. Chris Hartmire is an example that comes to mind. In Cesar's mind, this arrangement did not contravene his policy. For some, Cesar used the rationale that they worked for the National Farm Workers Service Center and not for the union. None of the exceptions were paid more than a stipend. We were given a lump sum of money once a month and had to make do. As you can imagine, there were times when these exceptions caused internal friction, but somehow Cesar was always able to finesse these situations. But he never wavered from the general rule—wouldn't even consider it! The other side of the coin is that some volunteers convinced themselves that they were not really being paid and therefore not be productive. And it is always difficult and messy to fire "volunteers."

The diary begins late in 1968 and continues for a few months into 1969. The afterglow of the fast in March, the Kennedy visit, and the publicity they brought were soon overwhelmed by events taking place in the United States and the world, for example, the murder of Bobby Kennedy, the election of Richard Nixon, and the ongoing war in Southeast Asia. At the level of organizational details, the work of the union proceeded without interruption, although, as Chatfield notes, new tensions were emerging within the organization, volunteers were struggling with burnout, and changes in the leader himself were becoming evident.

September 9, 1968

Today we left Cesar ill in the hospital. Last night he ate half a box of peanut butter brittle and his system was unable to digest it, leaving him constipated and with a splitting headache. To complete the comedy of errors, he had a terrible case of the hiccups. As I left the room, Dr. [Jerry] Lackner had just given him pills for the hiccups and an orderly was preparing to give him an enema. Two very old nuns were stationed at the door keeping guard. Their combined ages most certainly exceeded one hundred and fifty years but they still seemed up to frightening off friendly visitors. Cesar was completely dazed and so filled with sleep and pills that he could only grunt "yes" or "no."

Jerome "Jerry" Lackner (1927–2010) and his wife Yetta were among the earliest volunteers. Yetta recalls:

> It was December 1965. My husband Jerome Lackner and I drove to Delano from San José with our five young children. The older ones were on school holiday. We had heard about the most recent efforts to organize farmworkers. . . . We weren't sure what we might have to offer. Jerome was a physician; I was a school teacher/housewife then. It turned out that Jerome provided medical care and the children and I were on the picket lines. Sometimes, growers would single me out, come over and tell me that I didn't belong there, that it wasn't my business. I would explain that the conditions for workers who provide food for my table is my concern, it's everyone's concern. . . . After that first winter, we went to Delano whenever we could. Jerome continued to offer his medical services and worked with

many others, including Marion Moses, to establish farmworker clinics. . . .
As California State Director of Health he outlawed the use of the short-
handled hoe, got latrines in the fields, worked for pesticide and spraying
control. (FMDP, 2012)

Mrs. Lackner also served as a key outreach person between the NFWA and
Jewish communities. In March of 1965, Dr. Lackner had worked on the medical
team for the Selma to Montgomery marches; Governor Jerry Brown appointed
him as state director of health in 1975.

Paul Fusco of *Look* magazine called. I think he got the word from Zim-
merman that we are a little upset about *Look* still not running the article
and yet they keep coming to Delano to gather more pictures. Paul sounded
a little sheepish about asking to come back and get some pictures of the
Schenley workers or perhaps he is just more sensitive than most photographers and journalists. I suspect that Schenley Industries were responsible
for killing the last story; perhaps the editors hope to placate them this time
by giving them a boost.

We have orders from Cesar to corner Larry [Itliong] so that he can feel
the real pressure of responsibility. Guess Jim [Drake] and Jerry [Cohen] did
a good job the first day because Larry was at the office when Bonnie and I
came and then he returned again in the evening.

September 10, 1968

Dr. Lackner must be in his element. Taking care of Cesar also means
determining more or less who gets in to see him. Bill Kircher [AFL-CIO
director of organization], who is going to pay the bill, was told "no." Fred
Ross Sr. was given permission if he would go in the same time I did. I can
imagine Jerry really digging all this arranging and rearranging. Actually, it is
better for Cesar to have only a few, a very few, visitors. People mean well but
they can surely wear you out. Congressman Don Edwards called today from
Washington to say hello, to ask about Cesar, and to give him his regards. A
nice gesture but I had the impression his secretary had just given him his
daily list of important persons who were sick for him to call.

Paul Fusco of *Look* was here today doing some shooting. He picked a
gondola of grapes at Schenley just to see what it was like. He seemed genuinely impressed about how hard the work was and how fast the people had
to work. He didn't seem to be aware of what the latest developments were

with respect to the story or that Cesar had been asked to write an article for *Look*. I brought him up to date and asked him to tip us off when the article was going to appear, if it does, so we would have the opportunity to "key off" the story. He said he would.

Seemed pretty quiet today on the boycott front, at least not much was reported that I heard about. During the month of August our clipping service sent us about 1,350 newspaper clippings regarding the boycott. Clippings from all over the United States but especially from Minnesota, New York, Michigan, and California. The boycott has really become a national issue and it seems to be generating even more tension.

September 12, 1968

Bill Kircher came to Delano from Washington to ride up to San Francisco with me. Bill has accepted, I think, the role of a campaign director in California of the Humphrey presidential campaign. He talked at great length about some of his misgivings with the labor hierarchy and others and about what kind of a job it should be, etc. Then too, I think Bill is wondering if he really could cope or even understand the issues in California. The young radicals or anarchists or whatever seem not only to annoy him by what they do and say but he also feels helpless to deal effectively with them. And after twenty years or more of what he terms liberal activity, he sounds rather bitter that instead of being rewarded by being listened to he is really an outcast and considered part of the establishment and power structure that he has confronted. It is really a harsh time for older activists and liberals of another era. Especially if they need recognition and praise for their past accomplishments.

We stopped by the hospital to see Cesar. What a difference enforced rest makes. He looks ever so much better. Fred Ross was there too. Then Fathers McDonald, Garcia, and Corty came in unexpected and unannounced. Rules in Catholic hospitals don't apply to priests. Father McDonald is an old "radical" or "turk" who was exiled many years ago over the issue of organizing farmworkers. Since then he has spent time in Japan and South America. A very bright person, I am told, but now only a shadow of what he was or what people thought him to be. He strikes me as paternalistic, presumptuous, self-centered, and out of touch. He made over Cesar last night like a wise old man talking with a child. He recited the Our Father, Hail Mary, Glory Be, and Apostles Creed in such a way that all seven of us had to participate. He is one of those priests ever conscious of his priestly caste, a person set aside from other men and, whether he means it or not or knows it or not, he looks "down" on others. He cannot lead because he insists others must follow. That posture is so foreign in today's world. I fear he will die a broken and forgotten man.

September 13, 1968

The *Fresno Bee* had a good editorial on the boycott, calling on both the union and the growers to negotiate and to be willing to accept a third-party mediator. I can't imagine the *Bee* being so forthright if they didn't expect the inevitable, i.e., some talks to begin. As long as we won union recognition, I think we would be satisfied with any decent mediation.

Talked with Cesar at length yesterday on my way back from San Francisco to Delano via San José. He was very relaxed, in good humor, and without that tired look he has carried for so long. We discussed the possible "cessation" of the boycott—a planned and prearranged show of responsibility and morality. We don't want to ruin the industry, etc. We also discussed how to get O'Connor Hospital to remove the grapes from their menu. Cesar gave me the gist of a letter to the Sister Superior, which I wrote and had hand-delivered through one of the nurses. Today I found out from Dr. Lackner that Father [Eugene] Boyle called the archdiocesan priest in charge of hospitals and put it to him. He in turn called the administrator of O'Connor and suggested they not purchase grapes. One of the nuns came by Cesar's room tonight to say that all the grapes were gone and that all the hospitals in the archdiocese were getting rid of theirs too.

Dr. Lackner called at 3:30 this morning to tell me of a phone call that the hospital had received from a woman who said she was a nurse for a doctor who was to make an examination of Cesar the next day and could she please have Cesar's room number. The girl at the switchboard gave the number but then had the sense to let Dr. Lackner know what had happened. He immediately had Cesar transferred to another floor and notified the chief of police of San José. The chief conferred with the administrator today and they agreed to assign a policeman outside of Cesar's door from 12 midnight to 6 a.m. for the remainder of his stay in the hospital.

I guess I'm not one for meetings. Tonight was the Friday-night meeting and I decided to go. For one thing, Cesar was away and I didn't want Tony [Orendain] and Larry [Itliong] to jump to the conclusion that I don't respect their leadership, or more properly put, their positions. So I went. But at 7:55 p.m. the meeting still hadn't started and then I saw some visitors who came from out of town and who would trap me after the meeting to talk to me about working here in Delano so I split.

September 14, 1968

Dr. Lackner called a few hours ago to say that a reporter discovered the fact that Cesar had police protection. And though it is only from 12 a.m. to 6 a.m., it is newsworthy. But when the reporter called for confirmation, Jerry begged him not to report it. Well, you can imagine what happened.

My father phoned a few minutes ago to tell me he heard on the news that an attempt had been made on Cesar's life by a person disguised as a doctor and that two policemen were assigned to guard Cesar around the clock.

My inclination is to let the matter drop with a "no comment." The whole affair is now so confused and garbled that any attempt at clarifying it is impossible because no reporter is going to accept the truth—there isn't something that is being left unsaid. The most effective and truthful publicity is to decline comment. The reporters will naturally think we are trying to hide something, but if they report anything it will be the product of their own imagination and sense of prophesy.

God, will O'Connor Hospital be glad when Cesar leaves. Jerry also said that Ethel Kennedy and Ted Kennedy called Cesar. I hope that is true. We can hardly wait until we get to work for Ted Kennedy. Father [Roger] Mahony called to say that the Bishop is definitely coming back to Fresno on Sunday. And that he will be meeting with [John] Kovacevich and [John] Guimarra on Monday afternoon. He promised to call me immediately after the meeting.

I was reminded last February when mowing the lawn of some of the ideas that Cesar touched upon in his speech before he began his fast for nonviolence:

Building a union is not worth a single life of a grower or his child or a farmworker or his child.

How could we be so concerned about the taking of life in Vietnam and yet have so little reverence for life here in the United States.

I do this because I love you.

When we resort to violence, we lack the will to win.

Resorting to violence is really an admission of our lack of creativity and imagination.

I was so struck with Cesar's reaction when he heard that Bonnie was pregnant. His eyes lighted up and he spoke excitedly with genuine happiness. When I sort of shrugged and cautioned him that it was unofficial, he refused to be daunted and said, "I really like these sorts of things."

September 15, 1968

Cesar is creating a crisis for the leadership of the union. Better said, the officership. He is using the threat on his life, which has been blown up by the press, to force the officers to make a decision about whether they are going to see that Cesar is protected or not. He claims that they have to decide so that he can psychologically prepare himself. But it has the makings of a trap too, because if they do nothing—and they probably won't—then when the membership asks how come, the blame can be laid where it belongs. This whole affair leaves me emotionally frustrated because I have been trying to get Cesar to accept some kind of security measures and he has resisted, and now that he is pushing for a decision about such matters I cannot help but feel remiss. Obviously, the protection should come from the membership and I'm sure that we could recruit enough young men to cover the day.

I didn't go to the office today, Sunday, but I just don't relax either. My mind is constantly dwelling on what should be done. And I feel guilty about not doing more. But this is going to have to change because if I don't relax at least one day a week, it is going to affect my whole week. Especially during these times when there is so much tension and when we have such lazy people to work through.

I have decided to take up again the study of Spanish. It is so easy not to learn it but so foolish for failing to do so.

September 16, 1968

Bishop Timothy Manning and Monsignor Roger Mahony met today with growers John Kovacevich, John Giumarra Jr., Bergand, and Frank and Paul Deaner. The growers hope for legislation and are attempting to get the bishop in position to support them.

A bomb threat today on Cesar's house. Larry [Itliong] is finally getting the picture and José Luna, Philip Vera Cruz, and Tony Armington have been dispatched to San José to serve as security for Cesar. Little by little, I guess. [George] Zenovich from Fresno is trying to arrange a meeting with Caric and Setrakian about the union. He is concerned about the threats against Cesar's life and the possible reaction. What we need are a few threats against some of the growers in order to bring them to their senses.

September 17, 1968

Marion [Moses] and Manuel [Chavez] came back from New York. Picked them up at the airport about 5:15. Marion came over for dinner and was full of tales about the boycott in New York. By getting the community involved and really taking on those stores. I guess they have really raised hell. Whole sections of the city's poor areas are completely free of grapes, and the store managers are sick of the hassle it is causing them.

Born in West Virginia, Marion Moses first met Chavez in late 1965 while she was taking classes at Berkeley. Having already received her nursing degree from Georgetown University, where she had become engaged with the teachings of the Catholic Worker Movement, she left her position as head nurse of the surgical unit at a Kaiser hospital in San Francisco to volunteer for the farmworkers. Her initial meeting with Chavez made a strong impression on her: "I remember some of what he said but I mostly remember his gentle manner; that although he wasn't a particularly good speaker, he had a strong moral force, an inner quality which the often-used word 'charisma' cannot even begin to describe." She served as a nurse to both Dorothy Day and Chavez (especially for his lifelong back problems but also during his fasts), working full time for the union from 1966 to 1971, when she left to attend medical school. She returned to the union in the early 1980s and directed the farmworker clinics. Her research on pesticide poisoning was groundbreaking.

We had a sick meeting at noon of the pickets, office people, and the officers. Larry [Itliong] reported about the two threats to Cesar's life, one in San José and the other here, and told the group what steps had been taken: 1) he called Joe Luna but couldn't talk to him very well because Joe doesn't understand English, 2) he had Sally DeWitt talk to Joe, 3) he asked Philip Vera Cruz, who was sitting in the audience, to go to San José with Bob Armington, and 4) he volunteered Manuel Uranday and Joe Reeves to go to San José too. Then he asked if anyone had any objections to his course of action or if there were any suggestions. Candy said that whoever was assigned there should stand right by the door and not let anyone in who was not a member of the union and should even taste Cesar's food. Another man volunteered to go. Guarjado said that whoever went should be familiar with people who have business with Cesar so that an assassin would not get in.

The observations of these three were obviously sincere and they were genuinely concerned. Larry ran the meeting in a half-joking, half-apologetic manner, and it was quite clear that he did not give all that much weight to the problem. Larry also mentioned that he called Dolores [Huerta] and Julio [Hernandez]. I made the suggestion that perhaps it was the proper time to discuss what security policy the union should have when Cesar returns to Delano since it is a week from today that he will be released. Larry responded by saying that we have another week to give it some thought and besides there were only three board members left in Delano and we had decided upon the course of action for this week. As far as I am concerned Larry has had it. Both he and Tony [Orendain] instinctively react against the fact that Cesar is the famous man he is and they simply refuse to "let go," accept their limitations, and work from there. Larry just doesn't work, except when it benefits himself.

September 19, 1968

Yesterday, Marion and I traveled to Palo Alto, where I spoke to the Ministerial Association about the boycott. We spent part of the afternoon with Cesar. Bill Kircher was there. He is in California trying to build support for Humphrey. Of course, it is nearly an impossible job and he is frustrated at not being able to get Cesar to give it any priority. Bill reduces everything to a personal level, e.g., I've done this and this for you, why aren't you going to help me? But he just grunts and groans and whines his displeasure. Or he pouts and won't speak.

I complained bitterly to Cesar about Larry, Tony, and Bill Widman. Larry and Tony are very insecure people and are so afraid that Cesar is playing God. Then Larry is concerned almost solely with himself and fancies himself a lover, a playboy. At least Tony works, and works hard! Bill Widman is a two-faced politician who tries to say what he thinks you want to hear. He hates Delano and is here because Kircher ordered him here. He'll be leaving in December for the promised land, which is anywhere but Delano.

Cesar responded to my bitterness by saying that sooner or later he was going to leave the union and he had decided that it was going to be sooner. That he would like to organize a team to go from place to place organizing workers and once they were organized, to move on. Not to get involved with the politics that develop or to have to deal with officers day after day who don't want to move. Some of it is wishful thinking since the pressure of leadership will force him to remain in charge and in control. On the other hand, I wouldn't be surprised to see him resign very abruptly someday when the union least expects it.

September 26, 1968

When your days are guided by events and not the reverse, it can be very frustrating. Your thrust, your work has no direction, no goal. You are always on the defensive. These have been my kind of days for quite some time. Instead of building something, it seems that I am only responding. Very little satisfaction because there is little challenge. Theoretically, I could be busy about many things: clinic, co-op, Forty Acres, etc., but practically speaking all these take meetings of officers, including their time and attention. But with all our attention focused on the boycott, all of our expectations are centered there. The other union details and matters that come up are handled in such a way as to slide by them.

Throughout the month of October, Chatfield devoted his time to the painstaking work of developing the union's Health and Welfare Plan. This included multiple interviews with doctors, making cost comparisons with other plans, and constant travel, including trips to LA to prepare the union's activities there on behalf of Hubert Humphrey's presidential campaign. On October 12, he wrote: "Just impossible to juggle all of the things we have cooking. Seems like we just transfer them and or put them off until we simply have to act. Spread very thin."

November 19, 1968

Seems like ages since I have written anything and how many times have I resolved to do so. A diary is like a piece of old furniture, it can't help but grow more valuable—if not for its quality, at least for its sentimental value. Bonnie, Clare, and I spent four weeks in East Lost Angeles working on the Humphrey campaign. I found it very exhilarating. The long hours, the excitement of trying to build an organization. I guess it was kind of a relief to get away from Delano. It seems that when Cesar is away from Delano or out of the center of activity, Delano closes in on me. Petty differences, struggles for authority that don't mean anything, jealousies—all of these things seem to rage when Cesar is away. Perhaps it is because his presence is powerful enough to protect those of us who work around him and who become the butt for this activity.

Bonnie, Clare, and I went to Santa Barbara on Sunday to spend the afternoon visiting with Cesar and Helen. Cesar and I talked about [Ben] Berkov and the Health and Welfare Plan, some of the internal problems of the union, the bishops' statement, and about the money for the political education fund. Cesar bounced two ideas against me: how to use the ideas and techniques from the Liturgy of the Mass to enliven the union meetings, e.g., singing, a few rituals, scrolls on the wall with sayings, etc. The other thing was a retirement center for the Filipinos, a kind of co-op living where each one could raise chickens or a garden, where meals could be in common. You can tell Cesar is much better and his morale is good when he talks about things like this. I think he deliberately does this to stimulate us. He tries to have something for everyone. This forces us out of the doldrums and gives us hope and a spirit of achieving.

November 20, 1968

Today there was a news release that DiGiorgio was selling his 6,100 acres in Arvin and Lamont and that without a union successor clause, the union would be without a membership there. Building this union has certainly been a series of setbacks. I guess that is how unions are born and built.

Tonight, I put up a flood light in our backyard area. I guess we have been a little uneasy since someone fired a pellet gun through our front window last week and since our house was burglarized. Kind of shakes you up, at least for a while.

November 21, 1968

Spent most of today lining up appointments with doctors from Kingsburg to Sanger tomorrow. My hope is to get them to cooperate a little with their fees but really there is no hope of that, at least until we can build our own clinics or hire our own doctors. Some of these guys really flinched when I mentioned farmworkers or union. They just don't know!

Jerry [Cohen] announced a primary boycott of Bank of America today at a press conference in San Francisco because of their refusal to talk with the union about negotiating a contract. Jerry said that Larry [Itliong] came to the point of endorsing the student riots and lectured the press for fifteen minutes. That's all we need at this point—a call to violence!

Have begun to look for a space for a political action center in East Los Angeles. An abandoned church or synagogue or something along those lines. We need a place where we can build a base of operation, not only for the boycott but for political activity as well. I would hope someday to get involved in that kind of organizing. Time will tell.

Bonnie ran out of money for the month today. We discussed it at length. The question of buying—what and how much? But looks like we'll have to take money out of the credit union to make it through Christmas. And then we have the coming baby. We owe $100 more to the doctor and we will owe the hospital $150 at least. We still owe $340 to my folks for the furniture we bought, but if the insurance money comes through for our stolen stuff we will use it to pay them off. That still leaves our big bill with Sears for our washing machine and the one we bought Helen (Chavez).

Bonnie Burns Chatfield describes the daily life of a young couple committed to collective struggle:

> I look back with amazement at the way I was willing to live my life. When we were home together, LeRoy was usually on the phone. Every evening, beginning about 6, he made contact with every team leader throughout the L.A. area, including San Bernardino, Riverside, and Orange counties. He counted numbers at every store: How many contacts? How many turned away? The table was spread with charts. I prepared dinner, usually had some help cleaning up, bathed the girls, and put them to bed. Marriage and family life were not a high priority. But we did have a successful boycott. At some point during that summer, growers agreed to elections and the union called a temporary end to the grape boycott. (FMDP, 2004)

January 3, 1969

Once again, today was spent in discussing the Health and Welfare Plan with Cesar. He is a stickler for details—constantly probing and asking questions—many of which I have to answer with an educated guess. He is very concerned about translating what the alternatives are to the membership and making them understand, forcing them to understand. Cesar maintains that the union health and welfare plans are one of the major reasons why union members hate their union. Too often they accumulate millions of dollars in reserves and act like investment companies. Our latest idea is to put all the alternatives on colored cards and to let the leadership deal their own plan, limited of course by the restriction of what amount of money is available per month per worker. In this way they will realize the variables involved and the costs of medical care—which are fantastic!

Cesar seems to be regaining his strength and his buoyancy. He swims twice a day in David's pool. The temperature of the water is ninety-six degrees—psychologically perfect! Little by little, I am regaining my enthusiasm and capacity for work.

January 27, 1969

I am amazed. Just finished reading five or six union health and welfare plans and was horribly disappointed in what they offered. I remember reading the same plans a year ago and being terribly impressed with what they offered. Why my change of attitude? For one thing, I now know how much (approximately) each benefit costs and how much is available per hour to spend for the worker. And believe me, the worker isn't getting it all. Consultants, insurance companies, and administrators are eating a fair share.

Our plan, on paper, deals almost exclusively with outpatient care and those benefits are more substantial than other union plans. What is upsetting to me about these plans is that they pay a lot of "half-things": ½ maternity, ⅓ hospital, ⅓ doctor visit. They don't pay completely the usual everyday medical costs.

Aside from pride of authorship, we have the making of a solid, well-thought-out, master plan for family health care. Of course, since we are placing our premium costs (educated guesses) so close to our income, we will probably go broke! But what the hell! At least we will never have millions in reserve used in real estate or in the stock market.

February 12, 1969

I remember a talk that Cesar gave in the winter of 1966 at the St. Francis Hotel in San Francisco to a labor convention. Larry [Itliong] was also there as a speaker, representing AWOC. Larry gave his usual, "I'm not educated but . . ." and then used all kinds of flowery phrases and clichés. A typical labor speech, middle class, etc. Cesar completely won over the group with his straight, simple, and hard-hitting talk. A collection was taken and people gave generously. As soon as the formal program was over, Cesar motioned to me and whispered, "Try to find out what happened to the money." As I recall, the chairman of the program told me that it would be split in half between NFWA and AWOC. Later in the car, Cesar was furious that AWOC should so capitalize on our work and resolved never to be on a program again with Larry. I learned from that time on that when Cesar talked, we should have complete control or have an understanding beforehand about

FIGURE 24 Staff of Robert F. Kennedy Farm Workers Medical Plan, 1970.
Front row (left to right): Maria Robles, Jessica Govea, Maria Rifo; *back row (left to right):* George Catalan, LeRoy Chatfield. Photographer unknown.
Courtesy of Walter P. Reuther Library, Archives of Labor and Urban Affairs,
Wayne State University.

the money raised. Several times we have been burned, especially by the ACLU raising money at our expense, but not if I had anything to do with it.

I remember the night that Luis Valdez met Cesar. Luis was selling copies of the Progressive Labor newspaper at one of a series of meetings that Cesar was speaking at early in 1966 or late 1965 to raise money for the strike. Luis was capitalizing on our crowds and even asked us for a ride to Cesar's next speech so he could sell more papers. Someone did give him a ride because he was there when we got there. After the meeting, Cesar talked with him. In fact, I believe we gave him a ride back to San Francisco from our meeting at the Franciscan church in Oakland. Cesar explained to him some of his ideas about using theater and songs to communicate. Luis was very turned on and the next time I saw him was in Delano starting El Teatro Campesino. If memory serves me correctly, the last remark that Cesar made to Luis that night was "You, I like. Your friends, I don't!" (referring to the other Progressive Labor guys).

February 13, 1969

What a day! Driving for hours while Cesar talked to Eddie and Millie Lewis about "one hundred" different varieties of kibbutz. I was in the middle in the back seat, and was my rear end sore. After a while I became unusually impatient because I had been through it so many times before and I was ready for action. And Cesar can really go far out, though he rarely believes his own propaganda. At one point he told Eddie that he had two consultants for farming and raising cattle—Gil Flores and Katy Peake. I could hardly keep a straight face.

I remember once driving Cesar to a meeting in Oakland across the Bay Bridge and Jack Weintraub, a Teamster official, was in the car with us. Weintraub was explaining to Cesar how to identify the trucks and possible ways to mark them. Weintraub talked and talked and talked and Cesar listened and listened. I was ready to burst because Weintraub was so condescending and talking about things so simple that I was hoping Cesar would put him in his place. But no, Cesar just listened. Afterward, I started to commiserate with him about what he had to put up with but he simply shrugged it off as necessary. This happened in the winter of 1966 or late 1965.

I remember taking Cesar to speak at San Francisco State in 1966. Only a few people showed up, maybe fifteen to twenty. But faces that were new to me then I came to see years after, involved in some way or other. You can never tell from the size of the group about its quality. And some people always show up to get involved long before it is fashionable to do so. Of course they tend to drift away to something else but that's only natural, I suppose.

February 15, 1969

Cesar fell asleep on me. I left his house at 2 a.m. this morning and there were already four guards for the 12 midnight to 6 a.m. shift and Cesar was still awake. He had a meeting at 9 a.m. with the officers and then an audit committee meeting at 10 a.m. It must have been an exhausting meeting because when I arrived at 12:30 p.m. he was dizzy but still trying to focus on Jerry [Cohen] and me. But he fell sound asleep. That happened a few weeks ago too when we were having a Service Center meeting. He told me he fell asleep talking to Ann Israel too. The strain of decisions and problems must really drain him. I notice too that he does far more talking than before. He carries the ball more and his vocabulary continues to grow by leaps and bounds. He begins to savor phrases and examples. Some of us have also remarked about how repetitious he has become—same stories, same examples. But that probably is the result of having so many separate and subdivided meetings that it is almost impossible to keep track of what you told to whom.

When I was at the house this morning, I felt so sorry for Helen. Not able to go to bed, so little privacy day after day after day. And I mean I could really feel how difficult it was for her. I said, "How are you doing, Helen?" She said, somewhat wistfully, "Oh, fine." I said, "I'll bet!"

March 1, 1969

Cesar never ceases to amaze me. Yesterday I was urging upon him the necessity of permitting the union to celebrate the anniversary of his fast for nonviolence. He didn't say no but at the same time he said he would have to know what other things I had in mind. He talked about his proposed "Blessing of the Families Festival Day" and the victory celebration when the strike was over. He then revealed to me that on one of these occasions he was going to adopt the use of pajama-like clothing, similar to that used in Latin America and in Asia. Wearing this clothing would be an act of "sacrifice" until farmworkers had a union. Once again, a bold stab of genius—an act that cuts across all cultures, all ideologies, and creatively uses something as common as "dress" to communicate. And not mind you, the garb of the militaristic revolutionary but of the poor peasant. Clothes without pretensions but a powerful symbol of revolution.

Bonnie said tonight that she wished we were leaving Delano, that it was time. I probably have passed on to her my "blueness" about some of the internal bitching that has been going on inside the union. Or perhaps it is her intuition. At any rate I'm not ready to go yet, nor do I think it is "time." I am a firm believer of one phase leading into another.

March 2, 1969

As I see history made here in Delano and participate in decision-making that affects tens of thousands of people, I realize that written history is so shallow and misleading. The study of history or the explanation of the whys of an event are such a distillation and abstraction of the flesh and blood of the real happening that it is no wonder a college education is confusing and irrelevant.

Take the fact of the fast of Cesar a year ago. How fearful he was that it would not be received by the public correctly. How many times did he bounce the idea against me? How fearful he was that he couldn't do it. How he would dictate our next move with a nod, a wink, a phrase. When I began late in the fast to plead with him to end it on Wednesday, he simply said, "You won't be able to get the people until Sunday." How necessary the fast was to prevent the court hearing, which could have exposed union violence and marred our image. The fact that it was Lent, that the time of the year was slow and people did not have much work and could be organized. A very complex, sputtering, organized, plotted, and accidental event and yet history will neatly report the fact and the reason and the result. Will it also record the impalement of John Duggan, Fred Hirsch, and Tony Orendain by its point? Probably not, but yet in some ways they were the real ones responsible for his fast. Now when I read about events perhaps I will also see between, behind, and underneath.

Like Doug Adair quoted in essay 14, Hirsch, Orendain, and Father Duggan were among those who opposed the 1968 fast; many others were ambivalent. Bonnie Burns Chatfield describes her position:

> In the beginning, I was opposed to Cesar's fast. Not necessarily fast-ing—that was his business—but the use of the fast as an organizing tool. Using religious belief to manipulate people struck me as hypocritical. There were a few others, Tony Orendain among them, who were opposed. Since LeRoy, along with Marshall and Chris, was the organizer of the fast, I accepted it and became a participant in the nightly pageantry and week-end celebrations of hunger. It was staged as a Fast for Nonviolence. And it became a spectacular pageant. I began to understand its value, realizing that all of us are influenced by drama that plays upon our emotions and elicits action. (FMDP, 2004)

March 7, 1969

Bonnie is better and I am too. This time the whole family came down sick but Bonnie is worst of all—no voice, coughing, not able to sleep, sore throat, and all this late in the pregnancy. It could be dangerous.

Last night Marion came by to look after us and bring us some pills. I fixed her a drink. She looked ghostly pale. Tired and frustrated was my diagnosis. And we began to talk of Cesar's illness. She said Jim [Drake] seemed of the opinion that Cesar needed it. Her opinion was that it was definitely psychosomatic, at least at this stage. My view is that Cesar is experimenting with it. He knows he can get well because his Santa Barbara convalescence taught him that. He knows there is no quick and magic cure because our Carmel stay taught him that too. So he is using it to probe the people, to unify us, to force us to act more because he is helpless. There is a certain kind of power that can emanate from a "crippled" man when he speaks and acts with authority. I think there is a certain expectation among people that a great man should be physically handicapped—not deformed—but one who suffers and who has to overcome pain in order to accomplish something.

March 23, 1969

Sunday night. We are all moved in. Very comfortable. Folks came Thursday night and left today at noon. They gave Bonnie money for a clothes dryer. Paul Schrade and Doctor Janet Travell came to see Cesar today. Met with Fred [Ross] yesterday and today to do a taped interview for Fred's book about the union. So much has blurred in the year since the fast but I still remember some of the feelings I had at that time: uselessness and hostility and impatience toward those opposed. How sensitive I am. Too sensitive!

I have been mentally pacing for the past few days. My mind gallops and flits from point to point. My only outlet is work or sloth and thus far I have chosen sloth. Moping, sitting, puttering, watching TV, I just can't break out of it. Moving on Wednesday and Thursday was very helpful because the work was cut out and waiting and all I had to do was meet it. But now and for weeks past I seem to be in a situation where I have to create work, to marshal events in such a way as to accomplish something, but at the same time sensing that perhaps whatever it is I'm trying to create is useless and a waste of time. There is no direction or plan, or at least I'm unable to see through the maze. The employers are balking about the Health and Welfare Plan, Dolores [Huerta] is completely and totally disorganized, Coachella is opening up. I am confused!

The preparations for an action in Southern California were yet another item on an already-full agenda. Volunteer Hub Segur recalls: "The Coachella March in May 1969 was an appeal to workers in Mexico to support the table grape strike. Marchers took eight days to reach the border town of Calexico and stage a unification rally. . . . The following year the table grape growers signed contracts with the Union" (FMDP, 2006).

And my mind begins to race. I have doubts about my worth and my confidence wavers. I need more love and affection that I'm willing to give to others. To break out is simple: take one firm step and then a second. A form of overcompensation is trying to overachieve. The only way to accomplish anything is to start now and with something tangible. Stop juggling one hundred things—pick one.

March 27, 1969

Today I am giving a hand to Marion with Cesar's correspondence. Some of these letters received date back to September. Depending upon my mood, I write a letter that tries to say something and of course strikes a humble tone that befits Cesar. I much prefer doing this than writing an innocuous and bland response that could be used time and time again.

To give you an idea of the kinds of letters received:

> Ethel Kennedy
>
> Congressman John Tunney
>
> Senator Ralph Yarborough
>
> Archbishop Lucey
>
> Hubert Humphrey
>
> Leslie Dunbar

and add to these a few attorneys, professors, students, and a woman who writes from Texas asking for table grape cuttings for her garden.

I suppose Cesar gets a kick reading these letters and then reading "his" responses through Marion, Jim [Drake], or in this case, myself. I have done this for Cesar many times before but only with those letters in which I had a stake and felt that certain things should be said or not said. This is different, as I attend to each letter with a kind of dispassionate attention. I admit I sometimes get carried away and no doubt Cesar will kick them back to be toned down.

Dolores said she met with Brothers Frederick and Justin regarding me being named as the administrator of the Health and Welfare Plan. "We have nothing personal against LeRoy but our information is that these plans are administered by someone neutral." Maybe that's not exactly what they said but I'm not surprised if they took that attitude. I was good enough to work my ass off for them while in the Christian Brothers and to be entrusted with positions of authority. But now they can never forgive my change of allegiance, I guess.

The end came suddenly, without warning, seemingly from out of nowhere. The Delano growers agreed to recognize the union and sign a collective bargaining agreement. Just like that! Done! Finished! The nonunion grapes picked yesterday would become the union grapes sold today. The lives of the striking farmworkers and the boycott volunteers had for years been wrapped around the axle of strike picket lines in the field and boycott and picket lines at the nation's supermarkets. This unexpected development, this complete victory, was difficult to process. Sure, elation and victorious celebration today, but what do we do with the rest of our lives come tomorrow?

You ask: how was the Delano Grape Strike won? Was it the five years of farmworkers' strike picket lines in the fields? No, it was not. Then was it the four years of the volunteers' boycott picket lines at the supermarkets in the major cities of United States and Canada? No, it was not. Chavez was right! The growers had the money but they did not have the time. They did not have the time to contend with a strike zone that included both the grape fields and the parking lots in front of the nation's supermarkets. They ran out of time. Their only option was to sell union grapes.

The five-year Delano Grape Strike, a watershed event in the history of California, was over. Amen!

On July 29, 1970, twenty-nine table grape growers agreed to sign contracts with the UFW. Other growers and unions, however, were already plotting. Soon, lettuce growers signed a series of sweetheart deals with the Teamsters. Rev. Wayne Hartmire explains:

> In July of 1970 as the grape struggle was ending, the United Farm Workers (UFW) petitioned lettuce growers for secret ballot union representation elections. The growers ignored the request, sought out the Teamsters union and signed back door contracts. The workers were not consulted. Denied elections, they went out on strike on August 24, 1970, to demonstrate that they wanted to be represented by Cesar Chavez's UFW. 7,000 workers walked off the job in what the *LA Times* called "The Largest Farm Labor Strike in the U.S. History." (FMDP, "Straight Talk On The Lettuce Strike," August 1, 1972)

On December 4, federal agents arrested Chavez because the UFW disobeyed a court order prohibiting picketing. He was not released by order of the California Supreme Court until December 23. The so-called Salad Bowl Strike—

an unusually violent strike in terms of law enforcement and Teamsters tactics—ended on March 26, 1971.

NOTE

1. According to Matthiessen's notes on conversations with Chatfield and Marion Moses, "at a meeting of two hundred farm workers it was discovered that nine out of ten had never been to a dentist, and that only three had ever had X-rays of the chest. Most of the farm workers' complaints were based directly on deprivation, but the most serious illnesses were caused by exposure to agricultural chemicals" (339).

19 Letter from Delano (with Growers' Response)

As the actual author of the letter, Chatfield elaborates on its origins:

> It was one of the very few times in my life when I felt inspired to write. The ideas, of course, were Cesar's but not in the sense that he dictated them because he didn't have to. His ideas about nonviolence and its use as a strategic weapon developed gradually throughout the course of his career as an organizer. . . . He and I and many others often talked about nonviolence. I remember reading drafts of the "Open Letter" aloud to him a dozen times or more as I worked on it. He offered suggestions here and there but I could tell he really liked it. I hoped it would come off worthy enough to be compared to Martin Luther King's "Letter from Birmingham Jail" and would have a life of its own. It didn't. We put it out, primarily through our church network, and in a few weeks, it vanished forever. But the grower's "Response to an Open Letter on the Grape Boycott" is precious. If you read nothing else you must read that. It contains all the elements of the grower's public relations theme-strategy to defeat the farmworker movement. (FMDP, "Cesar 1968," 2009)

GOOD FRIDAY, 1969

Letter to E. L. Barr Jr., president, California Grape and Tree Fruit League, from Cesar E. Chavez

E. L. Barr, Jr., President
California Grape and Tree Fruit League
717 Market Street
San Francisco, California 94103

Dear Mr. Barr:

I am sad to hear about your accusations in the Press that our union movement and table grape boycott have been successful because we have used violence and terror tactics. If what you say is true, I have been a failure and should withdraw from the struggle; but you are left with the awesome moral responsibility, before God and man, to come forward with whatever information you have so that corrective action can begin at once. If for any reason you fail to come forth to substantiate your charges then you must be held responsible for committing violence against us, albeit violence of the tongue. I am convinced that you as a human being did not mean what you said but rather acted hastily under pressure from the public relations firm that has been hired to try to counteract the tremendous moral force of our movement. How many times we ourselves have felt the need to lash out in anger and bitterness.

Today on Good Friday 1969, we remember the life and the sacrifice of Martin Luther King, Jr., who gave himself totally to the nonviolent struggle for peace and justice. In his "Letter from Birmingham Jail," Dr. King describes better than I could our hopes for the strike and boycott: "Injustice must be exposed, with all the tension its exposure creates, to the light of human conscience and the air of national opinion before it can be cured." For our part I admit that we have seized upon every tactic and strategy consistent with the morality of our cause to expose that injustice and thus to heighten the sensitivity of the American conscience so that farm workers will have without bloodshed their own union and the dignity of bargaining with their agribusiness employers. By lying about the nature of our movement, Mr. Barr, you are working against nonviolent social change. Unwittingly perhaps, you may unleash that other force that our union by discipline and deed, censure and education, has sought to avoid, that panacea shortcut, that senseless violence that honors no color, class or neighborhood.

You must understand—I must make you understand—that our membership and the hopes and aspirations of the hundreds of thousands of the poor and the dispossessed that have been raised on our account are above all human beings, no better no worse than any other cross section of human society; we are not saints because we are poor but by the same measure neither are we immoral. We are men and women who have suffered and endured much and not only because of our abject poverty but because we have been kept poor. The color of our skin, the languages of our cultural and native origins, the lack of formal education, the exclusion from the democratic process, the numbers of our slain in recent wars—all these burdens generation after generation have sought to demoralize us, to break our human spirit. But God knows that we are not beasts of burden, we are not agricultural implements or rented slaves, we are men. And mark this well, Mr. Barr, we are men locked in a death struggle against man's inhumanity to man in the industry that you represent. And this struggle itself gives meaning to our life and ennobles our dying.

As your industry has experienced, our strikers here in Delano and those who represent us throughout the world are well trained for this struggle. They have been under the gun, they have been kicked and beaten and herded by dogs, they have been cursed and ridiculed, they have been stripped and chained and jailed, they have been sprayed with the poisons used in the vineyards but they have been taught not to lie down and die or to flee in shame, to resist with every ounce of human endurance and spirit. To resist not with retaliation in kind but to overcome with love and compassion, with ingenuity and creativity, with hard work and longer hours, with stamina and patient tenacity, with politics and law, and with prayer and fasting. They were not trained in a month or even a year; after all, this new harvest season will mark our fourth full year of strike and even now we continue to plan and prepare for the years to come. Time accomplishes for the poor what money does for the rich.

This is not to pretend that we have everywhere been successful or that we have not made mistakes. And while we do not belittle or underestimate our adversaries, for they are the rich and the powerful and possess the land, we are not afraid or cringe from the confrontation. We welcome it! We have planned for it. We know that our cause is just, that history is a story of social revolution, and that the poor shall inherit the land.

Once again, I appeal to you as the representative of your industry and as a man. I ask you to recognize and bargain with our union before the economic pressure of the boycott and strike takes an irrevocable toll; but if not, I ask you to at least sit down with us to discuss the safeguards necessary to keep our historical struggle free of violence. I make this appeal because as one of the leaders of our nonviolent movement, I know and accept my responsibility for preventing, if possible, the destruction of human life and property. For these reasons and knowing of Gandhi's admonition that fasting is the last resort in place of the sword, during a most critical time in our movement last February 1968, I undertook a twenty-five-day fast. I repeat to you the principle enunciated to the membership at the start of the fast: if to build our union required the deliberate taking of life, either the life or a grower or his child, or the life of a farm worker or his child, then I choose not to see the union built.

Mr. Barr, let me be painfully honest with you. You must understand these things. We advocate militant nonviolence as our means for social revolution and to achieve justice for our people, but we are not blind or deaf to desperate and moody winds of human frustration, impatience, and rage that blow among us. Gandhi himself admitted that if his only choice were cowardice or violence, he would choose violence. Men are not angels and the time and tides wait for no man. Precisely because of these powerful human emotions, we have tried to involve masses of people in their own struggle. Participation and self-determination remain the best experience of freedom, and free men instinctively prefer democratic change and even protect the rights guaranteed to seek it. Only the enslaved in despair have need of violent overthrow.

This letter does not express all that is in my heart, Mr. Barr. But if it says nothing else it says that we do not hate you or rejoice to see your industry destroyed. We hate the agribusiness system that seeks to keep us enslaved and we shall overcome and change it not by retaliation or bloodshed but by a determined nonviolent struggle carried on by those masses of farm workers who intend to be free and human.

Sincerely yours,
Cesar E. Chavez

In Reply to Cesar Chavez:

TO THE EDITORS:
The April 1969 issue of *Christian Century and National Catholic Reporter* (April 23) carried an open letter from Cesar Chavez to the president of the California Grape and Tree Fruit league captioned "Manifesto from a friend." We would appreciate it if *Christian Century* and *National Catholic Reporter* would publish our reply, which follows:

How are mere mortals to attempt to reply to the charismatic leader of the United Farm Workers Organizing Committee, who writes in flawless prose of his devotion to nonviolence, calls attention to his miraculous and marvelously publicized 25-day fast, and draws a comparison of himself to Gandhi.

How does one cope with an adversary so determinedly bucking for sainthood? With some trepidation, we try.

First, we must dispute Cesar's contention explicit throughout his Open Letter that UFWOC versus California grape growers is a struggle of the "poor" against the "rich."

The California Grape and Tree Fruit league represents growers large and small, many of whom employ no labor other than the members of their own families.

Writing on the grape boycott in the *Washington Post*, Congressman B. F. Fisk, an organizer of the liberal House Democratic Study Group, pointed out that "small growers as well as large are being attacked in an indiscriminate campaign that is the very antithesis of the justice which the Farm Workers union purports to seek."

Poor Cesar has few followers among farm workers, but he is blessed with many rich and powerful friends. The AFL-CIO, by its own report, has contributed $2,000,000 to Chavez's UFWOC and predecessor organizational groups. Chavez is a member of the board of California Rural Legal Assistance, established by a $1,276,000 grant of federal taxpayer funds. The Roger Baldwin Memorial foundation of the American Civil Liberties Union has contributed $85,000 in tax-free funds to the Chavez cause.

Recently, the *New York Times* featured a picture of a fashionably dressed Dolores Huerta, Chavez's chief lieutenant, conversing with her host George Plimpton of the best-seller *Paper Tiger* fame, at a party in Plimpton's spectacular East River Drive duplex described by the *Times* as "The Place to Be." "The Plimpton reception," the *Times* reported "was the last part of a $25 a person benefit" for "Cesar Chavez' striking grape pickers, a favorite cause of the New Left branch of New York society."

As to "nonviolence": Despite its name, the Students Nonviolent Coordinating committee—one of the many New Left groups with which Chavez actively cooperates—is not noted for its nonviolent approach. And despite Chavez's pious disclaimers, the UFWOC sponsored strikes and boycott are violent operations.

Farm workers who have been subjected to obscenities from Chavez's pickets and threats upon the lives of their children because they choose to stay on their jobs find Chavez's nonviolent philosophy hard to understand. Housewives who have been intimidated as they attempted to get out of their cars to enter supermarkets picketed by boycotters do not understand it either. Nor do store owners and managers who have been persuaded to remove grapes from their shelves because of fear for the safety of their employees and customers.

It would be hard to explain the nonviolent philosophy to the two New York grocery clerks who were seriously burned when firebombs were tossed into the store in which they were working. New York's fire marshal reported that the one fact that linked five stores subjected to firebombing was "that they all sold California grapes, they all have been picketed, and they all have been asked to join the boycott."

Chavez may disclaim responsibility for these violent actions, but the fact remains that the boycott is sponsored by UFWOC, not the Campfire Girls, and the head of UFWOC is Cesar Chavez, not Mary Margaret McBride.

Nonviolence is hard to define, but a valiant attempt was made recently by the Reverend James Drake of the California Migrant Ministry, an active member of the UFWOC staff, in an affidavit seeking revocation of a restraining order against picketing activities by the United Farm Workers Organizing Committee in the Coachella Valley.

In his affidavit, the Reverend Drake declares: "That I am a devoted believer in the philosophy of nonviolence and that it is the credo of our UFWOC. That human life and safety is held by the organizers of UFWOC to be of more importance than all other values except our rights which give us meaning in our society: the rights to organize, work, and exercise free speech to communicate our beliefs." By this definition, the rights of Cesar Chavez's UFWOC to organize, work and communicate come first—before secondary considerations as human . . . and the safety of others.

A recent issue of *El Malcriado*, a UFWOC publication, features a cartoon of a giant hand labeled "Big City Mayors, Labor Unions, Political Organizations, Religious Leaders" and others grasping a giant screw labeled "Boycott" plunged squarely through a dying farmer's middle. Hardly a sterling example of nonviolent Christian charity.

With the pronouncements of concern for the workers' welfare, we wonder why Mr. Chavez devotes his efforts toward table grape growers' employees who, according to Department of Labor figures, are among the best paid in continental United States, and who are not on strike and who have not seen fit to join Chavez's union and who are covered by more protective legislation than farm workers in any other state. Could it be that the real prize in this effort are the union dues that could be collected from the workers? This would account for an emphasis on organizing the Delano farm workers—among the most stable of the California farm worker groups. If the real concern is for the workers' welfare why not try to help the poorest paid workers rather than the highest paid workers?

From the standpoint of comparative wages and working conditions there is less justification for a boycott of California table grapes than for a boycott of any crop grown anywhere in the United States. Contrary to Chavez's propaganda, the easily verifiable facts are that farm wage rates in California are the highest in the continental United States; rates for vineyard workers are higher than the California average; and farm workers are covered by more protective legislation in California than any other state.

The California Grape & Tree Fruit league supports national collective bargaining legislation for farm workers that guarantees secret balloting in union recognition elections, and insures that the free flow of food to the American public will not be impeded. Chavez does not. His goal, as his Open Letter states, is "social revolution"—the same goal as that of his early mentor the professional radical Saul Alinsky.

E. L. Barr, Jr.
Past President
California Grape & Tree Fruit League

R. K. Sanderson
President
California Grape & Tree Fruit League

20   La Paz

Even as early as 1968, Cesar Chavez talked to me about finding a union headquarters outside of Delano.

He said the "ideal" place could also serve as a vacation area for farmworker families, especially those members of the union who were elected to ranch committees. I found a place in Santa Barbara—one of Cesar's favorite places in the world—and we went to look at. It was on a hill overlooking the city and the ocean but it was too fancy a neighborhood for our needs. Then there were a few hundred acres I found on the side of a hill overlooking the ocean, but the terrain was quite steep and it was bare ground. I looked around in the area of Mission San Antonio (near Monterey) because Cesar loved to come there for some of our retreat meetings—it was quiet and secluded. I could find nothing.

I found "La Paz" in Keene, California, a few miles down the mountain from Tehachapi, and Cesar Chavez wanted it. Frank Denison, our Service Center attorney at that time, structured the deal with movie producer Eddie Lewis, who bought it at auction from Kern County on behalf of the National Farm Workers Service Center.

Film producer Edward "Eddie" Lewis was born in 1920 in New Jersey and served in the US Army during World War II. He was active in the early years of television and then moved to producing movies with social themes, the best-known being *Spartacus* (1960), for which Lewis and actor Kirk Douglas

FIGURE 25 Nestled in the Tehachapi Mountains at Keene, California, the UFW compound was named "La Paz" by Chavez. Photo by Hub Segur. Courtesy of Special Collections, UC Davis Library/Hub Segur Papers D-605.

hired blacklisted writer Dalton Trumbo to write the script. Lewis and his wife, Mildred, continued to produce socially conscious films such as *Seven Days in May* (1964) and *Missing* (1982). The Lewis family supported progressive causes throughout the 1960s and 1970s.

It suited Cesar's purposes: there was a wide range of housing (duplexes, hospital rooms, single family homes, etc.), there were offices, there was a central kitchen and dining facility, it had acreage, it was in the mountains, and it was off the beaten track.

I take whatever credit is appropriate for the purchase of this property for the headquarters of the union and I was a most loyal supporter, but I still wonder if our relocation from Delano to Keene (renamed by Cesar Nuestra Señora Reina de La Paz or La Paz) was wise. I think a case could be made that this remote headquarters isolated us from the farmworkers' dirt and changed our orientation. But now that it is Cesar's burial place, it will serve a purpose in history that outstrips any second-guessing on my part about what was best for the farmworker movement.

Cesar Chavez has the last word, again!

Although a seemingly logical and innocent move at the time, the establishment of a headquarters in Keene, some sixty-three miles south of Delano, would be in retrospect one of the more controversial decisions Chavez made in the early years. For many of the union's most devoted supporters, it marked the beginning of a prolonged decline for the organization. As Marshall Ganz explains in *Why David Sometimes Wins*, "The move from Delano to La Paz, the site of a former public tuberculosis sanatorium, enabled the UFWOC leadership to create a full-time volunteer community, retreat center, and administrative headquarters removed from the daily claims of members in Delano. La Paz grew eventually to a community of over 250. Although it offered financial and managerial benefits, critics argued that its isolation encouraged a loss of accountability to farm worker constituents" (230). Chatfield adds additional background:

> I found La Paz only because, at Cesar's request, I had been looking for a place away from Delano. Santa Barbara was Cesar's first choice and we looked at a couple of properties I had found there but they did not fit the bill—AND they cost a lot of money. I can't say for sure that I was looking for a union headquarters because Cesar always put the emphasis on having a place where farmworkers and their families could come for recreational and educational purposes. That such a place would also serve as the national union headquarters did come as a surprise to me but he never emphasized that aspect with me. Thirty-five years later, I sometimes wish someone else could/would take "credit" for finding La Paz, but what can I say? (FMDPd, December 2, 2004)

Marshall Ganz captures the tension produced when an organization's leadership makes a physical move away from its primary constituency: "When LeRoy and I sat for a month with him [Cesar] in La Paz early in 1971 trying to restructure the union from there, the dark side of this choice began emerging as well. Having your breathing room can be beneficial, but allowing yourself to become isolated in the midst of a world you utterly control (or want to or think you need to) can be profoundly dangerous to everyone involved. And it was" (FMDPd, December 2, 2004).

Another key staff person at La Paz, Barbara Macri-Ortiz, offered her perspective:

> I was working in the Delano field office when Cesar made the move to La Paz in 1971. One of the reasons for his decision, which he shared with the field office staff, was that as long as he stayed in Delano the workers would naturally look to him for leadership, and it would be much harder for us to develop the local leadership—both staff and farm worker. Cesar was right about that, and after he left, whether we liked it or not, we all had to just do it. . . . Some of the staff may have been full of themselves, thinking somehow, they were it because they worked next to Cesar at the "head-quarters." But from my experience, the vast majority of the La Paz staff were hardworking people. (FMDPd, December 2, 2004)

Bonnie Burns Chatfield describes how the move affected daily life as well as the overall organizational climate:

> In 1971, in Delano, there was talk of moving farmworker headquarters to Keene, a tiny town in the Tehachapi foothills about 30 miles east of Bakersfield. LeRoy had arranged for the purchase of an old tuberculosis sanitarium. . . . I strongly objected. The union was becoming more and more cult-like, moving away from farmworker organizing. LeRoy, Marshall, Cesar, and others, but not Jerry Cohen, spent most of the spring at La Paz, the name that had been bestowed upon the complex. As I remember, many of us, including Helen, were opposed to the move of farmworker head-quarters from Delano to Keene. But more important, we were opposed to the beatification and glorification of Cesar, and to the increasing siege mentality that was overcoming farmworker leaders. We referred to LeRoy and Marshall (and probably too Chris Hartmire) as "true believers," those whose devotion and dedication to Cesar was complete and unquestion-ing. . . . On the positive side, as communes go, La Paz at that time was tolerable. And I can speak only about the year between August 1971 and August 1972. I did have my own home and individual family life. I was free to come and go, which I did often, to Bakersfield or Delano to visit friends. Demands to participate in union community activities were there, but they were subtle. And, since those activities were social, I was usually an active

participant. I can't speak for those "single" volunteers who lived, dorm-style, in the old sanitarium building and ate all their meals in the cafeteria. That seemed bleak. But of course, I was 30 by that time, "older" and more settled. I know, only through the accounts of others, that the psychological climate and conditions at La Paz changed drastically in the mid-1970s. Fortunately, I wasn't part of it. I don't recall what was going on with the union, as a labor union, during 1971. The boycott was in abeyance; strikes didn't seem in the forefront. Cesar was definitely in control at La Paz, which was becoming an isolated compound with security guards and police dogs. There was a lot of gossip; petty jealousies flared up. There were too many people with not enough real work to do. (FMDP, 2004)

It should be noted that the heightened security at La Paz was in response to a series of threats on Chavez's life, some of which, according to Chavez's FBI file, were deemed credible by state and federal law enforcement agencies. See essay 16 on the problem of security for Chavez as early as 1968. Jacques Levy's notebook captures the growing concern in 1971: "Toward the end of July, the union gets the most chilling news of all from US Treasury [ATF] agents who have learned there is a twenty-five thousand dollar contract on Cesar's

FIGURE 26 Map of Delano to Keene. For many members, the sixty miles separating Delano from the La Paz headquarters signified changes in the union's organizational character from its founding to later periods. Courtesy of the US Geological Survey.

life. . . . Top security precautions are taken immediately. Cesar disappears from sight, his location known only to his closest aides" (Levy, 438). Levy's book VII, chapter 1, includes a detailed account of less-than-robust state and federal investigations into specific assassination plots (a hesitancy more than likely born of the close ties between agribusiness and the Nixon administration). Also, an audio recording of a private press conference including Jerry Cohen and taped by Sam Kushner outlines the plot to eliminate Chavez. Cohen reports that a flyer with a photo of the suspected hit man was disseminated to union allies throughout California.[1] Chatfield and Cohen spoke about the plot to the various ranch committees during their orientations at La Paz.

Chavez's response to the potential dangers was classic: "As for the existence of a plot, I think it shows that nonviolence is working. They wouldn't go as far as trying to kill me unless they were very worried about our success" (Levy, 446).

NOTE

1. *The Cesar Chavez Assassination Plot*, directed by Sam Kushner (Los Angeles, CA: KPFK, 1971).

21   Jerry Brown Says, "I'm Not God!"

In the course of the United Farm Workers' statewide political campaign to defeat Proposition 22, an agribusiness-sponsored initiative on the California ballot in 1972, I discovered that voter fraud was used to qualify the initiative for the ballot. If we could prove it, I thought it might be possible to have the initiative legally removed from the ballot.

Proposition 22, created by the corporate grower–controlled California Farm Bureau and Republican legislators, was designed to roll back the clock on labor rights for farmworkers. If passed by voters, it would have prohibited consumer-led boycotts, regulated the timing of strikes, and stripped workers of collective bargaining on workplace issues. It would have begun the slow death of the farmworker movement.

In terms of the changing political climate of the early 1970s (of which the campaign against Prop. 22 was a prime example), historian Lauren Araiza's research is key. Araiza explains how Coretta Scott King and the Southern Christian Leadership Conference took an active role in supporting the farmworker position (unlike Dr. King himself, who had kept Chavez and the union at some distance during his life due to his funding from the Teamsters). She also describes the role of the Black Panther Party in turning out the African American vote against Prop. 22. See Araiza (in "Suggested Readings"), especially chapters 4 and 5.

The first evidence I received that something was wrong was from the uniform feedback our volunteers received during the door-to-door campaign work in the Los Angeles precincts. At our daily strategy/report meetings, dozens of staff volunteers reported that they were told by people who had signed the petition that they had done so only because the petition circulators standing in front of Los Angeles supermarkets told them the purpose of the initiative was "to lower food prices." In fact, many voters reported seeing a cardboard sign strapped across the top part of the petition that read, "Lower Food Prices."

Because of these reports, I sent my wife, Bonnie, to the Los Angeles County Registrar's Office to examine some of the certified petitions. This was really a fishing expedition, because none of us knew what, if anything, such an examination might show. At the very least, I thought we might obtain the names and addresses of thousands of Los Angeles voters who had been duped by the "Lower Food Prices" ploy, so that we could contact them by mail and by phone before election day.

Bonnie came back from the registrar's office with dozens of copies of signed petitions, but the names, addresses, and signatures on the petitions were all in the same handwriting. She said there were thousands of certified petitions filled with names, addresses, and even signatures—all in the same handwriting. It was obvious that the paid petition circulators had taken the voter registration rolls and simply transferred the information onto the petitions using their own handwriting. Because petition circulators were paid by the signature, it was the fastest way to make money. There was no attempt to conceal what they had done, and yet each petition was signed by the circulator, stating under penalty of perjury that the petition had been circulated among voters for their signatures. It is likely that hired petition circulators had used this process for years, and Proposition 22 was no exception. It was a stunning discovery!

I immediately called our campaign offices in the other major cities—San Francisco, Oakland, Sacramento, San José, and San Diego—and asked them to review the certified petitions on file in the registrars' offices in their counties. In less than twenty-four hours, we knew that tens of thousands of fraudulent signatures had been used to certify Proposition 22. But now what? With less than eight weeks before election day, how could we prove it? And how could we effectively communicate this voter fraud to the public throughout the state without sounding like political whiners? Even if we could prove it, so what? Would it make any difference in the election outcome, or would it simply be viewed as one of those last-minute campaign accusations?

We made a plan. First, we would gather thousands of statements from voters whose names were on the certified petitions but who had not actually signed the petition. We would ask them to sign a statement, under penalty of perjury, that they had not signed the petition; furthermore, they would petition the secretary of state to remove their names from the petitions. Statement forms were prepared overnight and hundreds of volunteers fanned out into the Los Angeles precincts to track down voters whose names had been fraudulently filed. In just three or four days, we had more than seven hundred statements signed, all under penalty of perjury, and more were coming in each day. Our campaign offices in the other cities also began to gather statements from duped voters. It was now time to meet with Secretary of State Jerry Brown, the only statewide officeholder who was a Democrat. In his 1970 campaign for office, he had used the slogan "I marched with Cesar Chavez and the farmworkers." It was time to collect.

I had only talked with Jerry Brown once before and that was by telephone. I forget the original purpose of the call, but I do remember shouting at him that he should not complain when farmworkers turned to him for help. Did he think they should turn to the likes of Governor Reagan, Lieutenant Governor Curb, or Attorney General Younger, all staunchly conservative Republicans? I doubt I even waited for him to respond before I hung up.

Tom Quinn, Brown's chief of staff, a young and brilliant campaign strategist in his own right, arranged the meeting. The meeting took place in a high-rise office building in Century City, where Brown had his Southern California office. I invited Jerry Cohen and Art Torres to come with me. We brought with us a couple of boxes filled with the declarations of voters who swore their names had fraudulently been used to certify Proposition 22. Jerry Brown came into the meeting not at all confident he even wanted to be there, and after the introductions he stayed in the background. Tom Quinn took charge and I began to explain what had happened with the certified petitions and that we needed help. But Jerry Brown broke in with a smart-ass remark to the effect that he wasn't God, and what could he do with these kinds of campaign-type charges? He proceeded in that fashion to discount any possible help he might be able to give. At this point, I stood up and said, "This is a fucking waste of time, let's get out of here." Jerry and Art hesitated a minute, got out of their chairs, and started to gather up their files when

Quinn stood up, extended his arms, and said in his friendly/firm Irish pol voice, "Now wait a minute, let's calm down here; let's sit down and see what we can do to help." I could sense his annoyance with Brown's flip remarks so I said, "Fine." The tone of the meeting was changed from "how do we get rid of these guys without hurting ourselves politically?" to "how can we help these guys and get something out of it?" The clincher were the hundreds of declarations, all signed under penalty of perjury, that we brought with us. A signed declaration from a voter about election fraud was something objective and tangible over which a secretary of state had some jurisdiction.

The plan that Tom Quinn and Jerry Brown cooked up at the meeting was masterful. First, we were to gather at least a couple of hundred additional declarations. Then Jerry would call a press conference to announce that declarations alleging voter fraud had been brought to his attention, that he was officially turning these allegations over to the Los Angeles district attorney, Joe Busch, to investigate and to bring criminal charges if the results of his investigation warranted such action. In turn, Joe Busch would call a press conference to announce that he had received these allegations from the secretary of state and he promised to open up a criminal investigation and bring charges if warranted. In turn, Jerry Brown would announce to the media that Joe Busch had informed him that a complete investigation was underway and he would await the results before taking any action. And so this public conversation would go back and forth in the media, first Jerry Brown, then Joe Busch.

After the meeting, Jerry Brown explained that he really had done nothing special except to publicly hand off our request to the Los Angeles DA, a Republican, who was running for reelection in a tight race and who, for his own election purposes, would publicly announce he had received the declarations, and so forth. It was all media smoke and mirrors, but it served the purpose of publicly smearing Proposition 22 in each of these ensuing press conferences. The final result came just three days before the general election, when the headlines of the *Los Angeles Times* screamed, "7 Indictments in Proposition 22," and the subhead line read, "Voter Fraud Used to Qualify Initiative."

True enough, Jerry Brown was not God. But you could have fooled me.

Chatfield on the organizing tactics that won the election for the proworker side:

Every aspect of a political campaign contributes to victory or defeat. It is impossible to know for sure which particular tactic was the most definitive. In the Proposition 22 campaign, Jerry Brown and Joe Busch played major roles in smearing the initiative with their allegations and indictments of fraud. Bonnie Burns Chatfield's discovery of voter fraud played a role; 30-second television commercials featuring a soft-spoken Cesar Chavez and the 60-second radio spots featuring Jack Nicholson and Warren Beatty played a role; Cesar's 30-second TV commercial . . . and Cesar's barnstorming tour was yet another piece which made up the Proposition 22 campaign puzzle. Remember, Proposition 22 was a life-and-death struggle for the farmworker movement in California; it was a political war, and no one is qualified, including me, the campaign director, to say who/what played the most valuable role. Winning campaigns are all of a piece.

I had developed a Proposition 22 campaign tactic, which we called "human billboards." Hundreds of union campaign volunteers were organized into squads of 50 or so, each carrying a placard approximately 2 by 3 foot. We started the human billboards in the last two weeks of the campaign. Our squads were deployed in the early morning (6:30 to 8:30 a.m.) to the major feeder freeway entrances in San Fernando Valley, Santa Monica, San Gabriel Valley, etc. By placing each human billboard 10 yards apart we were able to cover three or four city blocks on both sides of the street that led to the major freeway entrances. And then in the afternoon (3:30 to 5:30 p.m.) we reversed the process. . . . One Sunday right before the election we brought all the billboard squads together and completely surrounded (ten yards apart) the Memorial Coliseum for three hours before the L.A. Rams football game, which probably drew 80,000 spectators. (LC/PH)

Bonnie Burns Chatfield describes the status of union culture in the early 1970s, the impact of a political campaign on daily life, and how Prop. 22 was a decisive moment for the Chatfield family:

No one within the UFW was paying much attention to the growers, who in 1972 qualified an initiative for the November ballot that would have effectively destroyed the farmworkers' right to form a labor union and negotiate a contract. LeRoy was chosen to direct the No on Proposition 22 campaign from Los Angeles. Northern California was much more liberal and labor-friendly. The battleground would be the southern part of the state.

I was ready to leave La Paz and head back to an urban lifestyle, free of a compound.

FIGURE 27 "No on 22" "human billboards," 1972. Squads of farmworkers and supporters spread out every weekday throughout the Los Angeles area. Photo by Glen Pearcy. Courtesy of Susan Pearcy.

We stored our furniture, including my piano, in an old garage at La Paz, packed up the essentials, which of course included a few cribs and baby carriages, and set out again in search of a home—this time with four children under five. That aspect of farmworker life appealed to my sense of adventure.

I think that Chris Hartmire found the house for us on Yukon Street in Inglewood, very close to the Hollywood Park racetrack and the Forum, and directly below a flight-landing pattern at LAX. Those jets came through our bedroom where again we slept on a mattress. . . . But I was happy and anticipated becoming involved in the political struggle. Again, the UFW headquarters in Los Angeles for this campaign were joined with the Migrant Ministry office on Olympic Blvd. . . . At first I did the usual—making lots of telephone calls soliciting support. I worked under Chris's direction, soliciting ministers and church groups. His longtime secretary, Sue Miner, was so patient and tolerant of all of us. When I had to attend a meeting, Art Torres, at the time a full-time volunteer, later a state senator and longtime chair of the California Democratic Party, took care of our daughter Amy. When she awoke, he picked her up from her carriage and held her as he did his work and talked on the phone. At 5 p.m., I picked up the other girls and headed home through the L.A. traffic.

I can't recall the exact date, but sometime during late summer or early autumn, LeRoy and Chris became suspicious that signatures for the ballot initiative had been fraudulently solicited and possibly forged. The "[Lower Food Prices]" title on petitions and the misinformation proffered by the petitioners had misled many into signing. Actually, the fraud was much greater. I was the first to begin documenting the fraud. I went to the county registrar's office and petitioned to see the signatures. I was allowed into an attic warehouse room where the thick petition tablets, signature after signature, were stored. I began, one tablet at a time, to assess the possibility of duplicate signatures, and forgery. At the same time, I was copying down names, addresses, and telephone numbers.

Eventually, the registrar's employees allowed me to make copies. I discovered that the petition gatherers had been paid, a novelty at the time, and that they had canvassed and obtained signatures in areas where there had always been strong farmworker support, such as South Central and East L.A., and in pro-labor communities in the southeastern part of the county. It became evident that signature after signature had been done with the same hand—there was little attempt at real forgery. People had signed family, friends, and neighbors. There was not enough time for one person to read every petition. I solicited help from our volunteers and supporters. We had teams in the attic, pouring over names, addresses, and phone numbers. We began telephoning signers and documenting what they had been told about Proposition 22. They had been duped into believing that Prop. 22 was a pro-consumer ballot measure.

LeRoy, Chris, and others took our information and ran with it to the press and to Jerry Brown, then secretary of state. What absolute jubilation the morning we picked up our L.A. Times with the headline "PROPOSITION 22 FRAUD." LeRoy began a human billboard campaign on freeway on- and off-ramps, and put out leaflets and ads, including some television ones. Proposition 22 was defeated handily. What an election night party! But the defeat of Proposition 22 was the only political good news that November. Nixon began his second term.

Later that month, I accompanied LeRoy to La Paz where he was given a hero's welcome. We both understood that if Proposition 22 had not been defeated, he would have taken the fall. (FMDP, 2004)

22 Taking the Blame

Fortunately for me, I was not one of the key volunteers who needed to be pushed out of the farmworker movement. I left long before I wore out my welcome. But had I stayed, and I certainly had the opportunity to do so, the time would inevitably have come when my personal priorities would have clashed with the needs of the movement and I would be out—friend or no friend of Cesar Chavez.

I do not deserve much credit for my voluntary departure, because I had a foreshadowing of what lay ahead for me. After Cesar's funeral in 1993, I wrote a manuscript that I entitled "Cesar 1968." In this document, I recount a conversation Cesar and I had late in the evening the night before the 1972 California general election, an election that would determine the fate of Proposition 22, the anti-union initiative sponsored by California agribusiness to outlaw farm labor unions.

I wrote,

> So there we were, just Cesar and me, sitting in the big open room of our "No on 22" campaign headquarters looking out onto Olympic Boulevard five stories below. It was very late in the evening; everyone had gone home or back to our farmworker encampment at Lincoln Park to get some rest for another early morning of human billboarding and our "Get Out the Vote" drive. Cesar was tired and very nervous about the upcoming election. I was very uptight myself

FIGURE 28 Chavez speaking at a "No on 22" staff meeting at Lincoln Park in Los Angeles, 1972. Chatfield on stage at right. Photo by Cris Sanchez. Courtesy of Walter P. Reuther Library, Archives of Labor and Urban Affairs, Wayne State University.

and wondered if there was any last-minute campaigning that we could do. Just a few days before, with the help of our Hollywood media contacts, I had been able to arrange for a 30-second "Cesar No on 22 spot" to be aired on the Archie Bunker show [Norman Lear's popular *All In The Family*]. It was very expensive, I forget how much, but all the media experts said it was worth it and a coup to even break into the show. I remember being afraid to blink for fear I would miss it.

Cesar spoke very softly with a friendly but nervous edge to his voice. He simply explained to me that if we lost the election tomorrow, I would have to take the blame. I couldn't answer. I was totally silenced by the harsh reality of what he had said. I was completely helpless. My closest friend, almost nine years now, had just explained the political facts of life to me. I had worked on this "life and death" campaign full time since July, and barely had any time to even see Bonnie and the girls unless she was in the office working. I worked very late into the night plotting strategy on the telephone with my staff directors in other California cities and then worrying half to death about everything because of the high stakes involved for Cesar and his farmworker union. Now, to top it all off, I was expected to play the role of a fall guy, the person responsible for this historical defeat. I didn't answer Cesar. I just nodded and gave a shrug of the shoulders.

The union won! Proposition 22 was defeated 58% to 42% (Nixon beat McGovern 54% to 40%). I did not feel like coming to the victory celebration because I am very uncomfortable at those kinds of events, but I did make an appearance at the tail end of the party. But everyone was pretty drunk by that time, and thank God, all of the speeches were over. I didn't have to stay long.

Cesar tried to make it up to me. The farmworker union had a big "Welcome Home/Thank You" dinner party in my honor for all the staff and their families at La Paz. There was a banner in the dining room that called me a "Giant Killer," and Cesar made a big to-do about my work in the campaign and how I saved the union from the power of the growers.

But I was mature enough to know that just because Proposition 22 had been defeated, it made me no more a "Giant Killer" than if had it won. I would have been the person to blame. Winning or losing Proposition 22 wasn't about me or my friendship with Cesar. It was about him and his relationship with his vision, his farmworker movement. That was the only thing that mattered.

I remember this incident as clearly today as if it happened last night. And I'm grateful that it happened because it helped to spare me from the day, which surely would have come, when Cesar and I would have been forced to part company. I did not leave the farmworker movement because of this incident, but it certainly helped to lay the groundwork for my voluntary departure the following year. The conversation that evening, high above Olympic Boulevard, reminded me again that this was not my cause. I had only come to the farmworker movement to help Cesar with his cause.

The most difficult part of my decision to leave was the keen realization that I would have to give up my ten-year friendship with Cesar Chavez. Because of his all-consuming commitment to the cause of the farmworkers, he would no longer be a close friend. I knew it, I understood it, and I accepted the consequences of my decision. I felt a great sense of loss—and still do.

As Sandy Nathan writes in his post on the FMDP online discussion, many at La Paz believed the departure of the Chatfields was a result of burnout and the "sense" or understanding that, given the culture of the union at that moment, the future of the farmworker movement would be a difficult one. Chatfield offered a curious reporter four basic reasons for his departure:

> There were four reasons: 1) my oldest daughter (of four at that time, now of five) was just getting ready to start 1st grade and that meant we needed to decide where to anchor ourselves, 2) my father had died in 1970 and my mother was by herself in Sacramento. And I had been away from "home" since I was 15 years old, 3) my wife was from San Francisco and she missed Northern California, and 4) I had been asked by Gilbert Padilla of the Union Board if I would stand for the position of Secretary Treasurer at the first convention of this newly approved AFL-CIO International Union. This request while tempting (and should I admit, flattering) helped me to realize that it was time to leave because I had come to Delano, at Cesar's request, only to help out, not to spend the rest of my life there. If I now decided to become a union officer that meant I was making a long-term commitment.
>
> I could tell the reporter was disappointed because he was working on an angle. "Well," he said, "what did you learn from Cesar?" I answered, "How to organize." He went blank. I tried to spruce it up for him. "Cesar taught me how to make something out of nothing. He taught me how to take something that does not exist and make it exist. (FMDP, "Cesar 1968," 2009)

Bonnie Burns Chatfield offered her recollection of the departure:

> In the summer of 1973, LeRoy and I decided to leave the UFW. Our reasons may have differed but they coincided. Now that my children were beginning school, I wanted stability. We moved to Sacramento, where LeRoy's family lived. It was close enough to San Francisco that I could see my family and renew long-missed friendships. We both became involved

in California politics: LeRoy worked for Governor Jerry Brown, I for the Democratic caucus of the state legislature. I think there was shock and dismay on the part of some when we left the UFW. I have never regretted the choice. More important, I have valued my years with the union, from the 1965 summer teaching NFWA children in Memorial Park until now. I treasure all the friends I have from those years. . . . My life was enriched beyond measure during those eight years with the NFWA/UFW. I am forever grateful. (FMDP, 2004)

As the essays that follow demonstrate, their departure from the farmworker union did not mark the end of Bonnie and LeRoy Chatfield's committed activism on behalf of farmworkers and other disenfranchised communities.

23   Legislation vs. Movement

In my view, every significant piece of labor or civil rights legislation in this country has come about because of long-term social strife and
conflict. And while at first glance, the moving party— that is, the challenger
to the status quo—seems to be the beneficiary of such legislation, in fact it
is the historically conservative and entrenched economic and political establishment itself that benefits the most. This is because the legislation slows
down the pace of change and gives government-authorized bodies the tools
to manage and control it. Furthermore, the entrenched interests historically
opposed to change have the financial power to influence the day-to-day
government decisions interpreting and implementing the legislation.

I believe this opening statement is as true for the farmworker movement
in the 1970s as it was for the civil rights movement in the 1960s.

One may argue that legislation allows for change, but only in easier-to-
digest incremental amounts so that society might adjust more readily to
the desired outcome. In other words, legislative change is society's answer
to revolution. This may well be the reality, but it comes at a great price paid
over many generations by those who need social justice.

But the promise that social legislation lifts up the disenfranchised and
the underclass in society is rarely realized, even though it is widely held to
be the best remedy for such injustice. In fact, such legislation serves as a drag
on the momentum of those who seek social change. As an example, just
consider the astronomical financial costs imposed on both advocates and

adversaries in pursuing the protections afforded them by the Agricultural Labor Relations Act (ALRA). In the case of farmworkers and growers, who can better afford to pay for these protections? Which group has the financial staying power to impose its will?

One of the inevitable side effects of social change legislation, with its attendant legal processes, is to dampen the ardor of the movement and allow for the release of its pent-up energy through a series of calculated government-supervised procedures. Those who one day were breaking down the barricades that protected the injustice of the status quo were the next day trying to cope with new government rules and regulations that they neither understood nor agreed with. The movement leaders, who once could act with impunity because of the absence of law, now had to compromise their militancy because as responsible citizens they were expected to respect and accept the new law. And while this new change legislation never makes a complete return to the status quo that existed prior to the movement demanding change, it is close enough so as not to cause too much discomfort to the old business-as-usual policies.

The Agricultural Labor Relations Act is a case in point. Prior to the passage of the ALRA, the farmworker union in the early 1970s counted a dues-paying membership of more than eighty thousand members. In the summer of 1975, after the passage of the ARLA, more than forty thousand farmworkers voted in secret ballot elections supervised by the State of California. The vast majority of those voting selected the United Farm Workers union to represent them, but during the ensuing twenty-seven years the union's membership never again reached twenty thousand members. In fact, some large agribusiness employers have been meeting one day a year, now twenty-five years and counting, with the United Farm Workers in order to fulfill the letter of the legislation that seeks to provide for the "collective-bargaining rights" of their agricultural employees.

It must be said that these observations and conclusions are mine and mine alone. But it is also true that I learned many of these concepts from my ten-year association with Cesar Chavez. On the record, Cesar was always in favor of legislation, e.g., including farmworkers in the National Labor Relations Act. He was especially vocal in his support of such legislation when the growers were publicly opposed to it. The same was true for secret ballot elections. Off the record, Cesar was opposed to any legislation, including secret ballot elections. He knew that the government could not bring the growers to recognize and bargain with the union because only the power of the union, developed through the guerilla warfare of its strikes and boycotts, could accomplish this.

And yet in the spring of 1975, in the governor's conference room filled with grower lobbyists, attorneys, state senators, and union representatives, I heard Cesar's voice on the speakerphone agreeing to legislation. Of course, I knew in advance what his position would be, but when I heard his voice, I held my breath because I felt he should be opposed. But he wasn't.

What caused him during those intervening years to change his mind? The loss of the grape contracts, a flagging boycott, the Teamster invasion, pressure from the AFL-CIO, a *simpático* governor, the only alternative left since legislation is inevitable, cut the best deal you can under the most favorable circumstances? These are all questions for which I have no answers.

Was the passage of the ALRA the end of Cesar's momentum? In retrospect, with twenty-five years of hindsight, I lean toward the conclusion that it was the beginning of the end. Did it have to be? I suppose not, but once Cesar agreed to what he believed was a level playing field tilted toward unionization, it was too late for him to recover. In less than a year after the passage of the ALRA, the state's largest industry was able to tilt the field back to more than level.

For the sake of movements yet to be born, I hope history will explain the critical factors that led Cesar, against his better judgment, I believe, to accept legislation.

In 1975, Chatfield found himself no longer a principal actor in the farmworker union but rather a member of Governor Jerry Brown's staff. In February, the union had staged a march from San Francisco to Modesto to bolster boycott efforts. Chavez was surprised by the size of the rally at the end of the march and saw it as an opportunity to push on the legislative front:

> Before our convention in 1973, I had told the executive board "It's time that we go on the offensive on legislation, that we talk about a Bill of Rights for farmworkers. We gave the project to the legal department, and Jerry Cohen made a list of all the issues as he saw them. . . . As soon as Brown was in office, he made a lot of appointments . . . some of them very close friends of the Movement . . . LeRoy Chatfield as Brown's director of administration and Dr. Jerome Lackner as director of the Health Department." (Levy, 528)

Now working on the inside, Chatfield had to negotiate a series of difficult tensions—his distrust of politicians and the window for change that the new

governor represented, his ambivalence about legislation and the union's new drive to support it, the need to compromise on the proposed legislation, and his desire to remain faithful to the union's principles:

> I remembered how Cesar and Marshall Ganz talked about what legislation did to the Civil Rights Movement in the South. It seems to take the wind out of its sails. . . . I was looked to, in an ad hoc and informal way, to represent the farmworkers' viewpoint. . . . Sometimes I was very uncomfortable wondering how that would wash, so to speak, with Jerry Cohen, for example, or Cesar or Dolores or Marshall Ganz. Am I being fair to the farmworkers? (Levy, 529–30)

The California Agricultural Labor Relations Act (CALRA), signed by Governor Brown on June 4, 1975, declared:

> In enacting this legislation the people of the State of California seek to ensure peace in the agricultural fields by guaranteeing justice for all agricultural workers and stability in labor relations . . . It is hereby stated to be the policy of the State of California to encourage and protect the right of agricultural employees to full freedom of association, self-organization, and designation of representatives of their own choosing.

The ALRA was a milestone in labor legislation but enforcement mechanisms were soon underfunded and outcomes were uneven due in part to the huge backlog in complaints, the growers' use of scab labor, declining support from elected officials, and pressure from the Teamsters.

Sandy Nathan, a key player on the union's legal team, offers a nuanced appraisal of the ALRA period:

I was a full-time member of the legal department from January 1973 until some time in the middle of 1979. . . . I had been hired by LeRoy and Jerry Cohen initially to work on the Safeway legal attack in L.A. . . . It was well known and well understood by the leadership of the union in 1975 that the passage of the ALRA was only going to provide a window of opportunity to build the union. . . . It was not going to magically convert the union from an organization "fighting for its life" into a powerful force. . . . By the spring of 1974, we had even lost the Larson grape contract in Coachella, one of the last two grape contracts. The Gallo boycott was nice and kept people busy; the boycott apparatus was strong but organizing farmworkers into the Union was not a priority. There was very little infrastructure set up to do so. A change in the farm labor laws probably represented the Union's last best chance for meaningful survival. Certainly, the boycott apparatus could have continued indefinitely as a fund-raising organization, and as the arm of the "movement," but it could not organize farmworkers. With the departure of Ronald Reagan as governor in 1974. . . . and the dawn of the Gov. Jerry Brown era, it made sense to look for legislative solutions to turn things around. At that point it seemed like we really had nothing else to lose and everything to gain. . . . The rap against farm labor legislation, by the way, was that it would turn the "union" or the "movement" into a business union; that the sense of the cause would be lost. Ironically, the apparent effort to save the "cause" at the expense of the "union" in the late '70s may have resulted in the loss of everything, including the "cause," the "movement," and the "union." (FMDPd, December 23, 2004)

24 Eulogy for Cesar

Chatfield in 1993:

> I had come full circle. Twenty years after leaving Cesar Chavez and his
> farmworker movement, I was asked by the family to assist with the funeral
> services. One of my assignments was to work with Fernando Chavez on
> the eulogy that he, as the oldest child in the family, would deliver at the
> funeral. We worked hard to keep it short, to the point, and use everyday
> words. I was more than satisfied with the outcome, and Fernando Chavez
> delivered it flawlessly. I left Delano immediately after he finished speak-
> ing. My work was done. (FMDP)

DELIVERED BY FERNANDO CHAVEZ—APRIL 29, 1993

On behalf of my mother, my brothers and sisters, all the grandchildren, my
aunts and uncles, and all of our family, I want to say, "thank you" for being
here with us today on this very sad occasion.

All of you gathered here know that my dad dedicated his entire life to
help farmworkers in their struggle for justice, for equality, for dignity. And
I am proud to say that my mother and our entire family supported dad's
commitment in every way we could and sometimes, as you can imagine, at
great personal sacrifice. I hope and pray that we did our best.

My father chose to live a life of voluntary poverty and yet I believe that
his legacy will be rich. His legacy to our family, his legacy to all of you here,

FIGURE 30 Cesar Chavez funeral altar decoration with icons of the farmworker movement—Our Lady of Guadalupe and the Huelga Eagle—with Chavez portrait titled *RIP* by Octavio Ocampo. Courtesy of Susan Drake/FMDP.

and to the whole country is a legacy of nonviolence. A legacy in the tradition and spirit of Gandhi, Martin Luther King, and Bobby Kennedy.

My dad's life has proven to me that his nonviolent struggle for the rights of farmworkers was a true manifestation of his faith in God and his practice of the teachings of the Gospel.

Some people might say that my father was a "famous man" or that he was a "VIP." Perhaps he was. But for all of us who knew him, including all of you here, I can attest to the fact that he was never, ever, too busy to give his complete attention and interest to each and every person with whom he spoke. Be that person a field worker, a store clerk, a student, a grieving parent, or a complete stranger. He was that kind of man.

My mother and our family understand that Dad's life is finished. But we also understand that each one of you must carry on his spirit of nonviolence and continue his struggle for justice for farmworkers.

25   My Prophecy, 1993

Cesar Chavez is dead and buried. So, what does the future hold for his farmworker movement?

It's very simple, really. What Cesar Chavez was unable to accomplish during his lifetime, i.e., building a national farmworker union, will be accomplished over a period of decades through his death. But, in my opinion, this larger victory will be won from the "outside in," just as the table grape contracts were won through consumer boycotts waged thousands of miles from Delano. It will come about not because of any strike or boycott activities planned by the current union leadership, but because Chavez's life, through his death, will take on proportions that far exceed anyone's expectation and certainly far, far, beyond the bounds of the union.

This will be threatening and confusing to the union leadership, especially because the "public" and the media will expect Cesar's wife, Helen, and the Chavez children to speak in his stead and to attend memorials, participate in dedications, go to ribbon-cutting ceremonies, etc. The union, which after all has declined in recent years, will recede farther into the background. It will become more like the stage backdrop behind the development of Chavez's larger-than-life image. Their first—and understandable—reaction will be to bottle the genie Cesar so that he can be let out as needed.

It is a paradox. Chavez's mystique will grow exponentially larger and larger in the public consciousness—not only in North America but throughout the entire world—and the union's will grow smaller and smaller. And as his public legacy grows in public opinion centers of urban areas, outside the agricultural hinterlands, it will set the stage for farmworkers themselves to light the matches that will cause wave after wave of crippling agricultural strikes to protest their oppressive working conditions and to manifest their determination to have their own union. It is precisely at these flash points that the farmworker union must be prepared to intervene and provide leadership, support, direction, and the know-how to represent these workers.

I compare this readiness of farmworkers to act spontaneously with that of the residents in East Los Angeles in May of 1968 during Bobby Kennedy's campaign for president. Our presence as "Robert Kennedy for President" in these barrio neighborhoods was all that was needed for people—poor people, working-class people—to join our campaign to organize and vote for Kennedy. It was almost impossible for us to find enough campaign tasks for people to do. As for "get out the vote" activities, forget it! Many precincts had almost 100 percent turnouts. It wasn't any special campaign activity that "we" concocted that made the difference. It was simply the fact that people were responding to the brother of their slain hero, President John F. Kennedy. They wanted to be part of that special Kennedy family mystique that they believed stood for social justice.

How much more so with Cesar Chavez! A person who spent his lifetime working on behalf of farmworkers who were defenseless and without a voice. A person who sacrificed all his material possessions, lived in voluntary poverty, and disciplined himself and his movement with monthlong fasts. A person who preached with his deeds.

For those who think I exaggerate or who find this far-fetched, consider this: Chavez has not even been buried thirty days and already his life and death are taking on a life of their own in California.

Students at Fremont High School in Oakland have turned in 1,400 signatures to the school board to change the name of their high school to Cesar E. Chavez High. Parents in Union City are lobbying to name their middle school after Chavez. An Oakland city councilman wants to rename a major city street. San José officials want to rename Plaza Park, and the City and County of Los Angeles are just beginning to get into the "street-naming" act. All of this is in addition to a bill introduced in the California legislature by Senator Art Torres and Assemblyman Richard Polanco to declare March 31, the birthday of Cesar Chavez, a state holiday. This is only the beginning.

The pilgrimages to La Paz to visit Chavez's grave have already begun. It won't be long before the union bureaucracy will have to relocate, leaving

FIGURE 31 Gravesite in private cemetery at La Paz—final resting place of Helen and Cesar Chavez. Photo by Bobak Ha'Eri. Courtesy of Wikimedia Commons.

others behind to give the tours, to tell Cesar's story and sell the books, videos, and other mementos associated with these kinds of activities. But this outpouring of homage and respect will not, in my judgment, advance any particular boycott or strike activity on the present union's agenda. If packaged thoughtfully, however, it will create, over a period of time, an historical mystique about Chavez's life and work that will lay the groundwork to prompt a wave of agricultural strikes and farmworker union organizing activities throughout the country that will resonate well with national public opinion.

Even the growers, true to form, are doing their best to throw gasoline on the flickering fire. The *San Francisco Chronicle* (May 25, 1993) quotes one Bruce Burkdoll, president of the Central California Farmers Association: "I'm not at all in favor of renaming schools and streets, and a holiday is completely ridiculous. He (Cesar Chavez) was a labor organizer and a poor one. I don't see anything heroic about it." Deja vu! This is the same off-the-wall, anti-Mexican rhetoric that enabled us in the early days of the Delano Grape Strike to ratchet up the national debate over the rights of farmworkers. We could always count on the growers and their public relations firms to make our best case.

Do you think students care about the niceties raised by the school board over the renaming of a school for Chavez or that it will cost money to have new stationery printed and to have new listings in the telephone directory? Do you think thousands of Oakland residents, Latino and black, care that it will cost the city money to replace street signs that say "Cesar Chavez" instead of "East 14th St."? And a March 31 California holiday honoring Chavez's birthday is already a foregone conclusion. Not this year or the next, but you can bet it will be an issue in the next California governor's election or the one after that.

Cesar confided to me that he thought it would take twenty years before the first union contracts were won. They actually came in less than two. In retrospect, a case could be made that it might have been better for the union if it had taken longer, because a hundred-fold growth was not possible to digest. But since there are no choices in these matters, the point is academic.

Cesar Chavez was completely resigned to the fact that it would take a lifetime to build a national farmworker union—and now he gets a fresh start!

On August 8, 1994, President Bill Clinton posthumously awarded Cesar E. Chavez the Presidential Medal of Freedom. Helen Chavez accepted the award. On October 8, 2012, President Barack Obama established the Cesar E. Chavez National Monument. La Paz was now a National Historic Landmark. In his remarks, Obama said:

> Cesar believed that when a worker is treated fairly and humanely by their employer, that adds meaning to the values this country was founded upon and credence to the claim that out of many, we are one. And he believed that when a child anywhere in America can dream beyond her circumstances and work to realize that dream, it makes all our futures just a little bit brighter. It was that vision, that belief in the power of opportunity that drove Cesar every day of his life. It's a vision that says, maybe I never had a chance to get a good education, but I want my daughter to go to college. Maybe I started out working in the fields, but someday I'll own my own business. Maybe I have to make sacrifices, but those sacrifices are worth it if it means a better life for my family.

Chatfield updates his reflections that make up this essay in his afterword to the present volume.

26   Helen Chavez—A Tribute

This will come as quite a shock to you—even I have difficulty believing it—but at one time in my life, I was a young man.

It was during that time that I met Helen Chavez. She was a few years older than I was, the mother of eight children who ranged in ages from sixteen to six, and she was the wife of my best friend. Forty-five years later, I write of the Helen Chavez I knew and admired.

I remember the day I walked into her small, two-bedroom house in Delano to visit her husband. The house was spotless. Hospitality was extended. Her children were well mannered, courteous, and respectful to visitors like me. I knew immediately that in this family—and I include her husband—Helen Chavez was the no-nonsense organizer in chief.

There was no TV, I don't remember a radio, and there was no telephone, washer, or dryer. Helen and Cesar had no bank account. Cesar owned a small Volvo, but Helen did not drive. And if you can believe it, after the Volvo expired in late 1966, they never owned another car. Cesar and Helen Chavez, along with their children, lived a life of voluntary poverty because they wanted to be free to dedicate their lives to organizing and helping farmworkers.

In keeping with the spirit of the Documentation Project, in this tribute I use two primary sources: first, the account by Kathy Lynch Murguia, who began as an eighteen-year-old volunteer with the farmworker movement, and second, the account by Bonnie Burns Chatfield, an eight-year veteran of the movement. Kathy and Bonnie have written essays about their time with the United Farm Workers, and in them they include their experiences with Helen.

Kathy   I moved from the marginal chaos of a volunteer house to the Chavez's small, two-bedroom home on Kensington Street. The children were special. When Helen was absent, Sylvia, Linda, or Eloise was in charge. They seemed to be always cleaning and keeping the younger children in line. The sleeping arrangement was novel to me. Bobo, Birdie, and Titibet slept in the front room on the floor or the couches. The older girls—Sylvia, Linda, Anna, and Tota— slept in the other bedroom. Fernando slept in a covered porch area at the back of the house. The younger ones would compete for the couch. When I moved in, I got the couch. I have great memories of my stay with the family.

Bonnie   I spent a lot of time at Cesar and Helen's house on Kensington—a tiny two-bedroom cottage that housed eight children and all kinds of guests—room for all, pots of food on the stove, and repartee and laughter all the time, especially when Cesar was gone. I felt completely at home. Helen was my surrogate mother. If I had a "baby" question, I called Helen. Sylvia and Eloise were my primary babysitters but more like younger sisters for me, and beloved aunts to our daughter Clare. We had fun and they could always make me laugh. The Mexican women with whom I lived and worked were loving, patient, and generally relaxed mothers. I've looked back and been grateful for their influence.

Kathy again   During this time, I became good friends with Helen Chavez. I wanted to teach her how to drive. I thought it was a strain to take care of all the things she had to do—going to the picket lines in the mornings, working full time, and managing her family's needs. I often came over on the weekends to give her rides or to go shopping where we looked for specials on hot dogs or hamburger meat. At the same time, I became part of the office crowd, which included Esther Uranday, Helen Chavez, Fina Hernandez, Donna Haber, and Donna Childers. What a group. Helen, Cesar's wife, was in charge of the farmworkers' credit union. Her frank honesty and warm regard for others immediately drew me to her.

FIGURE 32 Truth be told, women were the backbone of the movement. Dolores Huerta, Helen Chavez, and Kathy Murguia on the picket line, 1965. Photo by Jon Lewis. Courtesy of FMDP / Yale Collection of Western Americana at the Beinecke Rare Book & Manuscript Library.

You talk about hard work? About being organized? You talk about bandwidth or multitasking? Managing the family, going to the morning picket lines, working full time managing the credit union, shopping on weekends for specials on hot dogs and hamburger, and mentoring other women—how on earth could Helen Chavez manage all this?

But there is more! Add forty-five years of marriage to the same person, especially if that someone is a *Time* magazine Man of the Year and an international celebrity who leads three-hundred-mile and thousand-mile marches, is jailed for a month in Salinas, travels throughout the United States and Canada for months at a time to raise funds for the cause and to promote the farmworker boycotts, and who periodically fasts publicly for a month at time during the course of your marriage. Living a life of such intensity and demands took great talent, dedication, commitment, and yes, maybe a little party time, too.

Bonnie again   Every couple of months, with Helen, her sister Petra, Kathy M., Esther, Fina, and many other women, we had a ladies' night

FIGURE 33 Cesar and Helen Chavez on the three-hundred-mile *peregrinación* (pilgrimage) from Delano to Sacramento, 1966. Helen played a key role in organizing the action and her presence empowered the other women on the march. Photo by Jon Lewis. Courtesy of FMDP/Yale Collection of Western Americana at the Beinecke Rare Book & Manuscript Library.

out—a beer party. "Don't tell Cesar that I smoked," cautioned Helen. God, did we laugh. About everything. My sides ached the next day.

Helen Chavez is the only woman I know who was arrested and jailed for three days for shouting "huelga!" on a farmworker picket line, had her picture taken with Charlton Heston, became close friends with Ethel Kennedy, had a meeting with the president of the United States, and secured a private audience with the pope.

In the program for a Tribute to Helen Chavez, sponsored by the Cesar Chavez Service Club of San Diego, it is written: "Without Helen by his side, Cesar Chavez could not have devoted his life to the struggle for social justice for farmworkers. While she never spoke in public, her steadfast and loyal presence was felt throughout the length and breadth of the farmworker movement."

What I write now will never be found in a book or in a documentary film or in any scholarly discussion about Cesar Chavez and his farmworker

FIGURE 34 Helen in charge of the food line, 1972. Helen Chavez spent countless days organizing the wives and daughters of farmworkers, along with visiting volunteers. A movement marches on its stomach. Photo by Gayanne Fietinghoff. Courtesy of FMDP/Yale Collection of Western Americana at the Beinecke Rare Book & Manuscript Library.

movement, but it is true. I ask you please, if you remember nothing else about Helen Chavez, please remember this: First, women were the back-bone of the farmworker movement and it was these women who looked to Helen Chavez for inspiration, modeling, and guidance. Second, Helen Chavez was a full partner with her husband in the creation and development of the farmworker movement. She was not a passive participant or a spouse who simply tolerated the full-time missionary work of a husband. She understood the need and she fully complemented the role of her spouse in their joint struggle to achieve social justice for farmworkers.

Let me give you one very concrete example of what I mean. In 1968, during Cesar's fast for nonviolence, farmworkers began to arrive in Delano from all sectors of California, Arizona, Washington, and Texas—at first, we counted their arrival by dozens, then by hundreds, and finally by thousands. They came because of the fast; they came to meet Cesar Chavez, the founder of the movement; and they came to pledge their support to him.

So, while Cesar Chavez was fasting and depriving himself of food for the sake of promoting nonviolence in his cause, Helen Chavez was spending her entire day preparing and cooking food to feed the hundreds and then thousands of farmworker visitors who came to Delano. She took charge. She organized the wives and daughters of the Delano strikers, as well as the visiting farmworkers and volunteers, into a workforce that converted the few loaves and fishes into a full course evening meal for the multitudes every day of the fast. These women were empowered by Helen and were swept up into the wake of her commitment to social justice for farmworkers and her willingness to sacrifice for it.

In the course of writing this piece, I have been trying to find a word or maybe two words that best describe the Helen Chavez I know. The words I have chosen are *noble* and *woman*. Helen Chavez is a noble woman. She carries herself with poise and great bearing; she has presence; she is gracious, approachable, and generous; she is blessed with God-given good common sense; above all, she was fiercely loyal to the work of her husband. In short, Helen Chavez is a noble woman—and she puts the rest of us to shame!

Helen Fabela was born in 1928 in Brawley, California, to parents from the Mexican states of Jalisco and Zacatecas. Her working life began at the age of fifteen after the death of her father. She met Cesar Chavez in Delano, California, where they were married in 1948. After working as a field laborer and in a variety of other jobs, Helen was active in the Community Service Organization, providing classes and workshops to migrant workers. She was a key player in the formation of the NFWA and beyond, administering the credit union and fulfilling other important functions. In 2012, Dolores Huerta told an interviewer:

> Because we didn't have any money when we started organizing the union, Helen worked in the fields picking grapes and still managed her household with eight kids. When we started the first credit union for farm workers in the United States, Helen became the head. Helen, who had a high school degree! She didn't want to do it but she was drafted, [and] we all voted for her. Cesar knew she was the one to keep our accounts straight. I think our credit union was started with something like three thousand dollars, but by the time that we merged with another credit union we had lent farm workers eleven million dollars of their own money. All those years, Helen directed the credit union, and with all of our audits, we never had anything wrong with the books in our credit union.[1]

FIGURE 35 Bonnie Burns Chatfield seeks to comfort Helen Chavez at the funeral for Cesar, 1993. In their eight years working together, a period that included the birth of four of the five Chatfield daughters, Helen and Bonnie developed a strong mother-daughter relationship. Photo by Carlos LeGerrette. Courtesy of Carlos LeGerrette.

Helen Chavez was arrested multiple times on the picket line. LeRoy Chatfield offers the following summation: "The historical record does not identify a co-founder for Cesar Chavez's farmworker movement. Some say Gilbert Padilla is a co-founder, other say Dolores Huerta is a co-founder, still others suggest Julio Hernandez. All three were Cesar's colleagues dating back to the Community Service Organization. . . . But I think a good case could be made to nominate Helen Chavez for co-founder of the Movement" (Personal correspondence, October 15, 2017).

NOTE

1. Dolores Huerta, interview by the International Museum of Women, 2018, http://exhibitions.globalfundforwomen.org/economica/stories/viewStory?story Id=3626.

27 The Organizer

An organizer is a person who knows how to create something out of nothing.

An organizer is a person who takes something that does not now exist and makes it exist.

An organizer is a person who creates their own reality.

An organizer is a person who knows how to create a path of forward motion moving from the known to the unknown.

An organizer is a person who knows how to shape chaos.

An organizer is a person who recognizes the blind alley, knows how to alter course, and pick up the pieces.

An organizer is not a person who does all the work, but a person who knows what work has to be done, why, and who can do it.

An organizer is a person who interprets for others the small victory achieved today, which will surely lead to a larger victory tomorrow.

An organizer is a person who recognizes the seeds of victory sown in today's defeat.

An organizer is a person who does not ask others to do what they will not.

An organizer is a person who leads not by fiery bombast but by example, by patient teaching, by their wits, and by a stubborn persistence.

An organizer is a person so convinced that others see the need to help.

An organizer is a person who organizes the march and not a person who leads the march.

An organizer is a person who does not accept "no" for an answer.

An organizer is not an administrator—that is another person.

A useful supplement to this list of axioms is Fred Ross Sr., "Axioms for Organizers" (1989) at the FMDP site: https://libraries.ucsd.edu/farmworkermovement/essays/essays/MillerArchive/064%20Axioms%20For%20Organizers.pdf.

PART THREE
WITH THE
HOMELESS

28   What Is the Answer?

How many times during the past twenty years have I been asked the question, "Well, what is the answer to homelessness?" Dozens of times, I'm sure, and often enough that I came to dread the question because my answer seemed to elicit little interest or understanding from the questioner.

I began to realize that the questioner did not expect an answer to such an intractable problem. In fact, the questioner assumed there was no answer. If I had simply responded, "Homelessness is a horrific problem, I don't have the answer to solve it," I would have received a more sympathetic and understanding response. At the very least, I would have confirmed the enormity of the problem. But you know me—I wouldn't allow the question to slip by without giving my answer, especially because I have the answer.

The question is not really a difficult one, which, of course, makes a simple answer even more difficult to accept, especially when the reporter, the Loaves & Fishes supporter, or the audience member presumes that the question about eliminating homelessness has no answer.

Think about it. The state of homelessness simply means that some people do not have homes. If every person had a home, there would be no homeless problem. What prevents a person from having a home? Exactly right, not having enough money to afford it. The fact is that every homeless person has some money, just not enough to afford a home.

There's your answer. People do not have enough money to afford 2004 rents. People who work low-skill, minimum-wage jobs, who are not even a paycheck away from homelessness, do not earn enough to pay the rent. And for those who are mentally and/or physically disabled and not part of the workforce, their government subsistence stipends do not include enough money for rent. If low-skill working people were paid enough money for their work, they would not be homeless or teetering on its edge. If the Social Security Disability Insurance included enough money for rent, disabled people would not be homeless.

Is this difficult to understand? I expect not. If a free market economy will not pay low-skill working people enough to live in homes, then it falls to the government to subsidize business by providing truly affordable housing, which means that no more than 35 percent of a worker's income should be spent on rent. In a 2004 California minimum-wage economy, this means $400 a month for rent, including utilities.

The answer to homelessness is simple enough: 1) set wages high enough to include payment for housing; 2) guarantee and provide affordable housing; or 3) both.

You ask, why don't free market employers pay low-skill workers enough to afford housing? Their answer is always the same—business will not make a profit if workers are paid more. No profit, no business. It is the use of this profit argument time and again that persuades government not to raise the minimum wage. Today's headlines make this very point: "Minimum Wage Boost Vetoed: Governor Says Increase to $7.75 an Hour Would Hurt Businesses and Cost Jobs."

Take a look at the profit argument from the perspective of a low-skilled, minimum-wage worker, a person always on the edge of homelessness. The conclusion seems inescapable—the viability of business depends on my being grossly underpaid, and my inability to afford housing supports the free market economy. In other words, homelessness subsidizes business profits.

Obviously, government at every level supports the profit argument used by business to prevent increases in the minimum wage, because the current shortfall in wages, not large enough to pay for housing, is $3.25 an hour, or 33 percent. Since government won't permit wage increases, why will they not subsidize business by providing affordable housing?

Dear reader, this answer is not a pleasant one. Local government, not unlike business-profit employers, considers minimum-wage working people to be relatively worthless. Truth be told, such people are considered to be a drag on the local economy, a negative influence on a desirable quality of life for the rest of the community, and insatiable consumers of social services.

Does this sound harsh and unfairly critical of local government? Yes, I'm sure it does. Is it true? Let me assure you, it is. Permit me to qualify—it is true here in the capital city of the state of California.

Understandably, no local elected government official talks publicly about these harsh realities. There is no need to talk; their policies say it all. Some examples: many hundreds of affordable housing units were razed in the downtown area to lay the groundwork for a more desirable, major league high-rise future; the city's own housing agency was forbidden to bring low-cost housing proposals forward for consideration; NIMBYism has been deliberately fostered in order to bury housing advocates and nonprofit developers; zoning codes were used to impede the development of affordable housing; and punitive special-use permits mandated astronomically expensive building requirements for midtown low-income housing. Dare I describe such policies as "cleansing"?

The bottom line for these elected leaders seems to be that people who have money are deemed to be moral and worthy citizens; those who do not are immoral and unworthy, and worse yet, unwelcome. This view is antithetical to and a corruption of our cultural Judeo-Christian religious heritage, which holds that because God created each person in His own image and likeness, each person is not only good in the eyes of his Creator, but also the recipient of His unconditional love.

Despite the inhumanity of such policies, I do not believe they constitute the social injustice that requires people to be homeless. The social injustice, as I see it, is the paltry sum of $3.25 an hour, which represents the difference between housing and homelessness. It is exactly this differential that our economic system deems necessary to guarantee business its profit. As a community, we cannot afford the human suffering caused by this social injustice of deliberately underpaying low-skill, minimum-wage workers.

Deep down within us, we know homelessness is not right. We know business and government should do better for the low-skill, low-income members of our community—but what? I submit that adding $3.25 an hour to the current minimum wage is the first step in putting our money on the side of our good intentions. The minimum wage should be the moral touchstone for our business economy and not the stranglehold that keeps people homeless or teetering on its edge.

Inspired by Dorothy Day's Catholic Worker movement, former Catholic priest Dan Delany (1935–2015) and his wife, Chris (a former nun), founded Loaves

FIGURE 36 LeRoy Chatfield, first executive director of Loaves & Fishes. He served for thirteen years. Today he is a volunteer organizer for the Homeless Breakfast Program. Photographer unknown. Courtesy of the Chatfield family.

& Fishes in 1983, a 501(c)(3) whose mission is to provide food and shelter for the homeless in Sacramento. LeRoy Chatfield became its first executive director in 1987. Bonnie Burns Chatfield was instrumental in the building of a volunteer pool to sustain the work. In 2001, Chatfield founded the Golden Day Project, which identified suitably zoned properties for nonprofit developers to build low-cost housing for disabled homeless people. For more on the role of Loaves & Fishes in the history of Catholic activism in Sacramento, especially the contentious relationship in the 1990s between the City and business leaders and Chatfield and his supporters, see Avella in "Suggested Readings."

As Chatfield describes above, the gentrification of downtown areas across California that began in the 1990s, and continues unabated today in 2018, essentially displaced thousands of poor people. Loaves & Fishes was one of the first organizations to fight back, with former UFW counsel Jerry Cohen on their legal team, and win an eventual lawsuit. (See essay 32 for more details on this story.) Today, Loaves & Fishes continues to provide food, shelter, and services to the homeless in Sacramento. See also https://www.youtube.com/watch?v=cpexzaadPt4.

In 2017, California increased its minimum wage to $10.50 per hour with the goal of reaching $15 by 2023. The massive redistribution of wealth to the top 1 percent nationally, however, has produced the radical gentrification of California's major cities and coastal areas—Los Angeles and San Francisco but also Oakland, San José, and San Diego—and an affordable housing crisis of historic proportions. Not surprisingly, California now has the largest home-less population in the country, including in rural areas, and with attendant public health consequences such as a serious outbreak of hepatitis A in San Diego in 2017. In April 2017, the *New York Times* reported on the dire situa-tion for homeless people in Sacramento following an estimated 30 percent increase in their numbers since 2015.

29 Guests, Not Clients

Loaves & Fishes serves guests, not clients.

Guests are made to feel welcome; hospitality is extended. Clients are expected to make (and keep) appointments. No appointment, no service.

Guests are accepted as friends, given the benefit of the doubt, and not kept waiting. Clients are expected to wait patiently, however long it takes, and then listen up when their turn comes.

Guests are treated as equals; they do not have to justify their presence. Clients must prove their need with ID and detailed questionnaires.

Loaves & Fishes
Homeless Survival Services
Since 1983

FIGURE 37 Loaves & Fishes logo, adapted from a Christian symbol dating back to the Roman catacombs of the first century AD.

Guests are free to kick back, relax, and catch a few rays. Clients have to be scrutinized, toe the mark, or seek services elsewhere.

Guests are free to ask questions, criticize, and challenge the system. Clients are expected to be grateful for any service rendered, and no talking back, please.

Guests are free to help themselves to seconds. Clients are notified that one is sufficient.

Guests are free to come and go as they please. Clients need permission.

The most challenging part of being a Loaves & Fishes staff member is to understand—and practice—the difference between *guest* and *client*. Some prospective staff members are inherently incapable of making the transition from client to guest because of a deeply held bias that they are different from, and therefore better than, guests.

Some of the measuring sticks a staff member uses to mark this difference are so superficial they could be called silly. Some examples: education ("my degree"); fashion ("Where did you get that cute outfit?"); lifestyle ("I'm going to work out"); mobility ("I'm going to LA for the weekend"); status ("What does your father do?"); and career ("Where did you go to grad school?"). Even the often-quoted scripture admonition "There but for the grace of God go I" is interpreted to mean "You poor bastards."

Finally, the Loaves & Fishes staff member must be nonjudgmental. Period. No exceptions. There is no latitude to say this guest deserves help but that one is hopeless. Or this guest is ready to reform but that one is a troublemaker. Or this guest is cooperative and needs my help but that one is a pain in the ass and can be ignored.

When Loaves & Fishes staff members begin to experience the joy of working with guests, not clients, they experience a newfound freedom in their daily work. This new relationship is honest, mature, and more like the values expressed in the Gospel.

These guests—formerly clients—now suddenly have ideas and points of view worth considering.

They can be wise beyond understanding and challenge us to live in the present moment now, today. Some have great talents bottled up within, trying to find expression. Many are generous beyond all measure. Most have suffered traumatic physical and/or emotional injuries and walk every step with pain that is relieved from time to time only by self-medication. They do not justify or make excuses about their shortcomings. They do not curse their fortune or the hand that has been dealt them; they live with such hope!

As one who has been fortunate to work at Loaves & Fishes for many years, I can sense when staff members have made the difficult transition to understanding the difference between client and guest. The refrain is nearly identical: "I have received from the guests much more than I gave."

30   Clean and Sober

I begin this essay with the general premise that each of us is an addict. But some addictions are more socially acceptable than others.

What little I know about addiction to alcohol and street drugs among homeless people I learned from my work at Loaves & Fishes. Perhaps the most important revelation for me was to understand that most substance abuse is a form of self-medication. People need to mask their pain, whether physical or mental, and drinking or using is simply a less expensive means to cope with this pain. Drinking is legal, using is not, but each serves a kind of medicinal purpose for people who are impoverished, marginalized, and forever hurting.

When alcohol and street drugs are viewed as inexpensive medicine, the rush to moral judgment is slowed and one can look beyond the outward, and sometimes raw, manifestations of substance abuse and begin to see the life of the addicted homeless person in a broader context.

The philosophy of Loaves & Fishes teaches us to accept—and not to judge—each person as the individual they are, and not who we might wish them to be—that is, more like us. But even more, it teaches not to require this person to be rehabilitated so that they become eligible for service or assistance. And because many, if not most, of the homeless guests who come to Loaves & Fishes for survival services are self-medicating substance abusers, it is not the mission of Loaves to render them clean or sober. The mission is to accept them and render service without any preconditions—unconditional love it is called, not tough love.

Even in such a lax and permissive environment, or perhaps because of it, some substance abusers wish to confront and overcome their addiction. They wish to be free.

Enter the Clean & Sober program. Originally begun by Loaves & Fishes staff members, some of whom were former addicts, the Clean & Sober program incorporated itself independently of its parent organization, housed itself in the same complex, and became an instant point of referral for addicts who had made the decision to stop drinking or using.

Ten years later, hundreds of homeless addicts had made the successful transition from addiction to living in recovery, leading independent lives, and being reunited with loved ones. At the anniversary banquet, which celebrated the first ten years of existence of the Clean & Sober program, I spoke to the assembled supporters and graduates of the program:

> These words are addressed to those who live in recovery, whether measured in years or months or even days.
>
> You have done what the rest of us are unable or unwilling to do. You have confronted your own addiction. You have been willing to do the hard work—the heavy lifting—of looking at yourself honestly, without self-pity or excuse. You have somehow managed to set aside your fear and personal insecurity about the unknown. You have made the decision to overcome.
>
> Why have you been able to meet and accept this challenge head-on while the rest of us are unable to do so? How were you able to make the decision to do something with your life while the rest of us do not even know we are in trouble?
>
> Why do we remain in denial while you are able to push forward with such courage? Why do we continue the delay, always looking for an easy way out, while you seek the truth of self? Why do we seek escape while you seek freedom?
>
> Where did you find the desire and the strength to choose the most difficult path of all? Where did you find the commitment to undertake such a life-altering change? What happened in your life that sets you so far apart from the drift of the rest of us? I cannot say. I have no answer. It is a mystery to me.
>
> What I do know, what I can say, is that your life of recovery gives us hope, and sets an example that one day we too will be confident and strong enough to confront our own addictions.

And if—or when—that day ever comes, we too will be able to come to you and say, "I just want to shake your hand. I want to say thank you, friend. You saved my life."

31 Cherry-Picking

I cannot be impartial. My bias about the criminal justice system as it affects homeless people in Sacramento is insurmountable. So much so that it prevents me from serving on a jury. I do not oppose law enforcement, the jury system, or the criminal courts. But I do oppose the crushing injustice inflicted on the poor and the homeless by these institutions through the criminal justice system.

Rest assured, I harbor no romanticized views about the innate morality of homeless people. They are people, after all, just like us—some good, some bad, some tall, and some short. The problem is that the criminal justice system does not treat the homeless fairly. Justice is not blind.

My bias undoubtedly took root forty years ago when I worked with Cesar Chavez and his farmworker movement. Agribusiness had stacked the cards against these Mexican workers trying to organize their union, and it counted on local law enforcement and the courts to protect the growers and preserve the status quo. And they did, or at least they made every effort to do so. Striking farmworkers were arrested for picketing and/or violating injunctions designed to make lawful picketing impossible. The workers were subjected to constant intimidation, courtesy of the sworn, armed, uniformed, and riot-helmeted police officers. Arrest wagons and police cars were always at the ready, camera surveillance was ongoing, and car license plate numbers were read into police cruiser radios for further investigation.

What, you ask, was new, unusual, and unexpected about using law enforcement to preserve the status quo? Not much, I suppose, except that its blatant unfairness made a lasting impression on me.

I do not believe my farmworker movement experience justifies my longstanding refusal to sit on a jury in a criminal case because farmworkers fought back against this injustice. They recruited their own civil rights attorneys, they sued the system, they tried their cases in the courts of public opinion, and they took their fight to the supreme courts of states and the nation. Over a period of years, the farmworker movement began to tilt the playing field of justice toward a semblance of equality and a sharing of power with agribusiness.

This is not the case with the homeless and the indigent poor in Sacramento. They are unorganized and powerless to fight back against a criminal justice system designed to criminalize and prosecute them because of their homelessness.

If there were a meaningful way to exempt certain police officers from the balance of this essay, I would certainly do so. They did not agree with the treatment accorded to the homeless, nor did they willingly participate, but the institutional reality in which they operated was not much different from that of being in the military: follow orders.

Cherry-picking is a learn-by-doing chapter in training programs used by law enforcement agencies in the Sacramento area. Young officers in training are assigned to patrol areas frequented by homeless people in order to practice such policing techniques as interrogation, investigation, arrest, and transport. Homeless people are selected as the cherries in this picking exercise because there is minimal risk to the officers and a high probability of finding so-called lawful grounds to interrogate, investigate, and make an arrest.

Officers in training do not feel threatened or personally at risk in confronting homeless people for several reasons—they are not armed, they are passive, they are tied to their possessions, they do not travel in groups, they are not gang members, and they have no effective means of escape. Better yet, there is the probability that a high percentage of those stopped and interrogated will have had a bench warrant issued for their arrest. In short, cherry-picking is a low-risk, high-arrest-probability training exercise.

Law enforcement personnel tell me that forty thousand bench warrants have been issued in the county of Sacramento for light-rail fare violations.

FIGURE 38 David Andre at a homeless protest in Sacramento, California, January 2016. Photo by Rich Pedroncelli. Courtesy of the Associated Press.

Imagine, forty thousand warrants in the criminal justice computer system, patiently waiting for the opportunity to ensnare an indigent citizen for non-payment of a $1.50 fare. Imagine the cost of such fiscal insanity. A light-rail user is cited for nonpayment (first cost); the citation is sent to the criminal justice system to be processed (second cost); the presiding judge schedules a hearing date (third cost); the judge assigned to the case calls the name of the defendant, who is a no-show for a variety of reasons, but primarily because they do not have any money to pay the fine and do not want to serve jail time (fourth cost); the judge orders a bench warrant to be issued for the no-show defendant (fifth cost); the bench warrant is issued and awaits acci-dental implementation by an arresting officer during cherry-picking time, or through periodic police sweeps to enforce anticamping ordinances or other "low life" cleanup campaigns (sixth cost); the arrest, the transporta-tion, and the booking at the jail take place (seventh cost); the defendant is incarcerated for several days (eighth cost); the presiding judge schedules the hearing date (ninth cost); the judge assigned to the case calls for the defen-dant's appearance, which requires police transport from jail (tenth cost); the judge conducts the hearing and imposes a sentence for time already served (eleventh cost); the defendant is transported back to jail and processed for release (twelfth cost).

What is the cost, then, of prosecuting a homeless person for the inability to afford a light-rail ticket? $6,000? $12,000? If the institutional overhead associated with the criminal prosecution of this homeless person is factored into the cost equation, I place the cost at more than $15,000. Imagine the cost if all forty thousand bench warrants were to be processed. Incredible! If Sacramento gave each homeless person an unlimited free transit pass, millions of dollars would be saved, and many thousands of hours of human suffering and humiliation would be avoided.

But my refusal to participate in the criminal justice system as a juror is not based on the fiscal insanity of the bench warrant system as it applies to homeless people. Rather, it is based on the rationale of the system itself, which is designed to criminalize and prosecute people who are so poor that they have to come to Loaves & Fishes for something to eat, so poor that regardless of age, physical condition, or infirmity, they are forever condemned to walk alongside the public transit light-rail tracks.

The criminal justice system is not simply misguided or corrupt in its treatment of homeless people. It is a highly evolved, complex, and sophisticated form of legalized cherry-picking.

It is unjust and I resent it.

32   A Public Fast

A public fast is a silent witness that religious and moral values need to be upheld. Its action is quiet, personal, peaceful, dignified, and non-violent. It doesn't argue with people. It is ongoing and unrelenting. A public fast needs only one person to make the witness.

One month in 2001, the executive director of Loaves & Fishes reported to the board about his efforts to secure a year-round shelter for homeless women and children. Every month thereafter, he faithfully reported the promises of the county staff to remedy the situation. He relayed to the board in great detail the results of his meetings with county officials, their plans, and their promised deadlines. Finally, in a stunning development, board members themselves heard county staff testify before the county board of supervisors that there was no need for such an emergency shelter—there was already enough shelter. In fact, they testified, no women or children were currently without shelter. A stunning development because it was not true!

One month in early 2002, the board of directors agreed that for the sake of homeless women and children, some direct and very public action needed to be taken to secure emergency overnight shelter. One of the senior members, schooled in advocacy during the 1960s, proposed a public fast, and so it was decided.

Swift feedback came back from county staff, the very same ones who testified that there was enough shelter—don't bother, it won't do any good, it's water off a duck's back, don't waste your time, county supervisors never respond to direct action from advocates.

No matter. Starting in Holy Week of 2002, Loaves & Fishes began a public fast in the posh waiting room of the Sacramento county board of supervisors. Taking turns, each board member faithfully fasted every day, and many others from the community at large joined in. In October of that same year, barely five months after the start of the public fast, the supervisors voted to open an emergency shelter for homeless women and children.

The county government building in downtown Sacramento is six stories high and covers an entire city block. It has operated according to its own rhythm for more than twenty years. A county government building can operate only when it is business as usual. In truth, this is what government does—operate the usual business as usual.

But the public fast altered ever so slightly the rhythm of the county building. Every person at every desk on every floor was conscious of the alteration in the rhythm of the building, and so it was not business as usual. The public fast made it just a little more difficult than usual to do the usual business. Every county employee or member of the general public who walked into the supervisors' chambers was immediately aware that the county was not doing business as usual. But what could the supervisors do about it?

The supervisors are the people in charge. They have the final say; they have the power. And yet, in the face of the public fast, they were powerless. They could not arrest those fasting, they could not make the fasters go away, and they could not afford even to be rude. They could only pretend to ignore the public fast, and that is what changed the rhythm and broke the status quo. It was no longer business as usual and doing the usual business. Their impotence reverberated throughout the entire county complex.

Water off a duck's back or not, the supervisors found a way to stop the public fast. They gave Loaves & Fishes what it wanted. Bittersweet, to be sure, but for the first time in Sacramento, homeless women and children were provided year-round emergency shelter.

The public fast is the scriptural knock on the door in the middle of the night at the home of the judge. Everything is locked up and secure. He does not have to answer the door. He says to himself, "I won't answer the door." The knocking persists. He shouts through the window, "Go away! I won't answer the door." Finally, because the knocking will not cease, he opens the door to deal with the supplicant.

Thanks to all who participated in the public fast by knocking on the door of the county supervisors.

Remember the lessons of the public fast—never forget its power.

An insightful feature news story from 1997 (when Chatfield was still the director of Loaves & Fishes) illuminates the consistency and contradictions of Chatfield's commitment to serving the poor. I include the complete story here (with corrections):

Say what you will about LeRoy Chatfield. The embattled director of Loaves & Fishes has stayed true to the cause. The main problem, according to those who have tangled with him, is his "to-hell-with-everyone-else" approach to it all. For Chatfield, whose agency is involved in a court fight with City Hall, the mission was spelled out more than 30 years ago, when Cesar Chavez, his friend and mentor, signed a commemorative portrait. "LeRoy," the legendary head of the United Farm Workers of America scrawled on the photo still hanging on Chatfield's office wall, "may your education be of benefit to the poor."

Even his critics, growing in number and intensity as more and more of the poor are fed at the North C Street charity run by Chatfield, would give him that much. At 61, with a religious commitment many of those critics consider zealotry, the former teacher in the Christian Brothers order has devoted much of his life to society's discards. In the process, Chatfield, blunt-spoken and fierce in his advocacy for the city's poor, has become one of Sacramento's most explosive personalities, a man people seem to love or loathe. It's a familiar role.

"This is not my only career where I've been a lightning rod," Chatfield said recently during his daily morning ritual of coffee and a roll at a Land Park espresso shop. "Maybe that's my bent. I'm not saying it's fun and games. But I don't shrink away from it. I've taken my lumps, deservedly so, and I'll take some more. But I have a clear conscience about all this."

For most of his life, Chatfield has championed the oppressed—with considerable success. Born into a family of rice growers, Chatfield left his home in the tiny Colusa County town of Arbuckle to join the Christian Brothers, a religious teaching order. He went on to become a confidant of Chavez, hero to farm workers but the bane of big California growers. Chatfield helped plan some of Chavez's most successful acts of civil disobedience.

That's why, when Chatfield was looking for something to do 10 years ago and signed on to run Loaves & Fishes for what he thought would be three months, he felt like he was coming home.

"I've had a lifetime of experience standing up for people who don't know what to do, who feel powerless or left out," he said. "I had one of the greatest mentors in history in Cesar. I learned a lot from my parents. I learned a lot from my monastic religious training about working hard, self-discipline. I'm not talking about sainthood, but am I fully engaged? Yes. It's part of my religious commitment, part of my religious value system that demands action. This is what gets me into trouble."

Some of that commitment was seen during a walk to lunch when Chatfield passed a very drunk man laid out in the bushes. Other passers-by were asking if the semiconscious man was OK, but Chatfield, recognizing him as a man who has eaten at Loaves & Fishes, called 911, gently scolding a dispatcher for not sending help quickly enough.

"I'm not doing the real work of Loaves & Fishes," he said later. "I'm not the one out there working with the poor and feeding them. I used to do more of that, but I'm the bureaucracy now. I'm in the office most of the time."

The public was given a glimpse of Chatfield's idealism in the late 1950s when he was a young man teaching at a Catholic high school in Bakersfield. Always outspoken on political issues, Chatfield lectured in public on the need to pass housing laws that didn't discriminate against farm workers from Mexico and other minorities, an unpopular position with many of the white growers whose sons were in his classes. "Sometimes when I look back, I can't believe I had the courage to do that, to walk uphill like that," he said. "I was so young. I was so naive."

Chatfield left the Christian Brothers order in the early 1960s because he wanted to work for Chavez and he spent 10 years with the farm workers movement before again changing careers. Following in the footsteps of his brother and father, he spent a few years developing condominiums in Sacramento but said chasing after a buck was distasteful.

Working with Chavez brought Chatfield to Gov. Jerry Brown's attention and he was appointed by Brown to the then-new Agricultural Labor Relations Board in 1975. He later ran the California Conservation Corps. He also coordinated Brown's quixotic campaign to wrest the 1976 Democratic presidential nomination from Jimmy Carter.

Both the political jobs and the development projects Chatfield undertook were motivated in part by wanting to finally make decent money, after years in the Christian Brothers and the farm workers movement. He and his wife Bonnie, a real estate agent he met after leaving the Christian Brothers to work for Chavez, had five daughters they wanted to put through college [Bonnie Burns was a teacher when she met LC. See essay 18]. At this point, having seen politics from the inside, Chatfield is not one to mince words. "I don't have a lot of patience for politicians who sit in swivel chairs in City Council meetings or other legislative halls," he said in his typically frank manner, "who seem oblivious to the reality all of us live with every day."

Reality today for Chatfield, a tall, thin man with a Marine cadet's haircut who keeps fit with morning walks, is that he is front and center in a controversy attracting national attention. "He is not a diplomat," said Tom Hoeber, a former Loaves & Fishes board member who is a friend of Chatfield's and publisher of the California Journal magazine on state politics. "His idea is to create the confrontation and let other people be the diplomats. The farm workers were successful not by being reasonable, they were successful by confronting the establishment with strikes and boycotts. This inevitably has shaped LeRoy's character and his approach to problems. He's almost itching for that still today."

Critics in the neighborhood around Loaves & Fishes and at City Hall are more pointed. "I was on the Richards Boulevard planning committee with him and the vote went against him and he stormed out," said Johann Otto, who owns property in the area and has criticized Loaves & Fishes for allowing people to "wander through the neighborhoods" after being fed. "I don't even remember what it was about, but it seemed awfully childish to me," Otto said. "It's his way or no way. He's proved it time and time again. He's just in your face."

Mayor Joe Serna Jr. has known Chatfield for years. As a young man Serna picked grapes and also worked with Chavez, and both men share a deep concern for the city's downtrodden. But while Serna opposed the city's lawsuit against Loaves & Fishes, calling it "a national embarrassment," the two men have clashed over style and personality. "LeRoy Chatfield is my friend," Serna said. "He's not my moral superior. We care passionately about the same people but government can go a long way toward achieving the same ends with a lot less animus."

In addition to being blunt and outspoken, Chatfield represents a segment of society—the poor and the homeless—that makes most people uncomfortable. And he has engendered a chorus of critics who live or do business in and around downtown who say he has thumbed his nose at city regulations. They complain that he has expanded Loaves & Fishes feedings without regard for trouble some of his "guests"—his name for the agency's clients—may cause through loitering, vandalism or other trans-gressions.

Some criticisms, including one particularly vociferous flier, have attacked Chatfield's record and personal integrity. Chatfield, who is paid $48,000 a year by the Loaves & Fishes board, much less than he made in development or politics, says most of the attacks on his character are attempts to deflect attention from the real issue—how a consumer-driven society takes care of its most unfortunate.

To escape the pressure, he recently took a 10-day retreat, alone, into the Arizona desert where he read, walked and filled his head with other thoughts. "I have a very active mind," he said. "I was just feeling really overloaded." Chatfield likes to think. He is the kind of man who, when he finds an author he likes, will read every single book the author has written. A recent example is Jane Smiley, author of "A Thousand Acres," winner of the Pulitzer Prize for fiction a few years back for a novel described as King Lear visits the Iowa cornfields.

"I have very fond memories of growing up in a small town," he said by way of explaining the profound effect Smiley's Iowa novel had on him. "I grew up in a town of 2,900 people. But there is this facade that people accept, we all accept. You have pillars of the community and all that. What she writes about is what's beneath the facade, the very real tragedies of a real personal nature. That all is not as it seems underneath that veneer."

Thoughtful as Chatfield may be, his critics have said he isn't above get-ting down and dirty when he feels provoked.

A few weeks before last Christmas, Chatfield infuriated at least one business neighbor with whom he had already been at odds when he sent a package with a note that said, "For your support during the past year. Have a happy holiday season." The package contained a dead salmon, its belly sliced and dripping messy fish eggs. "He says he meant it as a gesture of friendship," Hoeber said. "It strikes me as something anyone would see had the capability of being taken the wrong way."

But those who know Chatfield well—friends like Jerry Cohen, who was Chavez's attorney and is representing Loaves & Fishes for free along with local attorney Tina Thomas—say Chatfield is mischaracterized by those who resent what he does. "I have known him 30 years and never sensed any self-righteousness," said Cohen. "He just practices what he preaches. Some people see this as too good to be true, but I don't think it's a crime to be honest."

Then there are the reverent terms supporters use to describe Chatfield and his cause. "I have been in situations where people talk about LeRoy's arrogance and I say to them, 'I work with this man and I have never seen any sign of arrogance,' said the Very Rev. Don Brown, dean of Trinity Cathedral and a Loaves & Fishes director. "I would put him in a long line of people of passion, starting with the Old Testament prophets, with Jesus himself and the saints of the church, who when they take prophetic stands in the name of justice and mercy for the poor often aroused the antagonism of the established political—and sometimes religious—institutions around them."

Say what you will about him, Chatfield, like his old mentor Cesar Chavez, antagonizes the establishment.[1]

NOTE

1. Gary Delsohn, "Loaves Chief A 'Lightning Rod' in Homeless Feud," *Sacramento Bee*, April 13, 1997, B1. See also studies by Allahyari and Avella in "Suggested Readings."

33 There Is No OK Place To Be

NIMBY—"Not in My Backyard."

Friendship Park in Sacramento is at once an oasis of survival services for homeless people and a lightening rod for the city's NIMBYs because it symbolizes the religious principle that people who are down and out deserve care and assistance, not moral judgment.

NIMBYs, aided and abetted by local government officials, take the position that homeless people do not exist in our community. If they do exist, they should not be allowed to do so. There can be no excuse for being homeless, they say, unless the person has chosen such a lifestyle, and the policy makers of our community do not support or condone this kind of lifestyle choice. Be gone, they shout!

To fulfill their purpose of eliminating homeless people, they espouse the scorched earth policy; i.e., no allowable zoning will be permitted for siting emergency shelters or social services; for services already existing, new (punitive) special permits are required; the city's housing agency will be prohibited from proposing any new construction of affordable (very low-cost) housing; decades-old downtown single-room-occupancy hotels and hundreds of low-cost units will be razed in order to promote new high-rise downtown office towers; an aggressive law enforcement campaign will enforce the city's anticamping ordinance; there will be no feeding programs in public parks or at churches without special-use permits; and a

FIGURE 39 Gateway to Friendship Park—a safe place to be—in Sacramento, California. Showers, meals, and an array of social services are provided to the homeless. Photo by Rebecca (Becky) Reed. Courtesy of Rebecca (Becky) Reed.

so-called misdemeanor jail will be built for homeless people who commit such quality-of-life crimes as begging, camping on the river, or loitering in the downtown area.

In other words, homeless people, should they happen to exist in our community, are not welcome here, and they must be removed. Where? Anywhere else but here!

After many years of listening to the drumbeat of unchallenged public testimony by NIMBYs trashing homeless people, using unspeakable invective to urge their removal and/or incarceration, I came to understand how much they despised and feared homeless people. The silence of city council members in the face of such hateful attacks visited upon the most impoverished members of the community surely manifested tacit approval and provided encouragement for future ad hominem onslaughts. I hesitate to write this because it sounds so much like Nazism, but I believe it to be true. If the NIMBYs of the mid-1990s could have acted with impunity, they would have arranged for the vaporization of homeless people in our community. Harsh words, you may say, but believed to be true by homeless people.

The NIMBY collision with Loaves & Fishes was inevitable. I knew it was coming years before it happened because I had had enough experience working with impoverished people to recognize the distant sound of the drumbeat of hatefulness that foretold its arrival. Even so, I was not fully prepared, because it is not possible to predict what form such an attack will take and how the issue will be framed for public consumption.

It was a thriller! The City filed a lawsuit to close down Loaves & Fishes because of its proposed expansion of Friendship Park and the fact that it was feeding hungry people on Sundays. Both unlawful, they said. The next day, they sent swarms of building, fire, and planning inspectors to sweep through the Loaves & Fishes complex looking for code and zoning violations. City attorney employees arrived days later to "post" every building in the complex (including leased space) as "unsafe" and provided a forty-five-day statutory time period to file building plans for permits to correct code violations. The director of the building department posted a sign on the department's staff bulletin board, which reminded city employees that building permits were not to be issued to Loaves & Fishes. They locked us down pretty tight.

You have heard the expression "You can't fight city hall." But you can, and we did. It took us almost a year, but the lawsuit was settled out of court, through the services of a mediator, when the City agreed to give Loaves & Fishes everything it asked for and we agreed to drop our plans to expand Friendship Park. The most painful moment I had to endure was to appear with the council members during a hastily called press conference that announced the settlement. If you can believe this, we were all smiles and full of congratulations for one another. Other than that, as stressful as it was, I loved every minute of it.

Now, ten years later, the City tiptoes around Loaves & Fishes, the NIMBYS have dissipated, our redevelopment area developers have receded into the background, and Loaves & Fishes continues to expand.

Scratch that—I just heard the distant sound of the drumbeat.

The controversy in the usually sleepy town of Sacramento attracted national media attention:

Mr. Chatfield's energy and organizational skills—and, by all accounts, his compassion—are on display everywhere in the compound that Loaves and Fishes has built in an industrial area 10 blocks north of the State Capitol. In small offices that surround a park the group built over an old parking lot, Loaves and Fishes offers help for people wishing to visit relatives in the city jails, a health outreach program and a full-time lawyer. The organization, which operates on small, private contributions that totaled about $1.6 million last year, also runs a tiny mental-health clinic, alcoholics- and narcotics-anonymous meetings, a center for homeless teen-agers, a library, a dog kennel and an affordable-housing office. There are places for homeless people to take showers, shave and get their laundry done. The center of the operation is a pair of dining rooms, one of which is reserved for women and their children. The dining rooms are the outgrowth of a service that Mr. Chatfield's wife, Bonnie, and other Catholics started in the shell of an old skid-row bar, inspired in part by the Catholic Worker movement that Dorothy Day founded in the 1930's.[1]

In early July of 1997, both sides agreed to drop their lawsuits. The mayor offered to help raise money for Loaves & Fishes to obtain additional zoning permits, but the lawsuit had affected donations and Loaves & Fishes was forced to cut back temporarily on services. The NIMBYism described by Chatfield continued. The City and Loaves & Fishes established a task force to study the issues, and a cynical *Sacramento Bee* editorial opined, "The charity's executive director, Leroy [*sic*] Chatfield, called [the task force] 'a community-wide forum for people of goodwill to participate, to be positive, constructive.' Pulling that off will take goodwill, the wisdom of Solomon, the patience of Job and more. Good luck." In 2019, Loaves & Fishes continues to serve the homeless population in California's capital city.

NOTE

1. Tim Golden, "Sacramento Charity's Success Puts It at Odds With City Council," *New York Times*, March 31, 1997. See also https://www.youtube.com/watch?v=npvY3X3D29I.

34   A Bird in the Hand

If a bird in the hand versus two in the bush means the choice between a present opportunity and future possibilities, a homeless person wisely chooses the present.

When well-meaning but misguided (and in my view, disrespectful) church groups bring a load of used clothes to dump on a street frequented by homeless people, this pile always draws a crowd. People gather to paw through the clothes because they believe they will never have access to clothes in the future. These clothes piled up on this street are all the clothes there are or ever will be. The fact that there will be another pile tomorrow or the day after and the day after that, as there has been for years on end, makes no difference. This is the only pile that will ever be.

When Loaves & Fishes furnishes forty pounds of sugar every morning for the Friendship Park coffee breakfast program, at the end of the two-hour coffee period, all the sugar is gone. If fifty pounds of sugar are provided, that amount will be used. The same is true if seventy-five pounds were put on the table. It is all gone, for the simple reason that there will never be any sugar ever provided again, despite the fact that sugar has been provided for ten consecutive years for this coffee breakfast program. The sugar provided this morning is all the sugar there is or ever will be.

The same is true for the free noontime hot meal provided every day of the year in the Loaves & Fishes dining room, now in its twenty-first year. This is all the food there is. If enough food is prepared to serve seconds, all the food will be gone. If there is enough for thirds, all the food will be gone. If two hours are permitted for the noon meal, when the time is up, people will still be eating. If three hours or even four are allowed, it will be the same result. Never again will there be a hot meal served by Loaves & Fishes. This is all the food there is or ever will be.

Ten years ago, as the director of Loaves, I decided to confront and break this never-again-will-there-be cycle. A semitrailer of candy had been donated, creating a nearly inexhaustible supply of candy for the thousand or so people who gathered each day in Friendship Park. I ordered ten large buckets of candy to be placed in different park locations without any signs of restrictions. People would help themselves. With candy available every day, there would come a point when people would take only what they needed.

Ten large buckets were more than enough candy to satisfy every homeless person who might come to the park that day. Understandably, at first all of the buckets came back empty—and the next day, and the next day, and the next day, too. Two weeks later, the same story. After two months, I threw in the towel. It made no difference how much candy a group of homeless people could (or could not) eat. Whatever the amount of candy provided, that was the amount taken. Again, the simple explanation is that this candy is the only candy there is. There will never be any candy again.

Upon my retirement from Loaves & Fishes, I had occasion to reflect about this homeless state of mind during the course of the pilgrimage I made to Santiago de Compostela in Spain. Beginning in the Pyrenees village of St. Jean Pied de Port, I walked an average of sixteen miles a day for twenty-eight days to reach the cathedral that marks the end of the pilgrimage route. Each morning, hopefully by 7 a.m., with an orange or banana in my backpack, I was on the road walking. I planned to pick up morning coffee and something to eat en route. Rarely did it work the way I had hoped.

The restaurant bar would not be open when I arrived at a village. The guidebook showed another village a few miles farther along, but this village had no food services of any kind. I had to push on. It might be noontime before I came upon a place for coffee and food. Or the opposite would happen. After only thirty minutes of walking, I would come to a bar that had just opened for the day but it was too early for me to stop. I had just begun the day's journey, and sometimes the planned walk for the day would be close to twenty miles. I needed to cover some serious ground while I was still fresh and before the weather got too hot, but above all I reminded myself that I needed to make the prescribed destination before nightfall.

FIGURE 40 El Camino de Santiago. To mark the millennium, LeRoy and Bonnie Chatfield walked 450 miles of the pilgrimage route from St. Jean Pied de Port in the French Pyrenees to the Cathedral in Santiago de Compostela, Galicia, Spain. Illustration by Alfonso de Tomas. Courtesy of Alamy Stock Vector.

Not a good plan. Noontime would come and go, and I still had not come to a place where I could get coffee or food. After nearly three weeks of this sink-or-swim routine, I learned to think as a homeless person does. Wherever, whenever, or however the coffee-food opportunity presented itself, I chose to stop. I said to myself, this is the only opportunity I will ever have. There will never be another.

Even today, years later, I think twice before passing up present opportunities for the sake of unknown future possibilities. Perhaps because of my advanced age, I am naturally inclined to do this, but I doubt it. I prefer to believe that homeless people have much to teach us, and I learned this lesson from them.

35   Farmworker Movement Documentation Project

In the 1960s, Cesar Chavez had a saying I have used many times since: "If you do not know what to do, go out to the people. They will tell you!"

When I retired as executive director from Loaves & Fishes in 2000, I did not know what I wanted to do, so I walked 450 miles of the pilgrimage route called the Camino de Santiago. Gradually it came to me—as a former friend and associate, I felt called to document the thirty-one-year history (1962–1993) of Cesar Chavez and his farmworker movement.

Ten years later, I had assembled a digital archive that filled seven DVDs with photographs, oral histories, videos, personal essay accounts, out-of-print books, artwork, original documents, exhibits, commentaries, online discussion accounts, historical timelines, personnel rosters, and more—all immediately available 24/7 from anywhere in the world with Internet access. This Farmworker Movement Documentation Project (FMDP) is now housed online at the University of California San Diego (https://libraries.ucsd.edu/farmworkermovement/).

With the technical assistance of Cal State Sacramento graduate Jennifer Szabo, the FMDP became an online reality in 2004. On March 31, 2005, Chatfield dedicated the FMDP "to the volunteers who built the farmworker movement. It is but one way to say thank you for the years of dedicated and selfless service they gave to improve the wages, working conditions, and quality of life for exploited, impoverished, and powerless farmworkers." The site is now a major research and teaching tool for students and scholars seeking to learn more not only about the farmworker movement, but also the general political climate of the Vietnam War era. In 2014, the University of California, San Diego, agreed to host the site. The project has already facilitated the production of numerous books and articles, as well as several documentaries.

The project will never be finished, but I was finished! Now what? I was ready for something new! I remembered some personal unfinished business dating back to 1958 that I thought should be completed. As a newly minted high school English teacher in San Francisco, I decided to publish a literary journal that I would call *Syndic*. Open only to high school students, I gathered their submissions—stories, poetry, artwork, and essays—and published six issues, the last one in 1960. I was young, inexperienced, and insecure, and while the students who participated seemed pleased and even thrilled to see their work published, many senior faculty members objected: Students shouldn't be reading this "stuff," let alone writing it! Too dark, they said. Not morally healthy, said others. This beat continued unabated. No one ordered me to stop publishing *Syndic*. I simply stopped. Nothing happened. No one said a word. It was as if *Syndic* had never existed.

Now, fifty years later, I wanted *Syndic* to exist again, or better said, reexist. Bolstered by what I had learned from a decade of working on the FMDP about online publishing, I laid out my ideas about the presentation design to Jennifer, my tech whiz, and asked her to choose a digital platform, create a template, and teach me how to publish a new online version of *Syndic* (http://syndicjournal.us).

I published the first issue of the resurrected *Syndic* in August 2010. Nineteen issues later, July 2018, at the age of eighty-four years, I published what might have been the final issue of *Syndic*. Final because when one of my projects begins to feel more like work than a labor of love, I lose interest and my commitment wanes.

Nineteen issues, six hundred chapters, thousands of pieces of literary work—artwork, poetry, stories, essays, music, photography, filmmaking, performance—all written, created, and recorded by authors/artists of every stripe whom I met online and then worked with to organize the submission of their work for publication. Taken together, *Syndic* has become an incredible archive of literary work.

Time for something new! I felt housebound, hemmed in, out-of-touch with reality and aching for something new to tackle, something that would be personally meaningful. But what? I had no idea.

I tried to explain some of these feelings to the executive director of Loaves & Fishes but before I could finish, she said, "Would you consider volunteering to work for a year on my idea of creating a daily healthy breakfast for homeless people who come to Friendship Park? For years we have only been able to provide them with coffee and a day-old pastry. Essentially, we are feeding them sugar cake. We should do better than that! We need to give them a healthy breakfast ever day of the week." Given my own state of mind, I could not have selected a better project! "Okay!" I said, "I will give it a year to see what I can do."

I finished my volunteer year last month but barely made it to the finish line. I felt my age. I was tired and worn down; I was pushing myself. I needed a break! The fact that Becky, my homeless breakfast project partner, and I had organized nineteen volunteer groups during the course of the year to commit to provide a monthly breakfast to the three hundred homeless people who came to Friendship Park every morning was gratifying and personally rewarding, but I knew I had overreached my capacity. I was finished! For the fourth time in twenty-nine years, I retired from Loaves & Fishes. Now what?

My final homeless breakfast for 2016 was scheduled for Halloween. As planned, my volunteer group—forty in number—would bring their food donations to my home the day before the scheduled breakfast so the food could be sorted, organized, and made ready to be transported to Friendship Park at 6:00 a.m. on Halloween morning. The day was especially hectic, with volunteers coming and going and I trying to keep track of everything—it takes twenty large plastic storage bins of food to feed three hundred hungry and homeless people, so you can imagine my home turned into a staging area. One of my volunteers, a recently retired high school teacher, said in passing, "Are you still writing?" I hesitated, not sure what he meant. "Oh, you mean *Syndic*, my literary journal? Yes, I am still publishing it." He too hesitated, and then said, "I really enjoy reading your essays. I like what you write about." "Thanks," I said. He was out the door.

Then I realized what he meant! He was not referring to *Syndic*. He was talking about a series of very short essays I had written a decade ago and published on my personal website (leroychatfield.us). I called them "Easy Essays." Imagine that! He liked them!

Thank you for telling me what to do.

36   Management Maxims

At the age of fifteen, I was introduced to the world of maxims. As young trainees in religious monastic life, we were not permitted to talk during meals. The enforced silence was used instead to listen to prescribed readings from spiritual books. Every day at the noon meal, after one of the required readings was finished, the lector read a maxim of St. La Salle, the founder of the religious order to which we aspired. Now, fifty-six years later, even though I am unable to recall a single one of his maxims, I do remember how impressed I was with each one's forthright, succinct, and educational pithiness—the lesson for the day captured in a sentence or two.

In 1996, I wrote a set of maxims that captured my views about how to understand and manage an organization such as Loaves & Fishes, a private-sector charitable organization dedicated to feeding the hungry and sheltering the homeless in Sacramento, California.

Each maxim is set apart to visually remind the reader that each maxim is its own thought. It must read as a stand-alone principle.

Addiction We are all addicts. Some forms of addiction are more socially acceptable than others.

Generosity In general, you will find a more unselfish spirit of generosity and giving among the poor than among the wealthy.

Meetings More often than not, meetings with other agencies or organizations are a substitute for work.

Meetings 2 The most effective meetings, and those that achieve the most lasting results, take place at the work site, in the hallways, and in the lunchroom.

Mission Statement The philosophy and mission statement of the organization must be stated in capsule form and repeated constantly to new staff members, old staff members, volunteers, supporters, the media, and most importantly, to you. The words of philosophy and mission must be translated into the daily work of the organization.

Personnel Manuals Personnel manuals are developed to deny staff members agency, not to assist and affirm their needs.

Job Interviews To be effective in working with guests of Loaves & Fishes, staff presence must be active, not passive. The executive must know the difference. During interviews with prospective staff members, a judgment must be made whether this quality exists or not.

The Process The poor do not participate in the process, because they know from experience it will lead to no personal benefit.

Honor System The honor system and staff accountability can be nurtured only to the extent that traditional personnel control techniques are eliminated.

Staff Communication Everything you reduce to writing and everything you communicate verbally will be misunderstood by some staff members. It is always easier to unwind misunderstandings that are not the result of something written.

Memos Each time you write a memo to your organization, you should remind yourself that you have chosen the least effective method of communication.

Learning a Career Most careers are learned on the job through trial and error. Academic preparation for careers is the price of admission to learn the work.

Cleanliness Be firm about the need—and be willing to pay—for cleanliness. The return to the organization on the investment is sevenfold.

Job Seeking The easiest and fastest way to secure the paying job you want is to volunteer your services to the organization that has it.

Not Only One Way Be clear about it. Just because you do it one way and not another does not make it the best way, the right way, or the only way.

A Time to Be Magnanimous When a staff member decides to leave the organization, you can well afford to be magnanimous.

Recognition It is not possible to bestow enough recognition for the good work accomplished by staff members and volunteers.

Giving Orders You should avoid giving orders or insisting that something be done. Make suggestions, give advice, state your opinion, and let it go at that. Follow up to see what happened, if anything. Start over again.

Logo If it is possible for the organization to communicate its message to supporters by using only its logo, then its base of financial support is well grounded.

The Secretary If you must have a secretary, then you are not in charge of the organization. The secretary is in charge because you are always "unavailable," "at a meeting," or "tied up on the phone."

Moving River Despite what you might think, your organization is a moving river, and you must move with it by constantly changing and adapting to new conditions.

Inclusive Always err on the side of being inclusive.

Building Community When staff members talk about "community" or "building community," it means they resent autocratic authority and prefer decisions reached by consensus because at least they will have input. It frequently happens that when these same staff members are charged with achieving certain goals, they prefer decision-making "from the top down." Making decisions is a blend of input, touching base, making a judgment, and being willing to correct in midstream.

Telephone Systems Telephone systems that require the caller to make choices and punch buttons to attempt communication create the poorest possible image of your organization. Such a system has no redeemable features.

Making Time Don't kid yourself; you always make time for what interests you. When you say, I don't have the time, it only means you are not that interested.

Accountability It isn't fair to staff members at any level to put them in a position where they are not personally accountable for their work. Being accountable provides opportunity for affirmation, new direction, insight, correction, and taking justifiable pride in what has been accomplished.

The Only Difference The primary and sometimes the only difference between the homeless and the homed is their residence.

Leaving the Organization Some staff members are able to leave the organization only if they feel justified in doing so. Sometimes, it means they must pick a fight with you or the organization before they feel justified.

Working at Your Desk Stand at your desk to do paperwork and answer the telephone. Sit down to meet. You will work more efficiently, and your back will not bother you as much.

Using the Honor System Your commitment to use the honor system and hold staff accountable means that you must be willing to deal openly and honestly with staff members, even when it is painful.

Interruptions Encourage staff members, especially new ones, to interrupt you when they have questions, regardless of how trivial they might seem. It saves you time and prevents serious mistakes over the long term. It also helps you to assess the strengths of your staff members.

Your Best Ideas Some of your best ideas, some of the most important and far-reaching decisions about your organization, will come as a result of answering your own telephone.

Time or Money Your currency is either time or money. If you have both, you can spend both; if you have only one, you can spend one.

Asking for Help People want to contribute and support your organization, but they want to be asked first.

Personnel Manuals The primary purpose of personnel manuals is to take the decision-making authority away from the executive. The secondary purpose is to insulate the executive from the needs of staff members.

Daily Signals In the first hour of the workday, you must try to pick up the mood of the day and its early warning signals. It may be the only signal you ever receive.

Job Descriptions Written job descriptions stunt the development of your organization and create a barrier to change.

Open Door Policy Never close your door for a private meeting. You slow the growth of your organization by preventing staff members from interrupting you for a quick "yes" or "no" in order for them to continue building the program.

Grievance Procedures The purpose of written grievance procedures is to create time, distance, and insulation between the staff member with the complaint and the person in the organization who can do something about it. To avoid complaints taking on a life of their own, you must deal with complaints forthrightly, face to face, and in a timely fashion. It can be painful.

Needs of Supporters Supporters who contribute funds to the organization expect to be kept involved and motivated through frequent communications about the work of the organization, including its trials and tribulations.

Nonsense You can waste much time and emotional effort trying to make sense out of nonsense instead of just accepting it as nonsense.

Job Resumes Read every résumé that comes across your desk. Look especially for signs of hands-on work experience. This will tell you more about the individual than their stated career experience and their—sometimes lofty—stated goals.

Staff Recruitment The very first place to look for staff replacement is on the current staff roster. The next place to look is on the fringes of the organization for persons known to you. Next is through word of mouth. The last place to look is in a newspaper.

Telephone Systems Avoid centralized telephone systems. They do not promote communication; they prevent it. Everyone's time is wasted, including that of the caller. Centralized systems inevitably create a passive message-center system that is neither efficient nor manageable. Make sure that each program entity has its own separate number with enough lines and telephones to accomplish the work.

Doing More with Less Program directors constantly ask for more staff and more space. It is far less expensive to provide the space. It is less expensive still to rethink, rework, and reorganize the program itself to accomplish more with fewer staff.

Artists Artists need respect and encouragement to cope with their insecurities. Artists should be pushed to create what they feel reflects what you wish to communicate; otherwise, you will lose the benefit of their creative insight.

Time to Move On Even when a staff member realizes it is time to move on to another career or line of work, you have to help them make and implement that decision.

Thinking about Leaving When a staff member signals they are thinking about leaving the organization, do not under any circumstances try to talk them out of leaving. Should you be successful in temporarily reversing their decision, you must be prepared to take the blame when something goes amiss in their program, because they will be the first one to remind you that staying with the organization was your idea, not theirs.

Attrition Rate Staff turnover is good for your organization. It provides you the opportunity to bring new talent and high energy to the work.

Job Satisfaction Working only for money or because you need a job provides very little personal satisfaction; it will leave you restless and insecure.

Self-Interest Do not think otherwise: staff members will ultimately do what is best for themselves and not what is best for the organization.

Control You waste much time and emotional energy worrying about events you cannot control. Learn—and accept—the difference.

Government Funding If an organization accepts government money, a bureaucracy must be created to interface with government operatives. Inquiries must be answered, periodic and detailed reports must be filed, surveys taken, expenditures justified, and audits conducted. Finally, you must answer the newspaper headlines about the organization's misuse of taxpayer funds.

Personnel Policies Avoid written personnel policies, because the written policy seriously restricts your decision-making for the benefit of staff members.

Personnel Policies When staff members are sick, they should stay home and take care of themselves. When they need a vacation, they should take one. Written sick leave and vacation policies will not accomplish something as simple as that.

Job Prerequisites Organizations that do not recruit and interview staff applicants unless they have prerequisite academic credentials, required career experience, or state certifications cut themselves off from highly qualified persons.

Staff Recruitment If you have difficulty recruiting good staff members to your organization, it is an early warning signal. Pay attention.

Staff Recruitment You are the primary staff recruiter for the organization and should personally interview and approve each applicant before hire. This is important for many reasons, not the least of which is the opportunity to officially communicate the philosophy and mission of the organization to every new staff person.

What Could Be Done Learning from a résumé what others have actually accomplished helps you to realize what your organization could be doing.

Amassing Wealth Working to create and amass wealth is stressful and tends to be a life hollow at the core.

Ideas Your best ideas come from listening carefully to others in your organization. This creates the raw material for you to massage, reshape, and fashion into your own ideas.

Those Who Do the Work Try at all costs to structure your organization so that staff members who do the work do not have to report to you through a bureaucratic layer. It is a question of priorities; there would be no organization without those who do the work.

Unique Contribution Each person who presents themselves to work with your organization has a unique contribution to make. Your primary task is to recognize what that contribution might be and then be flexible enough to create the niche or opportunity to utilize it.

Management Presence Make your physical presence felt in every part of the organization. Be observant, ask questions as you walk from one place to another, offer opinions, and make observations as they occur to you. When your curiosity is piqued about something you have seen or heard, follow up and find out more about it.

Follow-Up After you ask a staff member to do something, it is best to assume that it will not be done in a timely manner and may not even be done at all. Follow up to see if it was done, and when, and how well. Ask again.

Accountability Staff members expect and need to be held accountable for their work. Give them that opportunity.

Budget Cutbacks There is no way for an organization to scale back its budget without decreasing the size of the staff. You must plan to cut staff even as you hire.

Talking About Finances When you talk about the organization's finances or controlling the budget, staff members will interpret your remarks to mean that staff layoffs are likely. When 75 percent of the cost of the organization's work is staff-related, their interpretation is not far-fetched.

Fund-Raising Events Fund-raising events sponsored by the organization should be avoided. Too much overhead and too much time will be spent for too small a return.

Donations Supporters who personally deliver items requested by the organization will also contribute funds.

Newsletters The use of newsletters instead of appeal letters to communicate with supporters is impersonal and seldom raises enough money to pay for the costs of printing and mailing.

Volunteering Volunteer orientation is critical. Regularly scheduled orientations work best because all telephone inquiries about volunteering can be funneled to a specific date and time. Volunteer orientation also represents that small decision-making step between "wanting" to do something and "doing" it.

Volunteers Volunteers are the lifeblood of your organization, literally. If large numbers of volunteers have a meaningful experience in the work of the organization, it is more likely that sufficient funds will be contributed to carry out the work.

Afterword
Cesar Chavez, 1927–1993
Twenty-Five Years and Counting

On April 23, 2018, Cesar Chavez had been dead and buried for twenty-five years and counting. "Counting" because his legacy lives on, seemingly without end, and the next twenty-five years will tell us whether or not he will be memorialized with a national holiday, taking his place alongside Martin Luther King Jr., Abraham Lincoln, and George Washington.

Soon after Chavez's death in April 1993, I prophesied (see essay 25, "My Prophecy, 1993") that Cesar's life, through his death, would take on proportions that far exceed anyone's expectations (certainly far, far, beyond the bounds of the union) and that his mystique would grow exponentially larger and larger in the public consciousness—not only in North America but throughout the entire world.

As I am writing in April 2018, I count 116 Cesar Chavez public memorials in California, Arizona, Colorado, Michigan, New Mexico, Texas, Wisconsin, and Utah; this does not count the US Postal Service memorial postage stamp, the US Navy *Cesar Chavez* cargo ship, and the US Park Service National Chavez Center in Keene, California.

And so, I take a deep breath before I dare write this: After the death of Cesar Chavez in 1993, more public memorials have been created to honor his memory than for any other citizen in the 168-year history of California. I believe this statement to be true but welcome any documentation to the contrary and will yield to the evidence.

On its face, this legacy seems inconceivable for a person who was born into an impoverished migrant farmworker family, received little formal education (Chavez told me he could count twenty-eight elementary schools he attended during his childhood), enlisted in the US Navy at the age of seventeen to serve for two years, and was then recruited and trained to work for the Community Service Organization (the Mexican American organization in San José, founded to help its members with voter registration and voter participation, housing and job discrimination against Mexican Americans, and the all-too-many examples of police brutality directed against Mexican American communities in California). So successful was his work that he rose through the CSO ranks to become its state director until he resigned in 1962 to found his own community service organization, the National Farm Workers Association, for the purpose of organizing farmworkers to fight for social justice and union recognition from the California table grape growers in Fresno, Tulare, and Kern Counties.

Chavez founded and built his farmworker movement (chartered by the AFL-CIO in 1966 as United Farm Workers of America) from 1962, the year of its founding, until 1993, the year of his death at the age of sixty-six years. He was married for forty-five years to Helen Fabela Chavez; together they had eight children and thirty-one grandchildren.

Without a doubt, Chavez lived a life of service to the migrant poor, but does this qualify him to now be the most memorialized Californian in history? What would motivate people in eight states to hold him in such high honor? Certainly, throughout California's 168 years, other Californians have lived a life of service to others but have not been so honored. Why Cesar Chavez?

The issue, as I see it, is not what Cesar Chavez accomplished or failed to accomplish during his sixty-six years, but those elements that made up his persona, his being, his life of voluntary poverty, and his commitment to serve others. It is what he stood for that made such an impression upon millions of people.

Chavez made famous this saying: "If you do not know what to do, go out to the people. They will tell you!" Yes, it's true! I myself have had this experience. The people will tell you.

Dozens of books have been written, documentary and feature films have been created, dramatic plays and musicals have been performed, muralists have covered walls throughout the state, and academics have poured over the thirty-one-year history of Cesar Chavez and his farmworker movement and have documented and dissected his life of achievements, his shortcomings, and his failures. But none of this explains why Chavez is the most memorialized Californian in history!

Why, you ask? Because no one—not even one person—has "asked the people." They are the only ones who can explain to us why the legacy of Cesar Chavez marches far into future generations with no end in sight.

The people I refer to are those who are organizing the powers that be to rename schools, university buildings, city parks and plazas, major roads, libraries, statues, and murals. None of these Cesar Chavez public memorials happen accidentally. It takes a groundswell of large numbers of organized people to make this happen. It takes tenacity and a lot of *¡Sí se puede!* It takes a long time to accomplish!

Before it is too late—people pass away, memories fail—who will take up the challenge to "talk to the people" and explain to us why Cesar Chavez is held in such high esteem twenty-five years after his death?

SUGGESTED READINGS

BY FARMWORKER MOVEMENT PARTICIPANTS

Day, Mark. *Forty Acres: Cesar Chavez and the Farmworkers.* New York: Praeger, 1971.

Drake, Susan Samuels. *Fields of Courage: Remembering César Chávez & the People Whose Labor Feeds Us.* Santa Cruz, CA: Many Names Press, 1999.

Ganz, Marshall. *Why David Sometimes Wins: Leadership, Organization, and Strategy in the California Farm Worker Movement.* Oxford, UK: Oxford University Press, 2009.

Hoffman, Pat. *Ministry of the Dispossessed: Learning from the Farm Worker Movement.* Los Angeles: Wallace Press, 1987. Available online at the FMDP site.

Meister, Dick, and Anne Loftis. *A Long Time Coming: The Struggle to Unionize America's Farm Workers.* New York: Macmillan Publishing Co., Inc., 1977.

Miller, Mike. *Community Organizer's Tale: People and Power in San Francisco.* Berkeley, CA: Heyday Books, 2009.

Nelson, Eugene. *Huelga: The First Hundred Days of the Great Delano Grape Strike.* Delano, CA: Farmworker Press, 1966.

Ross, Fred. *Conquering Goliath: Cesar Chavez at the Beginning.* Detroit, MI: Wayne State University, 1989. Available online at the FMDP site.

Vera Cruz, Phillip. *Philip Vera Cruz: A Personal History of Filipino Immigrants and the Farmworkers Movement.* Edited by Craig Scharlin and Lilia V. Villanueva. Seattle: University of Washington Press, 2000

SELECTED GENERAL STUDIES

Allahyari, Rebecca Anne. *Visions of Charity: Volunteer Workers and Moral Community.* Berkeley: University of California Press, 2000.

Araiza, Lauren. *To March for Others: The Black Freedom Struggle and the United Farm Workers.* Philadelphia: University of Pennsylvania Press, 2014.

Avella, Steven M. *Sacramento and the Catholic Church: Shaping a Capital City.* Reno: University of Nevada Press, 2008.

Bruns, Roger. *Encyclopedia of Cesar Chavez: The Farm Workers' Fight for Rights and Justice.* Santa Barbara, CA: Greenwood, 2013.

Dalton, Frederick John. *The Moral Vision of César Chávez.* Maryknoll, NY: Orbis Books, 2003.

Garcia, Mario T., ed. *The Gospel of César Chávez: My Faith in Action*. Lanham, UK: Sheed & Ward, 2007.

Kleiment, Anne. "Dorothy Day and César Chávez: American Catholic Lives in Nonviolence." In *Remapping the History of Catholicism in the United States: Essays from the U.S. Catholic Historian*, edited by David J. Endres, 119–44. Washington, DC: The Catholic University of America Press, 2017.

Levy, Jacques. *Cesar Chavez: Autobiography of La Causa*. New York: Norton, 1975.

London, Joan, and Henry Anderson. *So Shall Ye Reap: The Story of Cesar Chavez & the Farm Workers' Movement*. New York: Thomas Y. Crowell, 1970.

Matthiessen, Peter. *Sal Si Puedes: Cesar Chavez and the New American Revolution*. 1969. Reprint, Berkeley: University of California Press, 2000.

Pawel, Miriam. *The Crusades of Cesar Chavez: A Biography*. London and New York: Bloomsbury Press, 2014.

———. *The Union of Their Dreams: Power, Hope, and Struggle in Cesar Chavez's Farm Worker Movement*. London and New York: Bloomsbury Press, 2009.

Prouty, Marco G. *César Chávez, the Catholic Bishops, and the Farmworkers' Struggle for Social Justice*. Tucson: University of Arizona Press, 2008.

Shaw, Randy. *Beyond the Fields: Cesar Chavez, the UFW, and the Struggle for Justice in the 21st Century*. Berkeley: University of California Press, 2010.

SELECTED DOCUMENTARIES

Cesar's Last Fast. Directed by Richard Ray Perez and Lorena Parlee. Los Angeles: Monkey Mind Media, 2014.

Chicano! History of the Mexican American Civil Rights Movement. Austin, TX: Galán Incorporated, 1996.

Delano Manongs. Directed by Marissa Aroy. Burlington, VT: Media Factory, the Independent Television Service, and the Center for Asian American Media, 2014.

Fighting for Our Lives. Directed by Glen Pearcy. New York: Paper Tiger Television Inc, 1974. Available online at the FMDP site.

Huelga! Directed by Mark Jonathan Harris. King Screen Productions, 1966. Available online at the FMDP site.

¡Si Se Puede! Directed by Rick Tejada Flores and Gayanne Fietinghoff. Santa Monica, CA: Alturas Films, 1972. Available online at the FMDP site.

This Week: California Grape Strike. UK: ThamesTV, August 28, 1969. Available online at the FMDP site.

INDEX

Page numbers in italic text indicate illustrations.